Heredity, Race, and the Birth of the Modern

Studies in Philosophy

ROBERT BERNASCONI, *General Editor*

The Relevance of Phenomenology to the Philosophy of Language and Mind
Sean D. Kelly

Between Deflationism and Correspondence Theory
Matthew McGrath

Risk, Ambiguity, and Decision
Daniel Ellsberg

The Explanationist Defense of Scientific Realism
Dorit A. Ganson

New Thoughts About Old Things
Krista Lawlor

Essays on Symmetry
Jenann Ismael

Descartes' Metaphysical Reasoning
Roger Florka

Essays on Linguistic Context Sensitivity and Its Philosophical Significance
Steven Gross

Names and Nature in Plato's *Cratylus*
Rachel Barney

Reality and Impenetrability in Kant's Philosophy of Nature
Daniel Warren

Frege and the Logic of Sense and Reference
Kevin C. Klement

Topics in the Philosophy of Possible Worlds
Daniel Patrick Nolan

Understanding the Many
Byeong-uk Yi

Anthropic Bias
Observation Selection Effects
Nick Bostrom

The Beautiful Shape of the Good
Platonic and Pythagorean Themes in Kant's *Critique of the Power of Judgment*
Mihaela C. Fistioc

Mathematics in Kant's Critical Philosophy
Reflections on Mathematical Practice
Lisa Shabel

Referential Opacity and Modal Logic
Dagfinn Føllesdal

Emmanuel Levinas
Ethics, Justice, and the Human beyond Being
Elisabeth Louise Thomas

The Constitution of Consciousness
A Study in Analytic Phenomenology
Wolfgang Huemer

Dialectics of the Body
Corporeality in the Philosophy of
T.W. Adorno
Lisa Yun Lee

Art as Abstract Machine
Ontology and Aesthetics in Deleuze
and Guattari
Stephen Zepke

The German Gītā
Hermeneutics and Discipline in the
German Reception of Indian Thought,
1778–1831
Bradley L. Herling

Hegel's Critique of Essence
A Reading of the *Wesenslogik*
Franco Cirulli

**Time, Space and Ethics in the
Philosophy of Watsuji Tetsurō,
Kuki Shūzō, and Martin Heidegger**
Graham Mayeda

Wittgenstein's Novels
Martin Klebes

**Language and History in Theodor W.
Adorno's *Notes to Literature***
Ulrich Plass

**Diderot and the Metamorphosis
of Species**
Mary Efrosini Gregory

The Rights of Woman as Chimera
The Political Philosophy of
Mary Wollstonecraft
Natalie Fuehrer Taylor

The German "Mittelweg"
Garden Theory and Philosophy
in the Time of Kant
Michael G. Lee

The Immanent Word
The Turn to Language in German
Philosophy, 1759–1801
Katie Terezakis

**Discourse, Desire, and Fantasy in
Jurgen Habermas' Critical Theory**
Kenneth G. MacKendrick

**Volition, Rhetoric, and Emotion in
the Work of Pascal**
Thomas Parker

Heidegger on East-West Dialogue
Anticipating the Event
Lin Ma

**Gramsci and Trotsky in the Shadow
of Stalinism**
The Political Theory and Practice of
Opposition
Emanuele Saccarelli

**Kant, Foucault, and Forms of
Experience**
Marc Djaballah

**Hannah Arendt and the Challenge
of Modernity**
A Phenomenology of Human Rights
Serena Parekh

**On Mechanism in Hegel's Social and
Political Philosophy**
Nathan Ross

**Heredity, Race, and the Birth of
the Modern**
Sara Eigen Figal

Heredity, Race, and the Birth of the Modern

Sara Eigen Figal

Routledge
Taylor & Francis Group
New York   London

First published 2008
by Routledge
270 Madison Ave, New York, NY 10016

Simultaneously published in the UK
by Routledge
2 Park Square, Milton Park, Abingdon, Oxon OX14 4RN

Routledge is an imprint of the Taylor & Francis Group, an informa business

© 2008 Taylor & Francis

Typeset in Sabon by IBT Global.
Printed and bound in the United States of America on acid-free paper by IBT Global.

All rights reserved. No part of this book may be reprinted or reproduced or utilised in any form or by any electronic, mechanical, or other means, now known or hereafter invented, including photocopying and recording, or in any information storage or retrieval system, without permission in writing from the publishers.

Trademark Notice: Product or corporate names may be trademarks or registered trademarks, and are used only for identification and explanation without intent to infringe.

Library of Congress Cataloging in Publication Data
Figal, Sara Eigen, 1965–
　Heredity, race, and the birth of the modern / by Sara Eigen Figal.
　　p. cm. — (Studies in philosophy)
　Includes bibliographical references (p.) and index.
　ISBN 978-0-415-96479-1
　1. Social sciences—Philosophy.　2. Heredity.　3. Race.　4. Civilization, Modern.
I. Title.
　H61.F48 2008
　300.1—dc22
　2008003245

ISBN10: 0-415-96479-2 (hbk)
ISBN10: 0-203-89380-8 (ebk)

ISBN13: 978-0-415-96479-1 (hbk)
ISBN13: 978-0-203-89380-7 (ebk)

Contents

Acknowledgments   ix

    Introduction: Generating the Good   1

1   Legal Fictions of Genealogy   12

2   Mothers Have Animals, Fathers Have Heirs   25

3   Questions of Kind: The Human Species   41

4   Questions of Kind: (family) Race (species)   59

5   Genealogical Purification   85

6   Medical Police and Hybridization   105

7   Literary Insight: Brotherhood, the End of Tolerance   128

    Postscript: Heredity's Time   156

Notes   159
Bibliography   183
Index   197

Acknowledgments

This project has been many years in the making, and there are many people to whom I owe far more than I could convey by listing their names. I should like here simply to make public thanks for generous financial and intellectual support from Vanderbilt University, the *Deutscher Akademischer Austausch Dienst* (DAAD), and the Library of Congress. I also wish to thank the many librarians, directors, and resident and visiting scholars at the *Herzog August Bibliothek* in Wolfenbüttel and at the *Internationales Zentrum für die Erforschung der Europäischen Aufklarung* (ICEEA) in Halle for sharing their knowledge of bibliographic oddities and their passion for research into any and all aspects of the long eighteenth century.

Personally, I must thank Marc Shell at Harvard University, who has always asked me questions that sent me off into yet another disciplinary tangle; Peter Burgard and Judith Ryan of the Harvard German Department, whose encouragement saw me through and beyond my graduate-school years; Sara Friedrichsmeyer at the University of Cincinnati (my mother), whose patience in reading and responding to parts of this work (and everything else I have written) over the years was remarkable and sustaining; and my colleagues at Vanderbilt University, whose intellectual and personal generosity are unbounded. Finally I thank my husband, Gerald Figal, for his unfailing intellectual and emotional support, for his repeated editing of this manuscript during a busy semester, for his willingness to make breakfast for the kids so I could sleep in after late nights at the computer, for his continual reminders to avoid the passive voice and shorten my overly long sentences, for his occasional gifts of felicitous phrasing that I incorporated into my prose, etc. My debt to him is enormous and intimate, and I shall enjoy repaying it over time.

Introduction
Generating the Good

Heredity and its related concepts are visible everywhere: in the science of biological transmission (I am my father's daughter, because I share his genetic makeup); in folk and legal taxonomies of kinship (I am my father's daughter, and thus have implicit claims upon the social groups to which he belongs, as well as legal claims to his support); in metaphors of power (paternal) and love (motherly, brotherly). Stories of violence within hereditary lines—the violations ancient gods perpetrate on their sons and fathers, Cain's murder of his brother, the multiple betrayals and tragedies suffered by siblings of the Nibelungen saga from its Eddic roots through Wagner's *Ring*—are compelling and frightening precisely because they contradict a law that is at once moral, political, and "natural," a law uniting parents and children with love, loyalty, and shared identity. The earliest fragment of German literature, the ninth-century *Hildebrandslied*, is a tragedy because the blood that Hildebrand the father and Hadubrand the son share fails to speak clearly enough to prevent the son's death by the sword of his father.

Despite the powerful currents of meaning generated by Western culture's long history of presumptions about biological ties, heredity itself has no singular identity. It is my contention—my fascination, really, shared here in this book—that heredity should be understood as a Gordian knotted loop that splices together the real with the metaphysical, the institutional with the abstract, the historical with the transcendent. This book follows the tangled weave of these incommensurable and yet inextricable meanings and objects, suggesting in the process that we have to take seriously the role of heredity and its extended metaphysics of kinship in our understanding of the development of a particularly modern sensibility—if by "modern" we index the priorities of scientific analysis, rational progress, systematically justified racism, and the refinement of the academic disciplines that are associated with the Enlightenment and its aftermath. This study focus upon the confluence of heredity (in its range of biological, societal, and metaphorical guises) and the transmission of moral character, underscoring in the process the presupposition—embedded with the language of inheritance, heredity, and generation—that intellectual and spiritual value inhere in, and are transmitted through, kin relations at all orders of magnitude, be it the family, the nation, the race, or the species.

Certainly, a fully developed history of heredity in all its signifying guises would be both welcome and fascinating. However, I doubt that such a history can be worked out until specific, particularly resonant moments in the career of heredity have been observed, described, and ruminated upon. And so it is that I have chosen to focus upon the long eighteenth century and the German-speaking world, a time and place that witnessed new formulations of legal, anthropological, aesthetic, and scientific order much indebted to what was known about heredity. In approaching the problem from specific textual instances (legal structures, scientific claims, literary allegories), we will begin to appreciate the bricolage, a cobbled-together mix of fact, relationality, and metaphor that makes up any one manifestation of the heredity idea in the world. The German eighteenth century—within its broader European context—is an optimal source of material through which, via judicious juxtapositions, we might begin to trace the multiple functions of heredity at a moment when it began to acquire its modern dimensions.

The word "modern," as used here, has an edge to it, for I argue that heredity might best be approached as a particularly significant example of the "nature-culture" hybrid Bruno Latour describes in his critique of the unique claims made for modernity. Latour identifies—as an essential trait of modern self-styling—a critical imperative to reject hybridity by dividing the world's objects and ideas into separate components that are then assigned to multiple, mutually exclusive disciplines. In his introduction to *We Have Never Been Modern*, he writes: "the analysts, thinkers, journalists and decision-makers will slice the delicate network. . . into tidy compartments where you will find only science, only economy, only social phenomena, only local news, only sentiment, only sex. . . . By all means, they seem to say, let us not mix up knowledge, interest, justice and power."[1]

Perhaps the most significant hybrid divided and thereby denied by the self-styled moderns, so Latour maintains, is that of nature-culture: at every turn, we witness the claim that nature and culture are separate, that real things and power discourse belong to different discussions, that natural science and poetics might illuminate each other in charming or even provocative ways but are by no means constitutive of each other. It is as just such a hybrid—one that has been divided to be conquered by demarcated disciplinary turf—that I will engage heredity, recognizing that its nature-culture aspects are part and parcel of each other, existing as the result of myriad and ongoing translations within networks of mediation. These networks often intersect around textual engagements with new configurations of community that emerged around 1800, products of interconnected phenomena such as inheritance law, racial theory, and revolutionary rhetoric of brotherhood or fatherland. These domains are of a material and metaphysical complexity that is perceptible only once they are understood to be products of hereditary thinking. This book has, as its task, the making visible of such complexity.

It is with this goal in mind that I approach heredity not as an object but rather as a conceptual field that includes within its signifying range natural processes, social regulations, and cognitive metaphors. Thus, in pursuing the meanings and functions of heredity, I trace interactions among the normally discreet realms of scientific inquiry, historical cultural study, and literary analysis, examining texts that take various forms: scientific textbooks, legal documents, dramatic literature, philosophical papers, and essays that defy disciplinary boundaries.

Because heredity was (and is) at once a fact in the world, a social regulative structure, and a source of metaphor, it fostered the creation of further hybrid objects of knowledge: for example, the definition of a mother as a blend of science and law, or differentiated human races as a blend of knowledge claims by science, philosophy, and politics. These "quasi-objects" (Michel Serres's term, designating something that is both object and at the same time constitutive of the inquiring subject) emerged precisely because heredity functioned both as a structuring concept and a source of vocabulary that moved fluidly from technical terminology to metaphysically charged metaphor. This book demonstrates the conceptual and ideological paradoxes inherent in these creations, as very different fields of knowledge creatively drew upon each other's resources where profitable, while repressing structures of reasoning that were irreconcilable.

Such contradictions were made to appear benign or rendered invisible by a common figurative language of lineage and kin-relations. This further complicates any story we might tell of the impact of heredity upon the cognitive parameters within which Enlightenment (and subsequent) thinkers were able to formulate community. Eighteenth-century scientific knowledge about the biological process of generation changed the epistemological status of heredity itself, and thereby reconfigured the rhetorical power of the language used to represent the objects of this knowledge. Nonetheless, traditional metaphors linking heredity with community—such as "mother-tongue," "*der Eingeborene*" (native son), or "*fraternité*" (brotherhood), each deeply rooted in Western thought—continued to be used across discourses, shaping and limiting the ways in which claims to new knowledge could be represented.

The unmistakable presence of a moral law in metaphors of hereditary kinship—via the brotherhood of man, the debt of one's life to the fatherland, belonging to a regional or racial community as to a family—signals a compromise embedded within the secularizing and rationalizing tendencies of the texts in which these metaphors are found. Such moral law in figures of family ubiquitous to political and scientific prose reveals a displaced metaphysics that destabilizes the primacy of reason and objective observation in the construction of modernity.

In order to understand the relations among heredity ideas (rather than to separate and classify them), I have to begin with the language itself. Heredity and kinship function as primary cognitive models for Western thought—that is, conceptual structures that are intrinsic to cognition—from which both denotative and figurative language derive, and by which knowledge, beliefs, concepts, and images are formed. In making such assertions, I draw upon findings by researchers involved in the "cognitive turn" of past decades, people working in fields of cognitive neuroscience, linguistics, and psychology. Investigations in particular by George Lakoff, Mark Turner, Mark Johnson, and Gilles Fauconnier have advanced provocative theses of the embodied nature of human cognition; and Mark Turner, with his first book, *Death is the Mother of Beauty*, explicitly identified the centrality of kinship for both ordinary and literary language—and by extension, thought structures—in the West. These endeavors signal repeatedly the primacy of family and kin experience as a foundation for abstract thinking about and for linguistic representation of human relations at both biological and societal levels of interaction.

In attempting a conceptual cartography of heredity, any one particular legal argument, scientific debate, political concern, or literary topos might function as an initial point; regardless of the starting point, however, four interrelated conduits of meaning emerge:

1) A metaphorical relationship between family and political community;
2) A political relationship between family and state order;
3) A metaphysical relationship between family and a moral good;
4) A physical, objective relationship between family and race/species.

The chapters of this book might be thought of as different points on a circle: each leads to the others; each requires elements of the others as a premise. The beginning and the end that I have chosen for this book are just that: my choices, reflecting my confidence in the engaging narrative power of the facts and fictions of kinship. It is thus fitting that I shall now gesture toward a narrative beginning by evoking a drama of the period that invites all these considerations.

"It isn't flesh and blood, but the heart that makes of us fathers and sons," insists Franz Moor, the great dramatic malcontent of Friedrich Schiller's play, *The Robbers* [*Die Räuber*, 1781].[2] With these words, he evokes a sentimental belief in love as the essential component of the parent-child bond. Ties of mere "flesh and blood" are meaningless, arbitrary and hollow facts, as Franz argues at bitter length. It is, after all, his own sense of unfair exclusion, not only from his immediate family but also from the larger family of man, that to his mind justifies cruelty toward his father and brother. Feeling like a non-son because he does not possess the "heart" of his father, Franz strives similarly to orphan his brother by destroying the affection that his father lavished instead upon Karl.

Throughout the play, Schiller presents us with a character who struggles to separate the physical and emotional components of kinship. If we are to believe the tortured Franz, love and loyalty—whatever is included within the problematic signifying power of the "heart"—do not derive from a foundation of shared biological material with a parent or a sibling; such beliefs in the "natural" love of kin are scorned as pure idealism, rooted in a deceptive superstition. The morally inflected and emotionally compelling roles of "father" or "son" or "brother" are entirely the products of such superstition, regulated and sustained by nothing more than the capricious feelings of the "heart."

Convinced that he himself is an ugly aberration, or *Abart* betrayed by biology, Franz rejects both the claims of blood and love because neither successfully guaranteed his own inclusion within a social (familial) circle. In his experience, the facts of family (of lineage, of genealogy) are disconnected from their moral referent, leaving the blood-bonds exposed as material, scientifically identifiable facts and nothing more. Ideals of "brotherhood," of "fatherly love" or of "filial piety," each of which commonly represents structuring elements of the social order, are deceptive chimeras, masking the fact that human beings are merely "the work of animal desire."[3]

Franz's position does not liberate him in any way from the anger or pain that inspires his arguments; instead, he finds hell at the end of mechanistic argumentation. He may be able to expose the irrational foundations for granting love and loyalty to one's kin, but he cannot suppress his own intense longing for such bonds.

Schiller's play—the drama of a trained doctor with an interest in psychosomatic medicine, as we do well to recall—offers in dramatic form a glimpse into the spiritual impoverishment that results when biological connections are allowed to be mere scientific facts, severed from the emotional resonance of kinship. The separation of materialist and idealist positions represents, in the case of Franz, a thought experiment that fails to produce any tenable working relationship with the social world. On the contrary, *The Robbers* would seem to suggest that it is the irrational and indescribable combination of body and spirit, of blood and love that is capable of shaping meaningful relations among individuals.[4] Ultimately, the compulsion to understand the relationship between the blood and the heart, between biological kinship and love, is an expression of the urgent need to understand why people do or do not belong together, why they are or are not good to one another. It is a need that ultimately weighs upon the possibility of ethical community. I will suggest, by the end of this study, that a belief in the "natural" love of blood-kin which Franz disdains as unfounded and unreliable sentimentalism is, in some way, a vital component of a binding moral good.

One can trace folk idioms replete with wisdom concerning the de facto love—or the de facto animosity—that inexorably accompanies the flow of blood through a genealogical line. From a nineteenth-century compilation of German-language idioms, or *Sprichwörter*, we find variously: "The closer the kinship, the bitterer the enmity;" "The closer in blood, the more dangerous;" and the opposite sentiment expressed as, "Inborn blood calls out, even if it is only a tiny drop."[5] Blood is viewed as a faithful determinant of personality: "Good blood does not lie," a phrase elaborated upon by the collection's editor as, "the man of character shows himself for what he is. Blood does not deceive."[6] An eighteenth-century collection of idioms used in legal disputes includes the following: "Kind does not stray from kind. No magpie produces a dove." In this case, the editor is Johann Friedrich Eisenhart, an influential legal authority, who comments further: "Experience has sufficiently demonstrated that both the good and bad characteristics of parents are transmitted through the bloodline and are perceptible [*wahrgenommen*] in their children."[7]

For Eisenhart, the blood-bond bespeaks an origin: "The meaning of the word clan [*Sippe*] goes so far as to connote a source or origin. One understands thereby the bloodline; clan [*Sippschaft*] therefore means kinship [*Blutsfreundschaft*]." It also bespeaks a common body: "The entire kin-group is compared to a body."[8] The blood-bond is a kind of language, as in so many fictions of unknown or long-lost siblings, that speaks louder than convention;[9] blood cries out for revenge, uttering a truth that no one knew.[10] This idea of blood as an identifying ink marking human bonds is connected to its presumed function as a mediator between the real, physical world and a metaphysical realm of ideals. The knowledge of a blood-bond between people is assumed to be a guarantor of a higher affinity, with claims—for better or worse—upon the emotions, spirit, and reason.

Schiller, whose writing of *The Robbers* coincided with (or, more accurately, collided with) his medical practice, expressed through Franz's anguished doubts (concerning the relation between blood-bonds and emotional affinities) the limitations of a mechanistic philosophy in collaboration with the methods and vocabulary of early modern science. Franz's extreme view is not representative of any one branch of science in particular, but it is the expression of a tendency in the natural sciences to answer emerging and urgent questions of human history with a focus upon the observable and quantifiable physical body. Yet even as the body became increasingly an object of scrutiny, the "family" was still presumed to be both biologically and ethically coherent: biologically, because it represented the continuity of a genealogical line (a subject of interest to scientists investigating the natural processes of heredity, and a central idea for definitions of taxonomic categories like species and race), and ethically, because the origins of altruism and community-bound ethics were—and largely still are—more often than not understood to be a product of that line, evolving from the natural concern that people feel for their children and their extended kin. These issues were incorporated into many different discourses, traceable in the eighteenth century's legal preoccupation with the inheritance of property and "legitimate" (inherited) social position: in concurrent scientific debates about heritable traits and a perfectible species; in political essays that portrayed the state as a loving (or as a flawed) family;[11] and in literary works that explored the parameters of family roles and blood-bound obligations. These all share genealogy as their fundamental organizing principle. In each case, the primary representational figure is some version of the "family."

As we pursue the struggle by eighteenth-century writers to represent an organized, ethically inclined human kind based upon "natural" principles of affiliation, we shall attend to the different ways that genealogy functions both as a "fact" and as an operative "fiction." Genealogical thinking is a long-standing structural feature of Western writing and functions as a cognitive coordinate system: its governing axes are metaphors (such as "fatherly authority," "brotherhood," or "maternal love") and tropes (including dynamics of inheritance and generation) which together describe a subject of thought and dynamically structure how we think about it.

It is during the latter half of the eighteenth century that the notion of flesh-and-blood ties becomes increasingly invested with a material, historical, physiological reality. This reality is granted an epistemological status that is prior to and foundational for the ideas and the practices of social and ethical organization. We will examine the ways in which genealogy functions as a structural social ideal or fiction—the way that natural biological kin relations are assumed to have an ontological status—and we will trace the ways in which different discursive practices attempt to ground these ideals of cooperation and altruism in material, biological reality. We will consistently face some basic questions: Is genealogy simply a legal feint or fiction, albeit one with the singular power to shape a moral social order? Does it belong to the genre of myth? Or is it a biological fact subject to scientific verification? Might genealogy be always and at once both? And finally, what are the implications of our answer for how we are to understand the ways in which the writers examined in this book have understood community? In order to comprehend the full significance of genealogy and its role in the representation of community, we must regard it not just as a mechanism for the transmission of hereditary traits, nor only as a source of metaphors for human relationships; we must also recognize its prevalence as a representational system within an intricate framework of meaning.

In order to approach the idea and the function of genealogy in all its complexity, this study examines historical particulars—namely, specific textual artifacts from numerous discursive traditions—and theorizes their various relationships, based on common metaphors and rhetorical strategies. It engages broad terms like "the good," "family," "community," and "species," treating them as universal (if variously modulated) categories of human cognition and also as specific products of politically and linguistically contextualized discourse. In terms of its subject matter, this book examines networks of metaphor, scientific knowledge, and ethical concepts that are broadly applicable to Western cultures in the eighteenth and early nineteenth centuries. At the same time, in its particular examples, this book focuses primarily on German writers who, while contributing to a broader European dialogue, are all concerned on some level with an exploration of political, intellectual, and/or ethnic identity that is "German."

These various contributions all inform my larger concern with the connection between heredity and understandings of morality. My project seeks to bring together these various discursive traditions to examine the degree to which certain genealogical premises structure them all. Conversely, this approach seeks through a method of comparative textual analysis to distill what my diverse sources reveal collectively about the composition and function of genealogical thinking; this distillation, I hope, will convince the reader of the significance of the heredity complex for questions involving the material and the metaphysical components of human relations.

As an initiation into the practical workings of the conceptual complex of heredity, Chapter One begins on legal ground. During the long eighteenth century, European social structures were theorized, legislated, and even overturned using a language of family. Theories of the family as the natural (mythic) source of human cooperation and altruism—offered by such writers as Giambattista Vico, Charles Montesquieu, Anthony Ashley Cooper, 3rd Earl of Shaftesbury, and Adam Ferguson—provided eighteenth-century legal writers with justification for their emphasis upon the regulation of inheritance and legitimacy as a cornerstone of social order. By regulating the individual family (through marriage, legitimacy, and inheritance law) the well-being of the social "family" was guaranteed. That guarantee of political well-being extended into a moral and even spiritual realm. Nevertheless, juridical texts reveal a full awareness that legitimacy—and especially paternity—are fundamentally uncertain. The rhetoric that skirted this uncertainty reveals the capacity—not merely of an individual psyche, but of an entire culture—to sustain concurrent and irreconcilable beliefs, and to use rational argument to defeat reasonable conclusions when the need for particular mythic truths of human nature—the laws of the bloodbond—were threatened by facts. This first chapter engages in particular problems of legal codification evident in the *Allgemeines Landrecht* (the Prussian legal code) and key works by Johann Jakob Moser, Friedrich II ("the Great"), and Johann Friedrich Eisenhart.

Chapter Two pursues representations of illegitimacy and maternity, contrasting how the objects "bastard child" and "mother" are defined by medical science, how they fare within legal codes, and how they function as metaphors during a period of political and philosophical upheaval. Texts (including a compendium of folk idioms useful for legal argument, a forensic medical textbook, legal ordinances, political lectures, and dramatic literature) yield evidence of an anxious preoccupation with illegitimacy, whether in literal, allegorical, or metaphorical form. These various texts articulate primary concerns that reside in different social and discursive arenas. And yet together they reveal an increasing cultural pressure to credit science with the power to demonstrate the reality of the biological bloodline. The chapter analyzes not merely the causes and the consequences of this pressure, but the resultant paradoxes that come to constitute what is known about heredity, and how heredity can signify as a metaphor. Writers engaged include Adam Müller, W. G. Ploucquet, Immanuel Kant, and Johann Jacob Moser.

Chapters One and Two both begin with social and political problems and then, by following the traces of the heredity concept, they each demonstrate how conflicting methods and claims of science, moral philosophy, and metaphorical discourse all emerge as integral to a history of the social situation. Chapter Three begins with scientific inquiry into the real particulars of physical heredity, and examines its reliance and its impact upon available linguistic formulations, metaphors, and social structures in the interpretation of data and the creation of new knowledge. This chapter focuses upon the development of a concept of species, the scientific problem that has dominated the history of natural history. The genealogical species concept translates the metaphorical relationship between family and state into a physical product of reproductive history, literalizing—or materializing—the figure of the "family of man." The chapter reviews the eighteenth-century development of the biological (hereditary) species concept in France and Germany, paying particular attention to the role played by metaphors of family and the "great chain of being" in shaping the concept itself, as well as in delimiting the arguments that surrounded it. Key texts include works by Georges-Louis Leclerc, Comte de Buffon; Immanuel Kant; Denis Diderot; and Johann Friedrich Blumenbach.

Chapter Four pursues the scientific production of the race concept, the result of collaboration among botanists, comparative anatomists, philosophers, and traveling anthropologists. The race idea is a phenomenal hybrid product, a flawed extension of the logic of species that was intended to fill in a gap in the biological continuum between the hereditary family unit and the genealogically produced, familial species. Race, I maintain here, should not be studied simply as a cultural construct—though it certainly is one—nor as a natural phenomenon, although the variously assembled facts of racial difference continue to inspire sharp debate. Nor do we truly understand the problem if we treat it merely as a discursive construct, as the floating signifier that it so often is. This chapter traces the connections among these incommensurate identities of race as they were articulated first during the late eighteenth and early nineteenth centuries, and demonstrates the culpability of a morally charged language of heredity in making possible the conceptual shifts that seem to entangle permanently the facts and the fictions of race. This chapter focuses upon texts by Georg Forster, Johann Gottfried Herder, Blumenbach, Kant, and Christoph Meiners.

Chapter Five probes what happens when heredity is subjected to the microscope and dissected by science to expose its real, material content. The chapter examines the preoccupation of eighteenth-century writers with the problem of hereditary transmission, and follows the impact of its findings upon theories of urbanism, hygiene, and moral philosophy. As even the science writing of the era betrays, the knowledge of a blood-bond between people is assumed to be a guarantor of a higher affinity, with claims—for better or worse—upon the emotions, spirit, and reason. This chapter identifies a struggle by eighteenth-century writers to represent a socially organized, ethically inclined human kind based upon "natural" principles of affiliation and transmission—relying upon the blood-bond's presumed function as a mediator between the real, physical world and a metaphysical realm of beholdenness and mutual care. However, when bloodlines are presumed to transmit characteristics (physical, emotional, and intellectual) relatively reliably, then the consequential logic is eugenic: in theory, at least, family lines, and then ever increasing population groups including villages, nations, and ultimately the entire species can be perfected by controlling breeding. While following the development of this thinking during the late eighteenth and early nineteenth centuries, this chapter identifies crucial inconsistencies within scientific, biomedical, and political theories of human improvement. Writers include Richard Steele, John Gregory, Joseph Claudius Rougemont, Johann Peter Frank, and others.

Chapter Six investigates the practical application of theories of heredity at the turn of the nineteenth century, with a focus on the institution of the medical police and Johann Peter Frank's efforts to identify a political responsibility to perfect the human (familial, racial, national) species. Frank's work provides surprising evidence for the degree to which a proto-eugenic program might be advanced in the eighteenth century; it also reveals in its structural and rhetorical complexity an indication of the political profits to be gained by uniting an analysis of the biological and the moral good using arguments of kinship and heredity. Other writers, too, including Charles Augustin Vandermonde, Johann Daniel Metzger, and Herder, infuse their accounts of the new biological science with a moral metaphysics through the language of family, genealogy, and race, and consistently clouding any boundaries between the biological, the social, the aesthetic, and the metaphysical good.

Chapter Seven moves from the analysis of primarily systematic to primarily imaginative representation. Focusing on Gotthold Ephraim Lessing's canonical play *Nathan the Wise* [*Nathan der Weise*, 1781], the chapter examines the dynamics of kinship and blood relations that have long preoccupied critics of the drama. By emphasizing the function of illegitimacy, along with competing notions of fatherhood and of transmission, this reading presents Lessing's philosophically resonant position with regard to the ambiguous knowledge of parentage. Lessing's play offers a late-eighteenth-century meditation on the blood-bond as a fact as well as a fiction, as something equally able to unite people in loyalty and to divide them murderously; in so doing, he paves the way for a particular kind of ethical practice involving the constant interplay between an intellectual and an imaginative response to the knowledge of lineage. This points toward my conclusion, which raises questions not only about the significance of kinship for human cognition, but for the fate of "tolerance" as a mode of negotiation between groups of people.

The focus throughout this book is on the kind of language, the structures of argumentation, and the imaginative concepts that are devised and deployed in the eighteenth century to connect the idea of the heredity to something real and to an understanding of the good. Almost invariably, the "good" is connected to human compassion based upon ideas of kinship. This connection is then available for scientific investigation into the facts of heredity. While systematic writers concern themselves with the identification and representation of "facts," the facts they choose to represent all have social meanings. These meanings, which in turn lend moral weight to the genealogical "facts" at hand, are attributed—falsely—to "nature." Writers who wish to speak either of emotional or of physiological connections between people, it seems, cannot help but oscillate between representations of the material blood-bond and the metaphysical good.

These oscillations between the material and the metaphysical, however, do take on a cast slightly different from that of prior centuries. In the eighteenth century, many writers did not automatically begin their theorizing with a conception of the world as an imperfect reflection or translation of God. They instead began their inquiries by observing the world itself, claiming to find in its small kindnesses and beauties affirmation of an otherwise uncertain absolute. The connection between the material and the metaphysical was not affirmed in order to show how the world might or might not conform to an ideal good; rather, it functioned to demonstrate how manifestations of the good (exemplified by fatherly concern, motherly love, and brotherhood) were the cultural extensions of a transcendent nature. We shall see, however, that as scientific efforts increased over the eighteenth century to verify heritability and to prove its centrality in the determination of physical and moral character as well as social position through lineage, the imaginative resonance of genealogy and its potential effect upon the moral imagination were threatened with new surplus values, and thus with a corresponding loss.

But let us turn now to some historical particulars.

1 Legal Fictions of Genealogy

As an initiation into the practical workings of the conceptual complex of heredity, we shall begin on legal ground, focusing on that part of inheritance which intersects with the law, identifying what Michel Serres might have called a "regional epistemology."[1] Heredity, insofar as it concerned early-modern lawmakers, was a process and a pattern of movement indicated by the Latin terminology, *transmittere ad heredes*, literally, "to send across or beyond to heirs." The goods transmitted were primarily property and social identity, each of which relied upon the other to great extent for definition and legitimation. Over the course of the eighteenth century, a different kind of good—a moral, metaphysical good that was legible on the body and transmitted through the blood—joined the list of hereditary concerns. But this part of the story will occupy later pages.

The societal structure of early-modern Europe was to a great extent organized by laws regulating property and officially recorded identity through consanguineous, and specifically paternal, lines of inheritance. The right to own land, to practice a craft or profession, to study, to marry, to inhabit a particular region or city, even one's status as a freeman or a serf, was legally determined by one's pedigree. In sum, the position of an individual within a genealogical line mapped that person's regulative identity. Only within the confines of this identity, within the sweep of a social signature, might the expression of individuality have political reach—in theory. While this method of social identification through genealogical regulation appeared to be a transparent mechanism, considerable resources were expended to determine the legislative parameters of this "natural" order. The crux of concern was the paternal line, the material basis for all guarantees of legitimacy, the physical ground of the social order.

BLOODLINES AND THE LAW

In an influential legal text of 1778 entitled, *On the History of German Inheritance* [*Versuch über die Geschichte der teutschen Erbfolge*], Friedrich Christoph Jonathan Fischer identified the hereditary line as the sole

Legal Fictions of Genealogy   13

source of all law. The vast legal literature on inheritance, which for the most part remains buried in its many archives, suggests that the regulation of a smooth passage of goods and identities through time along genealogical lines was not only more complex, but also more important, than might be supposed. Turning our attention to these printed materials, we discover legal discourse to operate, alongside its more predictable roles, as an unmeasured and unacknowledged channel though which different meanings of heredity—the biological, the social, the discursive—were able to meet and exchange functions.

One recurring peculiarity to be found in books by prominent jurists is an inconsistency of priority between the law of bloodlines (the *Geblütsfolge*) and the convenience of the court. The internationally renowned Johann Jakob Moser's position on the compelling "truth" of the bloodline was typical: he deferred to its "reality" as the authoritative source of the patterns of inheritance law, and he maintained that position until he identified a reason for the law to preempt it. For example, when compelled to address the legal quandary, "Whether a person can be excluded from a bloodline, if he embraces or fails to embrace a particular religion?" Moser defended the priority of *Geblütsfolge* or bloodline in determining all inheritance decisions, even in the face of politically and emotionally charged opposition over religious difference.[2] In taking this position, Moser invoked nature's imperative to emphasize the priority of a blood-claim even over one of the most divisive issues of the early-modern era, confession, and he decisively identified the law of blood lineage not as an option but rather as an obligation, a debt to be paid to posterity, a *Schuld*. This decision, insofar as it curtailed an individual's right to pass down properties and privileges as he chose (and potentially circumvent the claims of family altogether), engaged a debate that had occupied thinkers during the prior century and continued to require eloquent defense during the following—as Hegel took up, for example, in his *Philosophy of Right*.[3] All differences in legal philosophy on the expression of free will aside, however, a consensus had slowly emerged on the overriding priority of genealogical integrity, or the preservation of a bloodline, as long as traces of that line were detectable. This dominant position posited a morally binding "truth" underlying the physical, emotional, and moral aspects of the blood relationship between parent and child, a socially structuring truth that was prior to the political state. This a priori status, as we shall see, made the parent-child *Geblütsfolge* available as a legitimate organizing principle of that state.

Paradoxically, however, the very bloodline that appeared inviolable in dictating the structures of inheritance (upon which the social order relies) was itself subject to the re-ordering power of "legal fictions." In discussing the possible challenges to a family line that illegitimate children posed, Moser related the following dilemma: A man who already had several illegitimate children with one woman married a different woman and had a second set of children. When his wife died, he married the woman with whom he had previously consorted, and he then officially legitimized his first set of children. Jurists were called to determine which set of children should be considered *legally* the first born (and thereby in better position to inherit): was it the elder children who were biologically the first born, or the younger children who were the first legitimately born? Moser identified the younger set of children as the "first born," and relegated the older, legitimized children to the category of *nachgebohrene*—literally, "born after"—as justified by the law per *aliam fictionem Juris*.[4] By means of this legal *Fictio*, the law assumed the power not only to legitimize bastard children but to re-order birth itself, thereby exposing *Geblütsfolge*, or the legal principle of blood-lineage, as a legal feint or fiction. The bloodline, as jurisprudence has it, is a malleable artifact, generated by the law in order to function as its own presumptive source for the authoritative structuring of both social and moral order.

The rhetoric of the blood-tie was powerful, however, and it was present in the ubiquitous figuration of the state itself as a family, according to which a ruler is represented as a father and the citizens are children, and which carries a corresponding moral code fashioned from metaphors of familial love, paternal care, filial obedience, and brotherly loyalty. The conceptual modeling of a state upon essentialized family relationships has a long and well-charted history. Plato figured the ideal republic as a family, albeit one newly configured in its practical functioning; and the Roman reference to the *patris urbem* was already weighted by nostalgia when Horace, in his odes, lamented the disappearance of its moral social order in favor of decadent self-interest. The family was not the only metaphor available: historically resonant alternatives include the state as a body, as a person, or as a machine.[5] However, the state-as-family configuration proved particularly useful to absolutist self-definition, whereby the metaphors not only structured patterns of authority and deference, but—more importantly—framed the "nature" of human loyalty to communities of any size. Accompanying absolutism's rise throughout Europe at the turn of the sixteenth century was the identification of the family as both the source and, according to Jean Bodin, the *vraye image* of the state. A necessarily generic idea of family functioned in this duel role for centuries, both as the state's model and as its reflection, both as the truth behind the institution and as its mask. Bodin's *vraye image*, expressed in his *Six Books of the Commonwealth* [*Les six livres de la republique*] of 1583, is generally interpreted to refer only to a correspondence between familial roles and structures of power, a correspondence that is said to involve only the performance of relationships and not the physiological basis of family relationships.[6] However, it is precisely the blood-relationship defining the family, the "natural" bond with claim to both soul and body, source and mask, that makes the family metaphor so compelling and so politically useful.

The equations presumed by the state/family analog are well-rehearsed: the relationship of a father to his family is the model for the relationship between a ruler and the state; the child's obedience within the family is compared to the citizen's within the state; the child and father share a relationship compared to that between citizen and ruler; the bonds of brothers in a family are the bonds of collective brotherhood among citizens under the paternal rule of the state. Both individual families and the state as a family are understood to function and flourish under the loving authority of a father; and the transmission of this authority from generation to generation is passed genealogically from a father to a son, who in turn becomes a father, and so forth through time.

Consider that a "family" was, even before the advent of its bourgeois nuclear incarnation in the nineteenth century, most elementally defined by the presence of a married couple and their offspring;[7] consider also that marriage law was functionally the prerequisite to any laws and theories regulating inheritance through a paternal line. A wife and mother, therefore, was an indisputable element in the family. However, there is no civil analog, no correlative "mother" position in any model of the familial state. The analogy, "mother is to the family as X is to the state," yields an absent value.

This absence did not go unnoticed, as much as uncorrected. One might observe with some cynicism that it corresponds well enough with Johann Gottlieb Fichte's famous and explicit justification of the married woman's exclusion from full legal and civic rights: in his words, she is "obliterated [vernichtet] in the eyes of the state through marriage."[8] Significantly, mothers are also largely—though not entirely—missing from German literary representations of the family generated by male canonical authors.[9] On the other hand, during the first decade of the nineteenth century, the conservative Romantic statesman Adam Müller identified the absence of the mother in models of the state in a lecture on the *Elements of Statecraft [Elemente der Staatskunst]*, delivered in 1810 to princes and diplomats. Müller's talk was entitled "How the living nature of the State expresses itself in the natural family contract, common to all peoples of the earth"; in it he pointed out that the much relied-upon theories of the state-as-family consistently failed to account for the significant power in the household—different from, but equal to that of the *Hausvater*—wielded by mothers.[10]

MOTHER AS *MITTEL*

The pedagogue Joachim Heinrich Campe also referred to maternal power and its roundabout civic resonance in his much-reprinted *Fatherly Advice for My Daughter* [*Väterlicher Rath für meine Tochter*] initially published in 1796. Acknowledging the inferior legal status and exclusion from civic life of a wife and mother, Campe consoled his daughter (and, by extension, the collective sisterhood of readers hearkening to his paternal wisdom) with the assurance that a wife and mother is, in practical terms, society's principal instrument. It is she who, as a mother, produces and socializes future citizens, and it is she who, as a wife, socializes her husband, translating him—in a kind of second, social birthing process—from a man into a citizen. Such a wife and mother, although not a citizen herself, is the precondition of and the underpinning for a state made up of citizens; she is, in fact, its *Mittel*. Given such acknowledgment that the mother figure is the generative force, both literally and figuratively, of the family, and given that this family—the product of a mother's body and a mother's love—is identified by jurists and philosophers alike both as a structural model for the state and as the source of the moral sensibility that makes possible civic virtue, what can we make of the fact that this medium of the mother is all but missing from the legislative center of society?

Let us sidestep this absent center, for a moment, to examine the traces of a maternal position in the theory and the law of the state which are legible in the discourse of legitimacy. The genealogically legislated state requires for its stability the integrity of the (paternal) genealogical line: that is, fathers have to know who their children are. Only with this knowledge are the political and social economies able to flow smoothly, based as they are on patrilineal transmission. The regulation of legitimacy, as an attempt to control those lines of transmission, was essential to a state like Prussia; it was considered essential to any monogamous society that regards marriage as a legal institution—which included any European state. Kant, commenting upon infanticide in his famous discourse on capital punishment, conflated "the law" explicitly with marriage, and argued that a child born outside of wedlock was born outside of that law: "[Such a child] has found its way into the commonwealth by stealth, so to speak, like contraband goods, so that the commonwealth can ignore its existence and hence also its destruction, for it ought not to have come into existence at all in this way."[11] The commonwealth [*gemeines Wesen*] need neither acknowledge the existence of a child born outside of wedlock nor, by extension, the death thereof.

Explicit discussions of the importance of legitimacy, or the knowledge of a child's legal origins, took place for the most part in the context of theoretical writing about the state, especially writing concerning its familial origins. Thomas Hobbes, in his "Dialogue between a Philosopher and a Student of the Common Laws of England," had written as a governing principle that "it is evident that dominion, government, and laws, are far more ancient than history or any other writing, and that the beginning of all dominion amongst men was in families."[12] This principle provided the basis for a model of civilization and its history that identified the family as a threefold source of political stability. Montesquieu's *Spirit of the Laws* [*Esprit des lois*, 1748] developed the model then cited by others for a century: first, the form and power structure of the (patriarchal) state was understood to have evolved from a primordial first family of father, mother and child; second, this hypothetical first family generated the capacity for virtuous behavior (effort expended not in one's self interest, but in the interest of one's children) that itself has evolved to be a part of the ideal nature of the state (as an ability to act in the interest of the general good); and third, the particular families that make up contemporary society are the units which comprise the state—they continue to be reflected by the whole, and they provide the moral socialization that is needed to produce citizens.[13] These families by definition are legally sanctioned, consisting of a marriage with legitimate offspring. Of course, there are significant differences in the regulation of legitimacy associated specifically with monogamous rather than polygamous societies. Such differences notwithstanding, the importance of legitimacy, argued Montesquieu, cannot be underestimated within a society concerned not only with the quantity of its citizens, but with the moral quality of each of them; such a society is required to degrade its bastards as "odious" reminders of legal infraction.[14]

The apparently simple requirement of a legal marriage for the general good of children, families, and states, was, in fact, qualified under the law. There were acceptable and unacceptable marriages in the German legal system. In order to qualify as a fully acknowledged union in which the offspring had comprehensive claims of relationship with both parents, the marriage had to be one between social equals and not a morganatic, or "left-handed" marriage ("*Ehe aus der linken Hand*"). This differentiation within the domain of marriage is another attestation for the priority of legal regulation over possible claims of blood-bonds. Marriage may literally flesh out the social genealogy, but any ultimate signifying authority over the hereditary line must be shared with a collective of other political and discursive forces.

In the case of non-conforming, inappropriate marriage, any offspring inhabited a social position halfway between legitimate and bastardy. The renowned historian and jurist Johann Friedrich Eisenhart wrote in 1759:

> German history makes clear enough that mistaken marriages [*Mißheyrathen*] have not been accepted placidly. . . Unequal marriages have been regarded as nothing more than concubinage. The woman thus had no share of her husband's social position, the children received nothing beyond what was established for their basic support. Entailed properties could in no circumstances pass to them.[15]

In stipulating here that, in the case of "mis-marriage," a woman would be excluded from the social position (*die Würde*) of her husband, Eisenhart exposed the presupposition that such alliances would always involve a woman of lesser standing than the man with whom she is involved. As Eisenhart was unconcerned with the possibility that a woman might marry a man beneath her socially, so he was unconcerned with the preservation or possible corruption of a maternal line. What occupied the legal community was strictly the integrity of the paternal line, underscoring the fact that regulated genealogy was a particularly male-oriented concern.[16] This is further evident in those passages from the *Allgemeines Landrecht* (the Prussian legal code) that treat illegitimate children, children from a marriage "*aus der linken Hand*," and children from a "legal" marriage ("*aus der rechten Hand*") differently. Both natural children, if conceived out of marriage, and children from a mis-marriage are illegitimate. If legitimized, each attains the *Stand* of its father but does not enter legally into the family of the father (thereby acquiring his name and coat of arms, and the various rights of relation with the extended family) unless a separate family contract [*Familienvertrag*] is constructed.[17] However, a child from a left-hand marriage is a member of the mother's family and has equal inheritance rights with any children born of a right-handed marriage, whereas a child born out of wedlock takes the mother's name and social position (as long as it is not noble) but is expressly excluded from the "family."[18] These strictures became even more severe under Friedrich Wilhelm II.

Building upon this tradition, the prominent German cameralist Johann Heinrich Justi defined the state both as a single family and as a composite of families, and argued that the quality of particular family life directly impacted the moral well-being of the state: "The well-being of the Republic is founded upon the peace and prosperity of the individual families that constitute it."[19] In a book of 1757 that concerned itself explicitly with the relationship between marriage laws and the well-being of the state, Justi turned the idea of the altruistically inclined family into an instrument for social regulation. Writing persuasively about the natural inclination on the part of a parent, and in particular the father, to protect the interests of family, he identified ways in which that inclination might be harnessed for the needs of the state. After affirming that a strong republic required the active participation of all members, he insisted that the regulation of the "family" was the only way to consistently inspire that activity:

> The more that a wise administration is able to provide motivation to productivity in its subjects, the stronger and happier the state will be. It is no small motivation to productivity, when men know with certainty which children were engendered by them. We work to great extent for our children, in order to leave them in fortunate circumstances after our death.[20]

Justi's schema is based upon the presumption of a natural love that parents feel toward their own children (albeit that fathers, by the same natural law, feel somewhat less)[21] and upon the natural interest in one's own genealogical continuance extending beyond one's child throughout the progression of the line.[22] This investment in the well-being of the succeeding generations, however, is entirely dependent on the father's feeling of certainty that his child is his own. It was based on this imperative that Justi drew a connection to the dangers of illegitimacy: a father uncertain of the identity of his offspring will fail to invest his efforts in the community for their well-being, and his subsequent alienation will thereby jeopardize the social order. This is the original justification for the societal regulation of marriage and propagation: "A commingling of both genders, whereupon the fathers are uncertain of their children, is in no way compatible with the prosperity and the responsible, basic law of the state."[23] Droll and dry prose aside, what we have here is paradox: Justi insists on the "nature" of love for one's offspring, but this "natural" love that he describes is an investment of imaginative energy that necessarily follows—and only follows—a confidence in the knowledge of shared (biological) nature. The love is a natural good (one that accrues to society at large), but it is a good that, for men, can only be manifest after some demonstration of its (natural) necessity.

The depth of this howsoever problematic belief in the nature of the love automatically extended to a child by its biological parent is further indicated by the demonization of step- and adoptive parents in legal adages, folk wisdom, and folk tales. These consistently depict the conditions surrounding a child without natural parents as dire and life-threatening. To warn against second marriages, presuming that a parent building a new family will neglect the children by a previous spouse, Eisenhart provided as a legal adage the following: "Whoever has a stepmother also has a stepfather" and similarly, "When the hen comes to the rooster, she forgets her young."[24] Johann Peter Frank, in his *System for a Complete Medical Police* [*System einer vollständigen medicinischen Policey*], published in 1779 and reissued throughout the following decades, insisted that "one has reason... to believe, that the raising of children by stepparents considerably increases their mortality."[25] These presumptions of non-nurturing or even hostile behavior characterizing a non-biological parent are also traceable within the language, as we see in the various definitions and citations offered by the Grimms' Dictionary: the term "stepparent" carries with it "the association 'bad parent'"; of "stepchild" the dictionary notes that "the word commonly evokes the sense of an 'unloved, mishandled child'"; and "stepmotherly" is a word that "nearly always bears a pejorative tone... 'unmotherly, hard.'" These notions are borne out by the collections of folk tales assembled during the turn of the nineteenth century, whether by the Grimms or by von Arnim and Brentano, which are replete with notoriously cruel and self-interested stepfathers and stepmothers who define in negative what a parent "should" be.

Conversely, the difference between the loyalty which a child owed a parent and a stepparent was publicly, visibly marked by the Prussian mourning decree, the "*Trauer=Reglement vom 7. Oktober 1797*," which stipulates that the official mourning of parents by their children is a six-week period of deep mourning with a dress code; for a stepparent, however, one need only wear a black arm or hat band, and that only for three weeks.[26] The *ALR* is blunt in its dismissal of any lasting or reliable bond between any but blood-related parents and children: "There exist no family bonds [*Familienverhältnisse*] between stepparents and stepchildren."[27] Similarly, an adopted child was significantly different from and not to be confused with an *echtes* or authentic child.[28]

THE BASTARD CHILD AS SMUGGLED GOODS

Bastardy is precisely where the question of the truth of the blood is most critical. Does blood account for bonds, or does the law, or does human volition? Or are the bonds that are optimistically called familial—motherly or fatherly love, brotherhood or sisterhood—just ideas, at times descriptive, but never prescriptive, of the actual practice of life?

The positions outlined above hinge upon the value of the blood-bond as the sole determinative element constituting a "real" family relationship. It was concern for community morals and political order, however, that explains the designation of an illegitimate child as an inauthentic or *unechtes Kind*. Within the Prussian familial state, Friedrich II consistently equated the family with virtue and virtue with much needed social order; since "virtue is society's most secure band and the source of public order," it is the goal of any state to produce simultaneously "good citizens, good fathers, good friends."[29] But, for all the metaphoric and sentimental inclusivity implied by the rhetoric of civic "brotherhood" upon which he so liberally drew, and despite his declarations of the equality of all before the law, Friedrich's state never reached so far as to include illegitimates in its encompassing familial embrace. Despite Friedrich's personal generosity in responding to particular instances of illegitimate pregnancies, and despite his inaugural efforts to decriminalize extramarital sex (thereby eliminating one motivation for infanticide, or so he hoped), the official state position on bastardy did not soften.[30] Under Prussian laws (as under the laws of the Empire) bastards were considered, in Montesquieu's term, "odious."[31] At mid-century, they could make no claims upon a father; they could neither inherit his property nor enter his *Stand*. They could not enter guilds,[32] had no claims to public support whatsoever, and in some regions were even barred from orphanages.[33] They were, for the most part, excluded from the rights-bearing human kind.[34]

One should note, in passing, that noble bastards as a rule fared somewhat better than did their common brethren. In his treatment of family law, Moser devotes substantial attention to royal "natural children," listing illegitimate male children from various princely houses who were given lands and titles (though never the titles of their fathers) and female children who were successfully married off. The identity of these children, all products of illicit affairs conducted by noble men, was no secret; on the contrary, legal commentaries developed better and worse ways of mapping these genealogies. Moser, for example, while writing about the complex status of bastards, writes: "One finds an abundance of reports from every corner about the many natural children of King August II in Poland. I will not dwell on these, however, because they are better reckoned separately among the natural children of sovereign crowned heads." Moser's list of bastard children spawned by roving noblemen fills twenty pages, at the end of which he concludes, rather merrily: "And what could I add as further examples!"[35]

By contrast, common illegitimates were scorned without clemency—and not only by the upper classes. The obloquy arising from the guilds, when they were threatened with including bastards into their ranks, is indicative of how thoroughly illegitimacy was linked to immorality and the taint of undesirability. Bastards were excluded by law from the guilds: as the Magdeburger *Polizeiordnung* clearly stipulated, "no apprentice shall be taken in by [a guild member] unless he is of legitimate birth, which should be verified by the presentation of a certificate of legitimacy."[36] When, in 1698, August Hermann Francke received royal permission to issue for his educated but illegitimate orphans a form replacing the otherwise required birth certificate, thereby enabling them to move from his Pietist schooling into a life of productive work within the community, he encountered ferocious opposition from the town.[37] Although many of Francke's projects were opposed by the guilds (his printing and chemist privileges, the annual funds collected from churches, his tax exemptions, not to mention his long-distance trading ventures, were variously resented by guilds and estates alike), it was his plan to admit illegitimate children [*Hurensöhne*, literally "whores' children"] into their ranks that proved absolutely unacceptable. And while Berlin tended to support Francke in his projects and privileges (the hostility between the court at Berlin and the guilds was overt and ongoing), in the case of the legitimization certificates, the Prussian state yielded to protests. Francke was forced to cease issuing the certificates of honor that would have made citizens of his orphans.[38] Why was this one project defeated? While Francke's other reforms might be understood to serve the Prussian state interests, the charitable blurring of boundaries between legitimate and illegitimate citizens, upon closer examination, clearly did not. Neither the defense of bastards, nor the erasure of the stigma they carried, was tenable.

This harsh and unyielding treatment of bastards was integral to the logic of the absolutist state. Even at the close of the eighteenth century, Friedrich Wilhelm II would publicize his decision forbidding requests made by soldiers and officers (including members of the nobility) to legitimize their "natural" children, asserting that extramarital relations threatened "the morality and the well-being of families" and thus must be discouraged in all ways possible, including a ban on post facto legitimization.[39] He specifically argued that "as a result of these legitimations, immorality will be served and the nobility will be debased."[40] Parallel to fears of counterfeiting, by which bad money drives out good, an artificial noble, minted outside of state controls, made rather than legitimately born and then smuggled [*eingeschlichen*] into the community, might very well degrade the noble currency altogether. As

Justi had declared with his considerable authority, "A civilized State must expect its population to come solely from marriage,"[41] so also Friedrich Christoph Fischer, in his widely-read book on the history of inheritance law in Germany, argued that *Erbrecht* was the simple source of the entire legal structure of political society. Both rhetorically and legally, the state needed to maintain vigilant control over the shape of the family and its relation to morality [*Sittlichkeit*] as well as over those figures—like bastards—who escape the family's parameters.[42] Justi pronounced: "Irregular procreation violates natural law and healthy reason: the natural consequences thereof lead to the greatest deterioration of morality; and it is equally detrimental to the populace itself."[43] Justi's work attempted to remove from the natural realm (and thence the law) any procreation that was "*unordentlich*," that did not follow the prescribed order thought to be at once natural and the source of civil, legal society. Natural law does not recognize the act that produces the bastard. Since this "irregular generation" is an act that is only made manifest by its bastard progeny (a progeny for whom, we recall, no father will provide social position or resources), we must understand that this progeny, a living signature of an illegal act, is a constant and legible threat to the moral underpinnings of the population itself.

Returning, then, to Friedrich and his reliance upon a familial structure to authorize the absolutist understandings of the power relations between state and subject: the understandable conflict with bastardy nevertheless contradicts somewhat Friedrich's enlightened pronouncements of equality for all under the law. Friedrich and his legal system were in fact caught in one of the many paradoxes produced by the clash between absolutism's particular language and the principles and the emerging democratic rhetoric of "enlightened" human rights. Friedrich, as *Landesvater*, had declared in a grand public performance of legal reform and benevolent concern for the least of his subjects, that "the lowliest farmer, even more, the beggar, is as much a human being [*ein Mensch*] as is His Royal Majesty" and that "all people are equal before the law: whether a Prince accuses a farmer or the other way around, the Prince is equal to the farmer before the law."[44] We could hear Milton here, declaring "if not equal all, yet free, equally free; for orders and degrees / jar not with liberty, but well consist."[45] Friedrich's rhetoric was dramatic and effective: with it, he defended human dignity before the law. He also, however, defended the objectivity of the law itself, focusing his criticism upon unfair practitioners of the law. Accordingly, it was not the laws themselves—including those which regulated the social difference between prince and beggar, legitimate and illegitimate—which required reform, but rather those lawyers who manipulated the law and practiced injustice, who were identified by the protective and corrective eye of Friedrich's *Landesväterliche Intention* (literally, "land-fatherly intention") and duly punished. The law itself, especially when codified—Friedrich's great project—was accepted as a thing pure and good, a necessary instrument for social and moral order; it required only the fatherly hand of the king to root out the evil passions of the corrupt and guarantee equal justice for all.

What Friedrich offered in his declaration that all men were equal "before the law" was an equality that no doubt sounded to his subjects like the harbinger of a new and fairer world. In essence, however, his justice consisted of a universal application of already existing rules of ownership, transmission, public conduct, and the like to the claims of any person, regardless of the social power that individual did or did not wield. This justice did not by any means redress the various privileges and restrictions that those already-existing rules conveyed upon the various estates or challenge the fundamentally hierarchical, undemocratic structure of the family as a social model implicit in the corrective authority of his own *Landesväterliche Intention*. We are reminded here that the idea of equality was, as Jonathan Israel has argued, one of the "most divisive and potentially perplexing of all basic concepts" of the Enlightenment era.[46] Friedrich separated his own position revealingly: in a variation of the traditional doubling of a king's identity,[47] Friedrich mentions himself both as "his majesty" and as the "father of the realm." Accordingly, his self as a majesty or king is the legal equal to anyone else in the land, deserving no better or worse treatment before the law. As a father, however, he is outside and above that legal system, guiding and correcting its application. Thus, although the law makes all members of the familial state equal, the family metaphor identifies the superior authority of the father-king, who reigns above the law where he must direct its application in the interest of his children.

Friedrich's commitment to codifying the law (resulting, after his death, in the *Allgemeines Landrecht*[48]) might be understood, in part, as a mode of resistance successfully applied by absolutism to the escalating discussion of and demand for human rights that characterizes the eighteenth century. It was an attempt to answer the needs of both absolutism and enlightened human rights. The codification, in an attempt to unify the Prussian territories under a single state authority and to stabilize an increasingly participatory society, makes of the law something objective and universally accessible to all "members. . . without regard to estate, status, or sex [*Geschlecht*]"[49] and offers unbiased protection of the rights and responsibilities it contains. At the same time, this law strictly retains and thereby perpetuates the traditional genealogical social structures that maintain the flow of resources in each of the estates within paternal lines.

During the 1750's, Friedrich corresponded with Major Borcke, the man overseeing the education of his heir, the young Friedrich Wilhelm. In a letter of September 24, 1751, Friedrich insisted that two lessons above all others be instilled in his successor: one is that all humans are equal; the other, regarding the privilege of birth, that "birth is naught but a chimera, if it is not supported by merit."[50] Had Friedrich written simply, "birth is nothing but a chimera" and ended his sentence, he would have heralded a meritocracy that did not really develop in Germany until the twentieth century. The conditional clause that follows, however, stipulates that meretorious action is able to make one worthy of one's birth—but not to raise one above or beyond it. Here is another example of a working fiction: noble birth, with its intertwined claims upon nature and social order, marks a superiority that is real if made real, chimerical if not. A chimera, of course, is a monster with mismatched parts; the implication here is that while birth might produce only such an incoherent, disunified collection of attributes, an individual is able to make himself less monstrous, and thus worthy of the patrimony, through the pursuit of virtue.

Noble birth, in fact, is identified as a very real category that is detached from the individuals who are identified by it, a category that regulates social order and identity. If the attributes of social position, honor, and intrinsic value are not realized, then birth is nothing but a value-laden symbol, a *Hirngespenst* (in its German translation) which haunts the failure as it inhabits the successful. Genealogy is thus not a descriptive category that evolves with the individuals ascribed to particular familial lines; on the contrary, it is prescriptive, a role which determines the identity of the individual who inhabits it. Similarly, social position is not the possession or the ornament of a particular person, but a station through which generations of individual lives pass. To attain and maintain social identity, an individual must adapt himself to the appropriate narrative of genealogy into which he is born; he must become that which was signified by his socially classified birth.

Friedrich seems to intuit—and to avoid—the consequence of focusing public scrutiny upon the fissure between the reality and the metaphor of family-identified privilege. According to the logic of his genealogically structured state, Friedrich places the burden upon the individual to embody the social signature attributed to him; only if the individual conforms (willingly or not) to the normative fiction of the genealogical family and state can that order be preserved through the changing times.

A bastard, however, has no such narrative, no "birth" to live up to. His blood is untraceable, it is silent and illegible; he has no starting point to his story. This is fertile ground for fiction, as the plethora of eighteenth- and nineteenth-century novels of foundlings attest. In the real places and times of emergent-modern Europe, however, this bastard was—to the extent that such a thing is possible—excluded from the social narrative altogether.

2 Mothers Have Animals, Fathers Have Heirs

How do we understand the measure to which some notion of "blood" accounted for the tangled bonds—physical, legal, emotional—that were called familial at the end of the eighteenth century? What does it mean, precisely, that a bastard was not a rights-bearing citizen as long as birth was of consequence, as long as parentage determined a child's identity?[1] A connection was presumed between socially and legally sanctioned procedures of generation, and the societal value of the product. A bastard did not inherit social identity: this legal circumscription was designed to close out the illegitimates with some finality. Nevertheless, there was increasing attention paid to what children—including bastards—might inherit physiologically. This natural inheritance issued an epistemological challenge to the functioning legal fictions of transmission and the attention to physiological heredity accompanied its shift from the realm of folk knowledge to the domain of science, where it was subject to an arsenal of laws more regular—because "natural"—than those the state defended.

The civil exclusion of illegitimates, with its legal dismissal of the bloodlines that otherwise constituted the societal foundation, did create a problem for the self-understanding of eighteenth-century absolutist states that relied upon a genealogical "family" structure to define the relations between ruler, citizen, and the collective populace itself. The legal scourging of illegitimates, which kept them safely stigmatized outside of the law of the land, failed to accommodate their claim to universal (if only vaguely defined) human rights. How to negotiate the space between exclusion from the law and inclusion within a *Menschengeschlecht*? There is a legal adage that conveys the solution: "No mother carries a bastard."

MOTHERS AND BASTARDS

In his *Foundations of German Law in Adages* (1759), Eisenhart explains this particular saying, stressing that, while bastards have no claims whatsoever upon their fathers or upon the state, to their mothers they are rights-bearing children equal to her other children in their entitlement to her love and nurture, and entitled to her name and social position.[2] Specifically, Eisenhart points out that an illegitimate child is called bastard only with respect to its father, who does not legally recognize the person as his child, "whereas it must be regarded as the proper child of its mother, because she carried the child under her heart."[3] By this logic, fathers have either child-heirs or bastards; mothers, who cannot have heirs because they are by definition external to the patrilineal succession, always have children—children whom they carried under their hearts, and for whom there is a natural bond of love. A father has heirs or bastards, in whom he either recognizes or denies the reinvestment of his own economic resources, social power, and political and legal identity; a mother has children, in whom she recognizes individual human dignity and a right to life that is somehow contiguous to, but not a part of, the legal state. Jurists and philosophers engaging this subject invariably mention that the Roman solution to illegitimate (or simply inconvenient) children was to expose them and let them die.[4] As an alternative to this no longer acceptable practice, they constructed a symbolic solution that divided precisely along gender lines: the male realm (including father and heir) was separated from the constellation of the female realm (including mother and child), an opposition of categories which essentially isolated two genealogical lines constituting each individual, and which opposed economic and political identity to the essential dignity of human life, placing this dignity, the intrinsic value of every individual, squarely within the domain of the mother.

By virtue of the "natural" connection of love that binds parent to child, a mother provided for her illegitimate child a link to humanity that the law could not afford. This is the same natural bond that, in theory, is the original and continuing source of civic virtue, the foundation of the society which the law protects. A bastard has only those *Menschenrechte* or human rights provided by the "natural" attachment to the mother, rights that are contiguous to, but not incorporated within, the law of the state. A bastard's humanity, therefore, may share its source with civil society, but it does not extend into that society's patrilineal public realm. However strained this might seem to a reader today, it apparently satisfied an "enlightened" conscience. Although debates challenging the ethics of slavery and serfdom abounded, and although public articulations of women's rights were increasing, there was no public discussion whatever about the unfair discrimination against illegitimate children.

The inclination to leave bastards in the care of their mothers, best unseen and unheard, required as an unchallengeable presumption the "certainty" that all mothers love their children, legitimate or not. This is, of course, a fiction, albeit a deep and abiding one shared by most cultures. Nevertheless, a pragmatic examination of maternal practice across cultures and historical periods suggests that "mother love" exists and sustains and socializes a child when conditions are right, but that infanticide or abandonment thrives when a mother finds it expedient to be rid of an infant.[5]

This realistic position, however, could not gain currency amidst the flood of representations of the nature of motherly love produced during the eighteenth century.

How did this period account for those mothers who kill their children? It is important to note that criminal law prosecuted all instances of *Verwandtenmord*, or crimes against one's "own flesh and blood," significantly more severely than it did a "normal" murder.[6] Nevertheless, even in the context of *Verwandtenmord*, infanticide—defined as a crime committed specifically by a mother against her newborn—was isolated as particularly horrifying in its assault against the natural inclination to nurture one's young, and thus was punished with particular severity. The notion that infanticide was "inhuman," an act that could not take place within the bounds of natural human behavior, was asserted repeatedly during this period of frequent occurrence. According to a Frankfurt policy conclusion of 1695, infanticide was identified as a crime which "absolutely contradicts nature itself, and the love implanted in all parents, including even the irrational animals"; a Nürnberg mandate of 1702 declared that infanticides in their monstrosity exceeded "even the most grisly, wild, beast-nature... which dedicates itself to nourishing and protecting the young it brings into the world."[7] Infanticide was one of the most frequent (and frequently prosecuted) crimes during the mid-century; in an influential 1781 essay on the topic, Johann Heinrich Pestalozzi wrote dramatically:

> Infanticide!—Do I dream, am I awake? Is it possible, such a deed? Does it occur? Does this nameless crime—no, not nameless, but named, this crime put to words—does it occur?... Hide your face, Century! Bow down low, Europe! The answer resounds from the seat of judgement: into the thousands are my children struck down by the hand of those who bore them.[8]

Whether the numbers of infanticides were actually increasing, or whether the perceived escalation was due to increasing vigilance on the part of official legal institutions cannot be ascertained. Although infanticide was always a crime and a concern of the church, Richard van Dülmen has noted that it only entered the secular legal jurisdiction in the sixteenth century, which he ascribes to "puritanical morality, which in the late sixteenth century began to permeate all levels of society; it not only resulted in harsher punishments and an increase in executions, but also influenced the number of child-murders."[9] It is not insignificant that this corresponded with the shifting focus upon marriage, which, during the Reformation, was loosed from the church's jurisdiction and became a matter of practical ethics and secular legislation.[10] Infanticide certainly entered the secular jurisdiction under the developing authority of the regional princes, the *Landesfürsten* during the seventeenth century, who increasingly assumed responsibility for maintaining not only the physical but also the moral well-being of those

28 *Heredity, Race, and the Birth of the Modern*

within their territory. This took the institutional form of a *Gute Polizey* directing and developing the *Gemeines Besten* (literally, the "common best") and the *Gemeines Nutzen* (literally, "the common use").[11] These institutional policing forces, especially in Prussia and Austria, developed as powerful control systems over the moral constitution of their residents.

In response to the prevalence of infanticide, Friedrich II felt compelled to pass an edict in 1765 specifically criminalizing not only its most overt form, but also those hidden births or even hidden pregnancies which could be interpreted as signs of an intent to commit murder.[12] He was neither the first nor the last to do so: there existed legislation in Nürnberg as early as 1598 requiring announcements of a pregnancy and financially rewarding denunciations of any woman trying to hide her condition;[13] and in the 1780's, Weimar extended its laws to severely punish the family and acquaintances of a pregnant woman without regard to social standing who failed to report her condition either to a city or to a religious official.[14]

The vast literature produced in response to the infanticide phenomenon varied in tone as in genre, but it uniformly reveals a double task. On the one hand, writers attempted to explain in rational terms the social conditions and psychological motives that propelled the crime, making of the woman a victim of circumstance and judgment-impairing despair; on the other, they emphasized the unnatural and inhuman quality of the deed which, in Pestalozzi's words, "shocks humanity!"[15] From a reasonable and critical position, writers increasingly advocated the identification and amelioration of social conditions that drove women to kill an infant. Encapsulated within his discussion of the death penalty, Kant famously offered perhaps the most dispassionate explanation for infanticide. Arguing that a woman will suffer irreparable damage to her honor, potential livelihood, and marriage prospects if an illegitimate birth is discovered, he identified her crime as one of self-preservation.[16] Alongside the reasoned debates, however, were—with perhaps the sole exception of Kant—insistent descriptions of the women's behavior as unnatural and inhuman.

One of the essay contests often cited in conjunction with studies of eighteenth-century infanticide literature, publicized in 1780 in the journal *Rheinische Beiträge zur Gelehrsamkeit* [Rheinish Contributions to Knowledge] challenged its readers to offer solutions to the following question: "What are the best possible methods to redress infanticide, without permitting fornication?"[17] The wording of the question implies that by removing the severe penalties for extramarital sex, infanticide would disappear; the challenge, therefore, is how to do so without seeming to encourage or tolerate lascivious behavior. The responses identified the stigma of bearing a bastard as the real cause of infanticide,[18] and this troublesome cause-effect relation—especially during a period that regarded legal reform with great optimism as a mechanism of social progress—was something that could be fixed. Pestalozzi reinforced this perspective, arguing outright that if the fear of punishment for fornication (made public by the birth of an illegitimate child) were removed, infanticide would disappear. Stressing that only the delirium of physical and mental anguish could prompt a "girl" [*Mädchen*] to kill her child, he insists, "A human being does not kill his flesh and blood when sane; and a girl, in her right mind, does not raise her hand against her child, and does not strangle her newborn until he is pale."[19] Since the crime was committed in a state of delirium and not in a state of rational consciousness, the threat of punishment for infanticide would never suffice to prevent the crime: "Without quiet madness, without inner, despairing rage, a girl does not strangle her child; and no one who is mad and despairing fears the sword."

This argument that, in killing their children, women acted somehow outside of themselves, that they had crossed a line and exited the condition of humanity to enter into a bestial insanity, was suggested also by Franz Heinrich Birnstiel. Writing in 1781 to assure his reader of the lack of physical and mental control experienced by such a woman, he described the "war between nature and honor" that arises in an unmarried mother. Citing the hopeless "battle of her will against blind and unacknowledged desires" and the "unrelenting visions" of the consequences she will face, the "natural bonds" that bind mother to child are dissolved, and she is literally "beside herself." The self that is mother is the self from which this poor woman is wrenched by terror. Because she is possessed by this terror, and thus unable to think clearly, her freedom to determine her actions is compromised. "Only in a state of clear thinking [*in dem Zustand deutlicher Vorstellungen*] do we have freedom of choice," he concludes.[20]

The implication that women only kill their infant children when deranged by fear and shame was given additional expression by the plethora of dramas and poems produced during the period—one need think only of Gretchen in Goethe's *Faust*, Evchen in Wagner's *Die Kindermörderin* (The Child-Murderess) Bürger's poem "*Des Pfarrers Tochter*" (The Pastor's Daughter), and the like.[21] These literary representations expand upon the story-structure found in legal summaries and essays, which relate the fate of a single mother, a good girl who is seduced and abandoned by a (single or married) man from a privileged class, and driven to murder her illegitimate child in a frenzy of despair.[22] The story is uniformly told by a male writer,[23] who—speaking from his position within the law—creates sympathy for the plight of the mother by explaining the conditions that drove her to her ghastly and unnatural act. Scholarly investigation of this topos has tended to accept the account of infanticide these works offer. While noting the discrepancies between the generally sentimental and middle-class dramas and the harsh realities of the poor and uneducated women whose cases came before the courts and the public,[24] historians have identified the sympathetic treatment (in dramas or in essays) of the unmarried mother's crime as both a call for social reform and a sign of the "enlightened" progress of a legal system (and a popular culture) that was beginning to consider the motives and the context of criminal behavior.[25]

Although one can understand the literary outpouring on the subject of infanticide in a number of ways, the concerted attempt not only to end infanticide, but also to explain it uniformly as something profoundly unnatural that could occur only under particular—and therefore remediable—circumstances, is indicative of the deeper issues that resonated alongside the crime. Friedrich II, in his speech of 1750 before the Academy entitled "Concerning the justifications for establishing or abolishing laws" (*Über die Gründe, Gesetze einzuführen oder abzuschaffen*), condemns the crimes of abortion and infanticide, calling the maternal perpetrators thereof "Medeas. . . brutal toward themselves and deaf to the voices of their own blood, who strangle the next generation."[26] At the same time, he de-fangs these monsters who are deaf to the voice of their own blood by describing them as the direct product of harsh conditions that must be ameliorated: namely, conditions in which mothers find themselves "required to choose between the loss of their own honor and the loss of their unfortunate offspring."[27] The movement, however, between an unwed mother afraid of the possible loss of "*Ehre*," and her purported transmogrification into a grisly Medea strangling the next generation, is excessive and willful—so much so, that a reader must ask from whence the will to represent in such a way might come.

With this question in mind, one may understand the expressions of humane sympathy for the victimized single mothers, as well as the dramatic portrayals of their madness and remorse, as a calming cover for the driving anxiety concerning the possible reality of a Medea: the fear that maternal love, believed to be a natural absolute and the origin of all social bonds, may in fact be conditional, equivocal, even a wistful myth.[28] It seems preferable to believe that *Mädchen* can turn into monsters rather than to accept monstrous behavior—at least, this particular kind—as potentially human. Such a preference is understandable especially for a culture that has accepted its own genealogical myth of origins and order: infanticide must be contrary to human nature, or it proves altogether too disruptive to the genealogical justifications for the transmission of legal and social identities through generations over time. The surface of eighteenth-century representations, despite differences between the focus of essays devoted to social reform and dramas engaged in their own social and aesthetic programs, is united in its portrayal of infanticide as contrary to human nature. By extension, then, it preserves the myth of mother-love as real, natural, and necessary. Parental love is a requisite for the complex moral and social order of the genealogical state modeled upon the immutable reality of familial bonds and hierarchies. If the father's investment is for any reason excised from the equation, there remains only the mother's blood and the love that flows in her veins to uphold the myth.

PROOFS OF PATERNITY

Mothers are resolutely understood to feel a necessary bond to their children, but this bond, allegedly stronger than and prior to all others, exploited by the law to justify an unmarried mother's responsibility for her disenfranchised child, may also directly threaten the patrilineal genealogical order of a particular family in a familial state. In a society that requires the regulation of family lines and the prevention of bastardy, a father must know that his children are his own. The problem, of course, is that fathers can never know this for sure; it is mothers who are presumed to possess the knowledge of the paternity of their children. The infanticide debates focused exclusively upon the unmarried woman, who often refused to disclose the name of the father of her child. Although courts did try to compel her to identify the man who was also guilty of fornication, the frequent failure to locate a father amounted to little more than a note in the file. As far back as Rome, people had repeated the adage, "*Mater certa, pater semper incertus*" (literally, "mother certain, father always uncertain"). In the case of unmarried mothers in eighteenth-century Germany, many a man was happy enough that this was the case.

There was another scenario, however, in which maternal certainty and paternal doubt was not convenient, one in which maternal certainty conferred a power upon the mother of a child that could potentially undermine patrilineal authority altogether. This scenario involved the uncertainty of paternity within a marriage. The issue of female fidelity lies at the heart of all of theories of the familial state. Justi was most explicit about this when he argued that fathers have to be certain of their children in order to work for and care for them. Philosophers, theologians and jurists had unified their efforts to "compel" female fidelity since the sixteenth century, from Luther's sermons on wifely obedience to the *Tugendideale* of the seventeenth-century *Hausväterliteratur,* and from the German juridical invention of the *ius mariti* to the attempts by Pufendorf and the later Thomasius to justify female fidelity in natural law.[29] As "nature" would have it, women were granted their own domain, namely, the nurturing of all their children. The genealogical line from father to heir, however, was no place for a mother—that is, as long as her generative role was both predictable and reliable. If such be the case, if she might act out of turn, then her power in the equation would be brought starkly to the foreground and the husband and father would be subject to the word of the mother that the child she bears is his.

Howsoever the legislating forces tried to ascertain the natural order of "wifely virtue" (and to seek out and punish those guilty of extramarital sex), the records of legal debate on how to handle paternity disputes reveal the not uncommon discord between rhetorical conviction and practical reality. Fears that women know, but may lie, creep into legal discussions. It is hardly surprising that there are no outright admissions of the control women have over family lines by virtue of their exclusive knowledge of paternity; such power would then be all too real. But an ever-present anxiety is legible in several sections of the *Allgemeines Landrecht (ALR)*. One example may be found in the conditions for a second marriage for widows and divorced women (that is, women with legally recognized sexual experience). These articles are solely concerned with ensuring that there are no children born to uncertain paternity and they identify mothers as the source of uncertainty requiring legal control in the form of physical policing: "Widows and divorced women who know they are pregnant from the prior marriage or are rumored to be so must await delivery before they can enter into a new marriage."[30] Since a woman might not confess to a pregnancy by a former marriage, rumor is an equally credible basis for legally denying her permission to marry again. Furthermore, only the physical delivery of a child marks the release of the physical bond not only between mother and child, but also between mother and sexual partner/potential father, and frees her to enter into a new relationship.

Even a widow or divorced woman not suspected of pregnancy still must wait a minimum of nine months before remarrying—implicitly to make sure she is not trying to disguise a prior pregnancy and pass it off onto her new and unsuspecting husband.[31] A torturously worded addendum stipulates what will be done in the rare case of uncertain paternity (that is, uncertain to the public or to the new husband) that occurs despite these precautions:

> If a widow becomes pregnant after the death of her husband and requests permission to marry the putative father of the child before the end of the nine-month post-mortem period, permission should be granted her, but only in so far as the child's legal rights remain suspended in case that the timing of the birth legally confirms the suspicion that the child might have been conceived during the marriage now ended in death; in which case it remains the responsibility of the responsible authorities to make a determination in the best interest of the child.[32]

The problems here are manifold: any pretense of a clear and certain resolution of the paternity problem is compromised by the string of relative clauses, by the "presumed" status of the father, by the indeterminate but nonetheless legally grounded conjecture, all of which must be distilled to reach a (subjectively determined) beneficial determination—a choice rather than the truth. In short, the paragraph announces that legal representatives have the authority (despite uncertainties) to dismiss the testimony of a woman whose honesty—and perhaps knowledge—are in doubt. A final decision is made, not with regard to any proof of the reality of the line, but according to the court's version of the best interest of the child. Prior to the *ALR*, as Wilhelm Gottfried Ploucquet described in 1779, a mother's word assigned the paternity of her child in such an indeterminable case, although it was admitted only when all other methods of proof had failed.[33] Even as a last resort, her verdict was officially supplanted by the 1794 legal code.

Actual legislation signals the (male) anxiety of pregnancies women falsely passed off onto their husbands, and thus into male lines, through a form of denial: rather than addressing the possibility that mothers control the narrative fictions of biological lines, the *ALR* replaces both the maternal voice and the bloodline with legal (patrilineal) control of the contractual line. Thus, when a married man denies that he is the father of his wife's child, he bears a heavy burden of proof to overcome the presumption of legitimacy. The mother, however, is not able to testify at all in such cases, either for or against.[34] The marriage contract itself serves as her testimony for the child's legitimacy. No hearing is granted, no legal language is available for a wife who might claim that her child's father is not her husband.

Legal commentaries are even more forthcoming in their admission that, while the preservation of familial lineage is indisputably necessary for social coherence, the biological reality of that line is of less consequence than the legal recognition of its integrity. Fischer inadvertently acknowledged this when he recorded, as a source of the legal family, not signs of a natural emotional bond but rather a historic social ritual: he recounted an ancient procedure the Romans practiced in which a father performed a formal *Aufhebung* of a baby, identifying the child as his own and thereby as belonging both to his line of descent [*Erbfolge*] and to the communal *Sammteigenschaft* (subsisting of God's world, the community's morals, and accepted customs).[35] Eisenhart, another pragmatist content with the mechanisms that make society work, refers to the anxiety over uncertain paternity with some cynical amusement, citing as legal tender the saying: "The mother says it, the father believes it, a fool pauses to doubt."[36] Fatherhood, he grants, can never be proven; that being the case, it is better for children as well as for society that people belong to legitimate families, and so the law identifies an apparent father—the husband of the mother—as the legal father and rests content.[37] There is no talk here of the value or the "reality" of biological connections at odds with legal relation—the function of the law is to simplify a complicated matter by determining fatherhood in the interest of the child and general social order. Children need parents, the most likely father will do, and only when its family has been identified does the child acquire an identity in the world. Eisenhart notes:

> It is not within the power of a son to prove who his father is. The laws have therefore determined that the man who appears to be the father of a child based upon a marriage bond shall be assumed to be the true father. The laws adhere only to the external and leave the invisible secrets of nature to Him alone who sees into all that is hidden and from whose eyes nothing remains hidden. [38]

If a mother says her child is legitimate, so be it; and if the legal truth contains a natural untruth—the moral consequences may be peaceably left to God. The biological truth of paternity, an "invisible secret of nature," is not a matter for legal concern; rather, it is the socially agreed-upon construction of the family line that must be supported. This is achieved through the identification of a child by something external, an outward appearance or *Schein* which is the product of a public marriage contract and the equally public acknowledgement of parenthood by mother and father. This outward, public identity of a child marks the limit of political concern. The implicit complement, a different or supplemental identity which is hidden, a secret, visible [*scheinbar*] only to God, is of no legal or political concern precisely because it is not visible to the public eye. As illustrated further in declarations by Kant and Friedrich Wilhelm II cited above, the legal system seems to reject what cannot be known and thereby controlled with some certainty, condemning the hidden, the *eingeschlichen*, the "*verbotene Waren.*" Eisenhart is explicit about the social/political investment in the identity of a child: "Children are not born only to their fathers, but also to the community [*"dem gemeinen Wesen"*]; from parents, they receive their property, but the social status of their person belongs more to the community than to the parents."[39] Thus two authorities govern the identity of a child: the father, who provides property, and the community, which provides social position.[40] Left out of this equation, of course, is the mother, whose testimony to the legitimacy of her child is the precondition for both paternal and civic engagement.

Eisenhart's justification for the law is pragmatic in the face of much dishonesty [*Betriegereyen*] which at times renders even a mother's knowledge questionable.[41] It seems that he is forced to shrug and say that, given our imperfect knowledge, all we can do is trust the mother to identify the family, even though we know she might be lying or in some cases, mistaken.[42] The biological "truth" of the matter is, as far as men are concerned, of importance only to a fool: what must be addressed is the profound need by legal social order for an acceptable construction of lineal identity. It does not matter whether or not we know, as long as we are able to make laws circumscribing that which must be controlled. From this perspective, the construction of legitimacy, upon which so much rests, is merely the product of an ordering principle; it is an artifice, a juridical fiction.

LAW AT THE TABLE OF SCIENCE: SEPARATING THE HEIRS FROM THE ANIMALS

A visible rift emerged in late eighteenth-century arguments concerning the importance of the "reality" of the bloodline, though its symbolic function was undisputed and its authority unchallenged. Many jurists argued along the practical lines Eisenhart suggested, ignoring the epistemological instability and accepting the authority of a legal artifice; others rejected any authority not grounded in "nature" itself, and rallied the medical community to try to redress the indeterminacy of the biological line, and to prove the reality of the blood-relationship upon which the law rested. This is the strain of argument that ultimately prevailed. By the nineteenth century, many prominent jurists no longer accepted the symbolic quality of the "bloodlines" they defended, but declared, like Johann Christian Majer, that there is "nothing more natural than that the greater degree of common blood and the lesser degree of mixture with foreign [*fremden*] blood should take precedence in issues of succession over the lesser degree of common blood and the greater amount of mixture with foreign blood."[43] Here the common blood—the *Gemeinschaft des Blutes*, literally the "community of blood"—is accepted as a reality that orders the law: it is the regulation of natural kind. This increasing attention to the reality of the bloodline was in part encouraged by research into generation and heredity by life-scientists, and was the use to which another branch of state legislation, the *Medizinische Polizey*, put their findings.[44]

Johann Peter Frank, in his *System einer vollständigen medicinischen Policey*, defined the medical police as responsible for "general promotion of health and the requisite hygienic order."[45] Explicitly concerned with ordering and determining the lines of generation that would be most beneficial to the state, the medical police attended in part to regulations concerning marriage and the welfare of small children. Hotly contested research into heritable disease (including diseases of madness and criminality) was of considerable significance to someone like Frank, who stated his agenda clearly in the first sentence of his book: the purpose of a medical police is the security of the familial state, and state security implies the active promotion and maintenance of conditions promoting the prospering of healthy generations in communities and states: "The focus of the medical police is, insofar as it is possible, to render nature and her powers effective, and to use them such that one can obtain from each human couple, under supervision by good laws, the best, healthiest, and most resilient of fruits."[46] Frank worked tirelessly to defend the medical reality of heritable diseases, or *Familienkrankheiten*, and to place their control at the top of the imperial political agenda. To substantiate his position, Frank provided an eight-page arsenal of answers to medical challenges that all facilitate his conclusion: namely, given the reality of heritable diseases (both physical and spiritual) which have no cure other than being gradually bred out of the population, the state should assume greater authority in regulating human propagation for the greater political good.[47]

Efforts such as these to control the quality of the genealogical state through the attentive monitoring of reproduction implied optimistically that such monitoring was possible, and that medical *Semiotik*, the science of reading the body, was sufficiently evolved not only to read, but also to interpret and classify individuals in order to determine their optimal relations with one another.[48] Similarly, this period saw a reinvigorated effort to employ this semiotic science on the part of forensic medicine [*gerichtliche Arzneiwissenschaft*] to determine the precise biological connection between mother, father, and child. Juristic medicine, described by Johann Peter Frank as that science which addresses the "fundamental answers to legal questions about natural occurences," was increasingly recruited to synthesize the continual advances (and regressions) in the emerging life sciences pertaining to embryology, fetal development, and pregnancy, in great part to testify in courts of law in cases of infanticide.[49] But *Semiotik* also played a significant role in the increasing attempts to assert legal control (via medical "proof") over the reality of the paternal bloodline. Already in 1751, Albrecht von Haller began his lectures on the uses and limits of forensic medicine for disputations concerning the status of a first-born child, the resemblance of children to their parents and to each other, as well as on assessing virginity and pregnancy; on determining the first moment of life; and on legal birth, among other things—all of which were directly related to questions of the medical/ biological legibility of a family line.[50] By 1779, Ploucquet was able to present a collection of medical "facts" in his [On the Physical Requirements for the Legal Capacity of Children to Inherit] *Ueber die physische Erfordernisse der Erbfähigkeit der Kinder* specifically for the use of jurists in settling inheritance and paternity disputes.

In his introduction, Ploucquet acknowledged that a child's legal capacity to inherit property [*Erbfähigkeit*] depended upon certain knowledge of paternity, and he attested to its paramount importance for the law, declaring that "fortunes, honor, power, even princely crowns depend upon it alone, and the importance of this legal question should not be underestimated."[51] Ruefully, Ploucquet acknowledged that positive proof of a child's paternity "is never possible except for those instances, in which a woman *could* not have come into contact with an other man."[52] If one could not isolate the mother from the first sexual contact until delivery, however, then science and the law would combine resources to provide sufficient presumptive evidence. Since the law was inclined to recognize the legitimacy of a child born to a married woman unless there were certain proofs against it, he identified the purpose of his book to be the compilation of such proofs for use by men disputing paternity claims, along with the strengths and limits of those proofs before the law. It is immediately apparent that such a book, resigned rather than hostile in tone, was written for the exclusive use of men, to protect male control of their lines; it in no way pretended to address the concerns, rights, or claims of women.

After treating the two physiological arguments available to disprove paternity, namely the proof of impotence (the discussion of which includes detailed descriptions of semen quality, penis shape, strength of erection, and the impact of the imagination upon the ability to have an erection or to ejaculate), and the timing of a birth (determining the age of an infant, the time of its birth, the use of statistics to measure boundaries between a child who is fully developed and one who is premature), Ploucquet turns the focus to negative proofs, or the detection of numerous possible female deceptions. He provides a sequence of elaborate accounts of such deceptions, elucidating their psychological motivations, their probable strategies, and the ways by which jurists can detect them. In addition to false claims of premature birth (if a woman was actually pregnant before she ought to have been) or of late birth (if she claimed to have conceived earlier than she did) in order to prevent the subsequent detection of adultery, Ploucquet identifies as problematic the "foisting off of a child, when the woman did not actually give birth"[53] for which he enumerates the predictable physical signs of having delivered. He follows a description of invented [*erdichtete*] conception with a discussion of the signs of pregnancy, how they may be falsified and how they may be detected.[54] There is also the problem of women switching infants at birth which is explained thus: "Where an actual birth has occurred, but the child was either stillborn, or died just after birth, or was a monstrosity or a freak or something else to that end, or when the child was a daughter when a son was needed for the line of succession, in these circumstances a woman might think about switching."[55] While a switched child can be difficult to detect, the bastard product of mixed races fortunately can, in many cases according to Ploucquet, be determined by the child's resemblance to the father:

> Nonetheless there are cases in which the resemblance to a different father uncovers the mother's adultery and thus the illegitimacy of the child, particularly when people of different races come together, as when a European woman who could have been with Moors, Negroes, Mongols, Americans, bears a child who differs so significantly from expectation in the color of the entire body, or even a single body part (there are examples of bastards springing from a Moor and a White who had only black genitals) or who so differs in the formation of the face that one must conclude that the European father is not the true father, even though the woman tries to attribute the phenomena to the workings of her imagination.[56]

Resemblance to its parents is important for more than just a child's claim to legitimacy; its very status as a human being hangs in the balance. "It is in accordance with the nature of things that the so-called bodily heirs [*Leibes Erben*] only earn this name, and that they are only thus able to inherit property, when parents see themselves quasi reborn in the child."[57] Extending the juxtaposition of one's legitimacy and one's capacity to inherit property with one's inclusion within the category of Menschheit itself, Ploucquet continues: "The heir must therefore resemble the parents in significant characteristics, and must be a true human being [*ein wahrer Mensch seyn*]."[58] The very condition of humanity is a visible sign (more particularly, a similarity, a partial reproduction of the parental corporeal signals) passed bodily from parent to child and detectable by science. The only troubling complication that might arise is the occurrence of miscegenation, the "unnatural mixing" of a woman and an animal: "Whenever a human body is born with a true animal head, the first question raised is whether it might not have resulted from unnatural mixing with an animal, like a dog, etc."[59] The belief in such unions was waning, perhaps, but was far from eradicated. Voltaire, in an essay of 1765 entitled, "Of the Different Races of Men," wrote in all seriousness of the possibility of monkeys enslaving girls in "hot countries." He also cites the Bible as a source of anthropological history, noting:

> It is forbidden in Leviticus, chapter eighteen to commit abominations with he and she-goats. These copulations must then have been common, and till such time as we are better informed, it is to be presumed that a monstrous species must have arisen from these abominable amours; but if such did exist, they could have no influence over human kind; and like the mules, who do not engender, they could not interrupt the course of nature in the other races."[60]

The anxiety here about the permeability of the human/animal barrier is kept at bay by the significant comparison with mules, the common example of a bastard animal—offspring of two distinct species, the horse and the donkey—who by definition is sterile and presents no threat to the genealogical continuity of established kinds.

The product of a union between a man and an animal is considered to be of no consequence, since there should be no danger of its passing into the human community. Ploucquet writes, "We shall overlook here those human births, which are brought into the world by dumb [*unvernünftigen*] female animals, and are presumed to have been conceived by men; for there is no question regarding the legal capacity to inherit in these cases."[61] Because the human community accepts only those animals born to human mothers, however, the paternity must be monitored to protect against not only the corruption of a family line, but the human species. Thus careful medical attention must be paid to all children "who are born of women, yet who resemble dumb animals in the formation of significant parts, particularly the shape of the head, such that they awaken suspicion that their father was not human."[62] Londa Schiebinger has observed that, in eighteenth-century rumors of hybrid matings, "it is invariably the male ape who forced himself on the human female. To my knowledge there was not one account in this period of a female ape taking a man or even of intercourse between a female ape and a male human."[63] Ploucquet's text offers a counter-example, the concern of jurists that must consider all possibilities because of the primacy of the birth moment for legitimacy purposes. A hybrid or *Mischling* sired by a man and emerging from an ape or a sheep was not horrifying, although it might well be an object of curiosity for science and the fairgrounds. Such a creature's actual birth from the body of an animal was sufficient evidence that, whatever the creature might be, it was not fully human and therefore was not *erbfähig*—no offspring of a ewe would ever threaten a genealogical line. However, a woman who bore a child sired by an animal might well lie about its paternity and try to pass it onto her husband as his heir. Ploucquet writes circumspectly, "it does not seem impossible that the Orang Outan could propagate with a human woman, a theory supported by the history written by Bauhin. Others also speak of some impregnated by dogs. This, however, requires more evidence."[64] Ploucquet reasserts yet again that the fundamentally suspect nature of a woman with her capacity for deception must be monitored and her progeny examined to prevent her from smuggling contraband, bastard goods (to borrow Kant's term) into the family.

Interestingly, both Kant and Ploucquet fail to take full advantage of the subject term, "bastard," neglecting the fact that the term also served as a scientific label marking the progeny of two species, a *Mischling* or mixed breed, a hybrid which by definition cannot reproduce.[65] Thus the monstrous progeny Ploucquet describes above is not only legally abject as a "bastard," but it is by scientific definition a "bastard," marking a critical intersection between the legal and the scientific terms, both of which involve the regulation of a system of kinds: a distinction is made—and termed 'bastard'—to mark individuals whose genesis is spurious and who are perceived therefore as potential contaminates of the parent kinds or classes, be they scientifically identified 'natural' taxa or social castes. A bastard—be it a plant, a child, an animal, or even an idea—is, by definition, that which represents, by virtue of its own generation, a threat to the purity or integrity of a system of kinds, natural or cultural.

From a man must come an heir; but from a mother's body comes an animal, whose bodily signs must be read by medical semiotic science to ensure that it is the correct animal. This process of deciphering the physiological code is necessary to translate the animal-child (the mother's issue) into a *Mensch* and an heir (the father's issue), or in Aristotelian terms, it identifies the animal as civilized, the *zoon politicon* existing both as an individual and as a member of the civic order. This division of a child into animal or heir, identified with the mother or the father, replicates in the language and in the authority of natural science the division made by the law, according to which a mother is bound by "natural" love to all creatures "carried beneath her heart," and a father responds to each such creature insofar as he either acknowledges an heir or rejects a bastard.

Ploucquet represents the united forces of law and science at the end of the eighteenth century, determined—in the interest of the integrity of the genealogies comprising the state—to detect and expose the lies women must certainly tell about the paternity (that is, the identity) of their children. This can be read as a fear of female control over the constitution of the family, presented as a female disruption of its integrity. Rather than accepting a female knowledge (and the power that accompanies such knowledge) and rather than granting the mother a place within the symbolic, genealogically constructed familial state, law and science rally to police the social order and the biological truth behind its familial structure.

Characteristic of a dawning age of positivism, the law learned to distrust the power of the symbolic order upon which it rested, summoning science instead to provide material proofs that would ground its metaphors and make facts of its fictions.

The seventeenth and eighteenth centuries had sought to rationalize social organization through an historical/psychological elevation of the "family" as a natural model. As an organizing fiction, patrilineal genealogy for centuries had wielded great power. The nineteenth century would assert the reality of the "family" in hereditary biology, in a truth of the blood. Although the Western politics of absolutism and its absolutely undemocratic familial hierarchy have given way in the twenty-first century to a political rhetoric of equal opportunity, individual autonomy, and the "self-made" man or woman, the ongoing investment, both economic and imaginative, in the semiotic science which we now call genetics (based upon a "code-script") is indicative of a deep lingering desire to identify who we are based on the identity of those from whom we come. Where this impulse will lead in our century is a story yet to be written. In the late eighteenth century, however, the increasing investment of law and medical science in gathering proofs of the cause and effect of human generation revolved around the absent center of society, the maternal generatrix, simultaneously focusing upon and denying her significance.

Ploucquet's book, representative of legal and medical discourses at this time of transition, contains eruptions of anxious misogyny which attest, despite themselves, to the power of a woman to disrupt and deflect that apparent line from father to child; they attest further to the possibility that patrilineal genealogy might well be a fiction. These possibilities were not included, however, in the enthusiastic reception of Ploucquet's work. On the contrary, the legal and scientific communities at the end of the eighteenth century redoubled their efforts to eradicate such doubts through the assertion of the priority of matter over idea, through an evolving set of "proofs" of the reality—and the legibility—of the bloodline.

3 Questions of Kind
The Human Species

It is well and good to talk about heredity in terms of power networks, anxious exclusions, societal niches, and metaphors; however—and here each of us bears physical witness—heredity is also real. We humans reproduce. Genetic science—or so goes the argument—proves that centuries of (howsoever muddled) belief in transmission intuited the right path. Is it not vital to acknowledge a reality of heredity that is not a power structure or a metaphor?

Certainly. But a problem immediately arises: as soon as the physical reality of biological transmission is identified and named as fact, its dissemination as knowledge returns us almost immediately to a confrontation with the metaphorically charged language of family and its attendant expectations of altruism. It seems that discussions of generation—whether in the eighteenth century or today—cannot help but engage also a problem of generating the good. Early scientific inquiry into the real particulars of physical heredity produced writing that relied upon and impacted available linguistic formulations, metaphors, and social structures in the interpretation of data and the creation of new knowledge. We might here focus upon one scientific problem, one that Georges Canguilhem rightly credits with dominating the history of natural history: that of species. The eighteenth century produced (albeit amidst fevered debate) a new physiological and historical understanding of species, one that is still largely operative today. According to what is now identified as the "biological species concept," a species comprises a set of organisms actually or potentially capable of reproducing fertile offspring.[1] Human kind—or kinds, depending on one's position with regard to mono- vs. polygenism—was, at the time in question, ascribed a physiological reality with a genealogical history. This reality was granted an ontological status that provided explanation for those ideas and practices of social and ethical organization modeled on an ideal of familial relations. In simple terms: With the species concept, the metaphorical relationship between the family and the state suddenly appeared to change, to have been one of literal extension all along. Subsequently, the theorizing of the species both permitted and required the re-thinking—the materialization—of the vaguer notions of "human kind," the "brotherhood of man," and other such potent formulations.

This language provides the foundation for emerging scientific definitions of the human species and its constituent races. The emergent sciences of man (nominally anthropology, but including embryology, physiology, and comparative anatomy) and the changes in "knowledge" that they issued had a profound effect upon the vocabulary and conceptualization of community, in large part because of reliance upon the language of genealogy. Heredity provided the metaphors, the analogies, and the objects for a scientific discourse on genealogy and its significance. As I will show, however, the language of science could not contain all that genealogy—with seeming inevitability—would signify.

AN INITIAL EXCURSUS

Denis Diderot's criticism of the Paris Salon of 1767 includes an imaginary walk through various settings depicted in Joseph Vernet's landscape paintings. One scene in particular provokes a tangential discussion about the meaning of virtue and the relativity of customs. Diderot asks rhetorically why "the most general, the most revered, the most widely used words— law, taste, beauty, goodness, truth, custom, morals, vice, virtue, instinct, mind, matter, grace, beauty, ugliness—though uttered so frequently, are so little understood, so variously defined?" There is irony in the question, in the baroque excess of his list, and in the repetition of "beauty" at its end, suggesting that even for the questioner, such terms are uncertain, multiple, even distracting in their numbers. The terms, according to Diderot, are at once general and fragmented, universal and particularized. He continues to explore the relationship between the general and the particular, taking as a point of departure Pope's identification of the "proper study of Mankind":

> In undertaking such an inquiry, what should be the first object of study? Myself. What am I? What is a man? ... An animal? [....] How is one to formulate precise notions of good and evil, of beauty and ugliness, of goodness and wickedness, of truth and falsehood, without a preliminary notion of Man? ... —and if Man cannot be defined? ... —Then all is lost. How many philosophers, having failed to make these simple observations, have prescribed ethical teachings suitable for wolves to Man, which is as stupid as prescribing human ethics to wolves! ... Every being inclines towards its own happiness, and the happiness of each being differs from that of every other. A given ethical code is applicable only within the boundaries of a given species.—What is a species? ... —A multitude of individuals organized in the same way ... —So organization provides the basis for ethics? ... —I believe so ... —So Polyphemus, whose organization had almost nothing in

common with that of Ulysses' companions, did not act any more atrociously by eating Ulysses' companions than they did by eating a hare or a rabbit? . . . —And what about kings, and God, who are the only ones of their kind?[2]

All in all, this text is playful and provocative, and it leaves the reader with a series of unanswered questions that, despite their levity of tone, in turn allude to deeper concerns with the interconnections between the biological, social, and discursive components of human existence. A chain of associations links the facts of organization (of humans as a species) to ethics and thence to the definition of abstract ethical and aesthetic ideas. The presupposition that commonly shared humanity involved both physiological and ethical components is an old one: the Stoics were perhaps the most concerned with arguing that the very fact of being human should elicit a species loyalty in each individual sufficient to require that each individual actively promote the good of his fellow man. This belief is the foundation for a classical ideal of cosmopolitanism embraced by the European Enlightenment. But a fundamental difference in the reasoning process is evident if we look to one of the Roman thinkers most influential to eighteenth-century cosmopolitanism. Marcus Aurelius, in musing upon the consequences of common humanity, writes: "If reason is common, so too is law; and if this is common, then we are fellow citizens. If this is so, we share in a kind of organized polity. And if that is so, the world is as it were a city state."[3] Even as Marcus constructs a logical sequence to join a common species-nature to cultural organization, it is important to note that the fundamental species-nature he admits is that of reason. Humans are a distinct species for the Stoics precisely because they have the capacity for rational thought. The endurance of this legacy is evident in the taxonomic designation for modern man: we belong to genus *Homo*, species *sapiens*, nominally distinguished by our capacity for thought. Nevertheless, while this capacity was cherished in the eighteenth century as a definitively human attribute, the investigation of 'species' *per se* was becoming a science of physical form, of heritable morphology and anatomy. Maintaining the connection between physical phenomena that defined 'humanity' and ethical norms commonly associated with 'humanity' was thus a very different project.

Diderot's text suggests that all of its questions can be answered by a sufficient knowledge of organization. However, it is unclear whether that organization is primarily physiological, political, or conceptual in nature.[4] Although elsewhere (notably in the *Encyclopédie*, itself a product of the classificatory impulse, complete with its textual-graphical tree of knowledge[5]) Diderot does seriously engage the scientific species concept, this passage delivers a satirical jab at naive systematics and the uses to which it might be put. In this particular case, the narrator is concerned ultimately with social questions and the patterning of discursive meaning. Nonetheless, he is a product of his time in turning to the emerging life sciences and their accounts of the collective human kind for insight into particular riddles of human behavior.

Musing on grand questions of the general and the particular, of linguistic meaning and its fragmentation, Diderot's narrating persona deploys the clarifying power of organization via a notably disorganized, stream-of-consciousness narrative style. The progression of his observations, following a logic that is associational rather than methodical, exposes a fundamental problem that inhered all too often in systematic science: namely, how does one identify precisely the exclusive and necessary criteria that signal "organization" of a species? This, of course, is precisely the question that would lead science from system to method, from the construction of logical, atemporal, associational networks (like Linnaeus's classification, or Diderot's tree of knowledge) to the search for natural patterns that were themselves products of a natural, genealogical process occurring in time.

Diderot's initial frustration with the "variously defined" terms essential to civil society shifts to an interrogation of the individual, and then shifts again, under an injunction to "know thyself," to the question of the generic nature of man. After admonishing the reader that "all is lost" if "Man" should elude definition, the narrator begins a process of elimination: a man, though he may be an animal, is not a wolf (although some men fail to distinguish the two philosophically); further, a man is not a Cyclops. What exactly does Diderot hope to accomplish with these comparisons, which all serve as the basis for exclusion? The rhetoric pendulates between the general and the specific, becoming more inclusive as it moves from "Myself" to "Man" and on to "animal"; it then begins a process of differentiation, separating animal-man from specific animals (the wolf), from man-like beings (Polyphemus), and finally from particular, unique men (kings). The process of specification, conflated here with speciation, seems whimsical and arbitrary. It functions more to illustrate the flaws that compromise various possible affiliations than to isolate the unifying characteristics that might define the species and serve, thus, as a reliable basis for knowledge.

Diderot's evocation of Polyphemus—not merely a generic monster, but a particular character familiar to the educated reader—is in this sense revealing. Because the narrator insists peremptorily that Polyphemus and Ulysses' companions share no significant organization, we may be provoked to examine the qualities that they did have in common, and to question what it means that these particular commonalities do not serve to unite them. As any reader of Diderot (and Homer) might be expected to know, Polyphemus shares with his human counterparts (the unfortunate, ingested companions of Ulysses) specific qualities—including language, the capacity to reason, and an upright stance—which, in eighteenth-century scientific discourses, were identified as the characteristics of man that clearly placed his species above and distinct from all other animals.[6] And yet these qualities of speech, thought and stance, purportedly unique to humankind and here stretched by Homer's fiction and Diderot's example to include the monstrous nearly-human Cyclops, do not suffice to characterize "species" as Diderot wishes to define it. We are told not the reasons for the distinction, but simply the consequences: Polyphemus and Ulysses' companions, being of different species, cannot be held to the same behavioral norms. The fundamental difference that is implied in the organization of the two types returns us to a discussion of ethics, although not to the initial discussion of normative understanding, but to the relative judgment of behavior. Yet it is not behavior associated with the good or the beautiful, or any of the other lofty concerns with which the narrator began. It is, in fact, a logical reversal of the Stoic model of species loyalty, which, according to Marcus, should prevent feelings of anger or hatred toward any other who is of the human kind.[7] In this case, the knowledge of species difference becomes the defining parameter of acceptable aggression, identifying who or what may be killed and consumed. Diderot's narrator is ultimately unable to do more than call upon obvious difference in kind: he offers humans, hares, and Cyclops as examples of species-difference that are reassuringly commonsensical. This excuses him from a methodological account of what any particular species is, and he resorts instead to a description of what the knowledge of the species boundary *does*: in his initial discussion, it provides the basis of ethics; in his example, it serves as the limit of ethics and the boundary for acceptable aggression. Thus we learn by implication that eating a member of one's own species is an atrocious act. One may however feel free—at least free from any breach of ethics—to devour a creature of another kind.[8] But what happens when the borders of "species" or "kind" remain unclear? If the species difference separating men from hares and Ulysses from Polyphemus is the same as the difference in kind between ordinary mortals and kings or God, then might not kings, by virtue of the passage's last turn, be morally free to feast upon their subjects—or, as soon would prove the case, vice versa? The separation of kings is not entirely lacking a biological component: consider the tradition of regarding a king as distinguished from the populace not only politically but by the biological historical fact of his belonging to a particular genealogical "House" or bloodline.[9]

The potentially revolutionary aporia produced by the text's jumble of literary, philosophical, and scientific associations provides more of a conceptual provocation than an answer to the questions raised about the knowledge of species. Nonetheless, it is precisely the narrator's inexact use of "species" that illustrates both the limits and the expectations of the popular understanding of the term. When the narrator commences his search for a basis of denotation to make possible (and legible) a reliable definition and application of ideas, he rejects the purely subjective ("What am I?") for the presumably objective (the scientific collective "species") as the structural foundation for a signifying authority. If the Enlightenment had dismissed Marcus Aurelius's "human portion of the divine" as the compelling basis of community orientation, then communal values of ethics and aesthetics were instead to be derived where the truth of species lay: in the facts of human nature.

Of course, the narrator's presumption of "species" as something real and identifiable is challenged immediately by his recourse to an imaginative, literary example in order to pinpoint the "facts" of organization. This need to sift through nuanced products of the imagination highlights the impossibility of a simple statement of facts and underscores the lack of an answer to his questions. It is also a critique of a particularly unscientific mode of investigation: Diderot's narrator is unable to derive general meanings from the specifics of species, because the specifics with which he does proceed are so variously individuated that they cannot be brought together to signal a consistent general principle. His associational process (really, his lack of method) triggers a *mise-en-abîme*, so that, instead of discovering a dependable system that might unite people in both physical and metaphysical realms (clarifying both human kind and human good), Diderot can end only with a rhetorical question focusing on difference and individuation. In the end, we face a paradox: while defending the natural mandate of species, Diderot's narrator unwittingly demonstrates that species is just as "little understood" and "variously defined" as the other abstract (ethical and aesthetic) terms which he sought to pin down. Should we take this as an invitation to consider the possibility that species, like those other terms, is also a concept rather than a thing, an organizing, prescriptive idea that is as much a product of culture as ethics and aesthetics?

Canguilhem observed quite rightly that the question of species has dominated the history of natural history.[10] A central element of the debate is the question of whether there is such a real thing as a species, or whether it is an artifact of the organizing mind, conceived for scientific and philosophical convenience. Throughout much of the eighteenth century, classificatory categories like "species" were to a certain extent accepted as conceptual artifacts. While by no means arbitrary, they were organizational mechanisms by which scientists tried to cope with the overwhelming numbers of bewilderingly diverse plant and animal specimens that were amassed during the Age of Exploration.[11] Efforts of eighteenth-century scientists and philosophers to devise *methods* of inquiry rather than *systems* of arrangement, in order to produce an account of the history of nature rather than merely a description of its bounty, produced the first 'scientific' articulations of species as something that demarcates real and historically distinct groups of life-forms—a position still dominantly held today. Following closely upon this debate must be the question of what purpose the identification of species is to serve. As Diderot's passage dramatizes, the species category tends not to remain within the signifying domain of the natural historian but is all too eagerly seized as a potential bridge between physical and metaphysical knowledge—conveniently replacing religion, as in Diderot's text, when God is finally subsumed *within* the natural system as yet another, if solitary, specimen belonging to yet another unique, if indefinable, kind.

DETERMINING THE SPECIES

What constituted a species in eighteenth-century Europe? Despite (or in addition to) the quandaries and reservations communicated by the particular vignette we have analyzed, Diderot not only shared with many of his generation a new physiological and historical understanding of "species;" he was instrumental in propagating it. As editor of the *Encyclopédie*, Diderot offered to his readers an entry on species extracted from Buffon's *Natural History*, which defined it not merely as a collection of living beings with common traits, but rather as consisting of "the constant succession and the uninterrupted renewal of those individuals who constitute it."[12] This succession is further specified as genealogical, as it is produced and restricted by reproduction. Different species, the reader learns, are invariably distinct—one can draw "a line of separation" between them—because their individual members reproduce only amongst themselves and are unable to crossbreed. While Buffon is elsewhere skeptical of the "lines" that scientists were all too apt to identify for the project of classifying nature, he maintained his case for species distinction. This insight, that species were most accurately identified by their discreet genealogy rather than by observable morphology (and much less than by behavior or a common "portion of the divine"), became the standard premise for further inquiry and debate.[13] This point, according to Buffon, "is the most stable [*le plus fixe*] that we have in natural history."[14] Any other resemblances and differences used to compare living beings, Buffon continues, are neither constant, nor real, nor certain.

We must detour for a moment to examine the implications not of Buffon's assertion, but of his reservation. When he writes, first in 1749, that the genealogically determined species is the *most* stable (*le plus fixe*) point available for the field of natural history, he raises the question of just how reliable this fulcrum will prove to be for a science that is, after all, new. Buffon's qualification becomes apparent in his formulation that it is a "chain of successive individuals which constitutes the real existence of the species."[15] That is, the "real existence" (as opposed to an arbitrary linguistic convention) is not just an aggregate of individuals, but is brought into being by the actual generation (and modification) of successive generations. And yet, the species only can be said to "exist" as the totality of all generations, on whose entire genealogy one can but speculate.[16] Buffon writes—and Diderot cites: "Species is thus a word that is abstract and general, for which the thing does not exist except when considering nature in the succession of time, and in the constant destruction and just as constant renewal of beings."[17] Thus, species is first (and last) an abstract word; and the thing or matter it signifies (a *chose* which stands in a subordinate relation grammatically to the *mot*, as if the species-thing were just one attribute of the species-word) exists only "during consideration," during the process of imagining the succession of time and the constant processes of destruction and renewal that are constant for all life forms. By this formulation, the species-thing—if it is a "thing" at all[18]—exists materially in space and time only as an imagined unity of past, present, and future generations, a provisionally situated ideality. In fact, however, it is precisely the complete succession of generations, the entire physical genealogy, which gives measure to space and time.[19]

At any given moment, or in any individual lifetime, a species is something that exists only during thought, *en considérant*. In other words, its material existence, while undeniably real, can nevertheless only be intuited and invoked; it cannot be directly experienced or demonstrated. The "real" genealogical species, which provides an epistemological foundation for natural science, is, in fact, apprehensible only through (and constituted by) the genealogical species *concept*. Phillip Sloan has written that Buffon's theory implied "a distinction to be made between an abstract and ideal order of *ideas*, and a *real* order of bodies in relational time and space, and that genuine science would seek to grasp this real order."[20] I would add to Sloan's observation, however, that Buffon's awareness of the impossibility of separating the real from the ideal, particularly when dealing with genealogy and time, infuses his text with one of its many ironic resonances.

Such philosophical qualifications of the reality of species are left, for the most part, with Buffon. None of his successors confront the possibility that there might be more to the concept of a genealogical species than consistent scientific thought can contain.[21] For his contemporaries and the immediately succeeding generations, the identification of the genealogical species was increasingly accepted as a real point of departure for the sciences, providing for Kant the conceptual and physical foundation of what comes to be known as the "history"—and not merely the description—of nature.[22]

Following Buffon's stress upon the composition of species by reproduction over time, Kant systematically differentiated this new method of classification from the previous, morphologically focused tradition. He asserted that classification, to be scientific, must acknowledge and discard its practice of organizing knowledge based upon academic conceptual edifices which could at best produce systems of what Kant dismissed as *Schulgattungen*, descriptive, logical categories based on morphological similarities, which were functional but could not convey knowledge of the world. Instead, knowledge had to be derived from nature itself, which organized living beings according to its own "laws." For the task of writing natural history, the classification of life forms had to be arranged and labeled in accordance with their *Naturgattungen*, the natural species divisions determined by genealogical lineage. Susan Shell explains:

> What unites a species, for Kant, is not merely the temporal succession of fertile generations (in which case the species would be a mere aggregate), but the invariable passing down, from one generation to the next, of a *common seed*. It is the invariability (and hence, implicitly, necessity) of this inheritance according to what Kant would later call a rule

that marks the species as a real, rather than merely nominal, whole. In short, Kant's definition of a natural species is not merely descriptive, but 'historical' (in the special sense of securing a collective identity over time) and hence 'scientific.'[23]

As for human beings, all were to be recognized as members (and products, and producers) of a single *Gattung* or species descended from a single line. At the same time, their marked physiological, cultural, and geographical differences suggested that further subdivision into races or varieties was also "naturally" (and purposively) dictated.[24]

Johann Friedrich Blumenbach, a naturalist, anthropologist, comparative anatomist, and professor of medicine in Göttingen whose work in the natural sciences established terms and debates that reverberated well into the twentieth century, also argued that all people(s) are the product of a single, real, historical human species. His *Handbook of Natural History* [*Handbuch der Naturgeschichte*], issued in 1779 and revised repeatedly for two decades as an authoritative text on natural history, reveals much about the fundamental instability of the scientific formulation of a species concept. Blumenbach wrote in the 1791 edition of the *Handbook*:

> There is only one species [*Gattung (species)*] in the human kind [*Menschengeschlecht*]; and all known peoples of all times and places [*aller Himmelsstriche*] stem from a common racial line [*Stammraße*]. All of the national differences [*National-Verschiedenheiten*] in the form and color of the human body are not a whit more significant or mysterious as those among other species of organized bodies, for example domestic pets, that change [*ausarten*] under our very eyes.[25]

This sentence can be read as an apparently simple statement of fact (there is only one species in the human genus) followed by a logical conjecture (all peoples may derive from a common ancestral race). It can also be read as a set of morally charged associations. Blumenbach does not write that there is only one species belonging to the genus *homo*, which would have been more precise, but instead deploys the term *Menschengeschlecht*, effectively connecting the scientific category with a popular term. This word signals not merely a universal human collective, but the presence of *Menschlichkeit*, a moral, empathetic, humane quality that makes of the *Menschengeschlecht* a coherent body of human ideals and the potential to realize them.[26] The reference to an inclusive "us" builds upon the species' unity reported by the sentence to stir an individual sense of unity among readers as well as the writer; the *Himmelsstriche* is a poetic term that effectively extends the geographical totality to include all peoples ever existing under the heavens—presumably God's. Thus the sentence functions to connect a scientific idea that might find resonance with a familiar ideal of human moral unity built into both Christian and Enlightenment rhetoric.

This morally homogeneous *Menschengeschlecht* is also unified biologically, something communicated overtly by Blumenbach's statement and intensified by a further set of associations the term evoked. Long before the word *Geschlecht* was adopted for taxonomic use, it was used synonymously for *Art, Stamm, Volk, Nation*, "*die blutsverwandte Familie*" or *Sippe*, the *Geschlechterstaat*, a caste-determined group of families (*Stand*), a tribe, both natural and grammatical gender, and simple *Verwandtschaft*. Except for grammatical gender (translated from the Latin as *Geschlecht* as late as the seventeenth century), all of these synonyms designate groups related genealogically to a greater or lesser degree.[27] Luther, whose work on the German language remained authoritative in the eighteenth century, had himself insisted upon a genealogical definition for *Geschlecht* as "the natural issue from father to child's child, that each member of the same issue is called a '*geschlecht*.'"[28]

In terms of the scientific language used in the above-cited statement of the singular identity of the human species, Blumenbach employs the terms *Gattung, species, Menschengeschlecht*, the collective *Völker* (also refered to as nations, or *Nationen*), and *Stammraße*. While some sense of difference among them is indicated, both in terms of scale and of historical time, the sentence communicates their mutual participation in a single genetic process. First, the *Gattung* or genus, a category that contains one or more species, is in the human instance materially the same thing as the species.[29] This species comprises all of the various peoples, here called *Völker*, and elsewhere in the same text called *Rassen*, and *Varietäten*. These, we are to understand, are groups also identifiable by their national differences [*National-Verschiedenheiten*]. These variously identified subsets of species collectively *are* the species. Furthermore, they are all (ergo, the entire species is) descended from a singular *Stammraße*, which thus, at some moment in the past, was also the material equivalent of the species. Blumenbach's formulation leaves the reader with the sense that all of these terms are more or less equivalent and that the differences between, say, a species and a race or a nation are less significant than their shared genealogical nature.

Although—or perhaps because—the writings of systematic thinkers like Kant and Blumenbach are replete with these confusingly multivalent terms, they and others recognized a need to stabilize scientific nomenclature. Blumenbach was concerned specifically with the imprecision of scientific terms, as well as with the practical task of standardizing a German (rather than Latin) vocabulary. The real problem, I suggest, lay not in the lack of scientific standardization *per se*, but in the use of terms that had such a rich and complex folk usage.

As indicated above, an attempt to develop a precise science of species through terms like *Geschlecht* could not help but invite a blurring of the concepts involved—and in particular, critical ways. As scientists tried to depict the true and distinct "nature" of human kind, the terminology selected conceptually linked the entirety of human beings with particular family lines and with ethnic, racial, and national populations, implying that all were genealogical products with equivalent scientific and historical validity. Ultimately, the language of science itself invited an understanding of family, race, nation, and species as merely different orders of magnitude of the same genetic thing.

NATURE'S LANGUAGE

Aware to a limited extent of this language problem, Blumenbach offered the following in the preface to his *Handbook*:

> When, in referring to organized bodies, I always translate the word *genus* as "*Geschlecht*" and *species* as "*Gattung*," I do so with an eye to the authority not only of our most exacting German linguists, as well as the German classics in the field of new German literature, and Herr von Haller, among others; however I also have two quite different authorities before me, namely the common conventions of language and effectively nature itself. Nature demonstrates (at least in the common course of things, *de regula*) that only animals from within one species propagate with each other.[30]

Scientific language, according to this passage, is authorized by precedence, common parlance, and "nature itself." Nature's process is evidenced by the products of generation; the motor of generation is the verb *gatten* (to mate) and thus nature is evidence for the appropriateness of the term and its definition. Blumenbach attempts with this passage to vanquish a sense of arbitrariness not only with regard to the organizing facts of science, but with regard to its language as well. To do so, he argues that the natural system generates the sign system, that scientific language, properly derived, is as "natural" as nature itself, and is therefore reliable. But while Blumenbach claims to educe the term from nature's own demonstration, it is not empirical observation, but the etymological relation between the verb *gatten* and the noun *Gattung* that authorizes the terminology in question.

Nature shows or indicates generation, and only animals within a given species *gatten* or mate—at least legitimately. Blumenbach notes several times that there are instances of inter-species procreation, but their progeny, according to zoological convention, are labeled "bastards" and supposed to be infertile—thus ensuring that they (like their legal counterparts) remain anomalous and do not corrupt or redefine the species/family line. In fact, bastards, notes Blumenbach, are a result of degeneration (like hermaphrodites, monstrous births, races, and *Spielarten* or varieties) that demonstrates how the *Bildungstrieb* itself, the generative force responsible for each individual's epigenetic development, can be disturbed or modified by a number of factors and thus forced to deviate from its proper destined path. Whereas races and varieties reproduce their like, establishing their own continuities over time, bastards (among which the mule was a favored example) were understood to be sterile.[31] When in 1800 the zoologist and first director of the University of Berlin's Museum of Natural History, Johann Karl Illiger, published his compendium of natural history terminology, he standardized scientific vocabulary for the German language and confirmed this meaning for the term bastard through three interlinked statements of "fact." He first defines the species as the collective embodiment [*der Inbegriff*] of all individuals who together produce fertile offspring (xxvi); he then reiterates as a law of nature that animals of different species either produce no offspring, or occasionally infertile offspring (xxvii-xxviii). Finally, he defines the "bastard-kind," or *Bastardart* (also called a *Mittelart* and a hybrid) as a product of the interbreeding of a male and a female of different species—which is already, by previous definition and by the "law of nature," necessarily infertile.[32]

The intersection between the zoological and the legal use of the term "bastard" is significant: both the biological and legal uses of the term identify and exclude the progeny of mixed kind from the genealogical continuum of the lines in question. The use of the term "bastard" by scientific writers concerned solely with botany or zoology (excluding human animals) in all likelihood did not have consequences beyond reinforcing through a popular term the need to stigmatize idiosyncratic divergence from a standard kind. However, the use by eighteenth-century philosophers and natural scientists who were also anthropologists has to be more closely evaluated. When Voltaire wrote in 1765 that "mulattos are only a bastard race of black men and white women, or white men and black women, as asses, specifically different from horses, produce mules by copulating with mares," he made clear through his use of the term an antagonism toward miscegenation.[33] His defensive—and rather inept—construction of an analogy between mulattos and mules, turning on the figure of the bastard, resonates multiply to render the subject sterile, isolated, and illegitimate. Similarly, because figures like Kant and Blumenbach write of both the biological history of human life and its potential intersections with the development and constitution of ethical community, we must be alert for terms like "bastard" which, when they are based in "natural" processes of differentiation and exclusion, carry ideological weight, and reappear all too easily in discussions of, for example, racial difference and miscegenation.[34]

Returning to Blumenbach's exegesis of species and *Gattung*: since propagation is naturally reserved for animals within a given species, the *Gattung* by nature ensures its own continuous purity—not because the genealogical continuum precludes bastards or hybrids, but by the fact that such bastards are excluded as monstrous exceptions.[35] *Gattung*, however, is also philologically justified. According to Blumenbach's argument, it is actually the verb *gatten* that generates the noun *Gattung*. This pattern of linguistic generation is important to note: one word is acknowledged to be the source for, or the generator of, another; here, the verb (the genetic action or process) generates the related, second-generation term, the noun. This neatly establishes in a grammatical system the genealogical dynamic that Blumenbach attributes to the natural order. We have to wonder about the priority of the elements in the cognitive matrix: Blumenbach claims to observe patterns of generation in nature, and he claims further that the process of generation or *gatten* produces *Gattung*, both physiologically and grammatically. He argues, obviously, for the priority of nature as the model for grammar—but he is not entirely successful, and nature ends up functioning as an illustration or manifestation of the concept. At the base of Blumenbach's thinking about nature and about the language that represents it is a pattern of generational argument that is fundamentally cognitive.[36]

Within the cited passage, Blumenbach ostensibly wishes to justify his choice of German words to translate Latin words, the meanings of which are assumed to be clear. However, his rhetoric not only uses the Latin language to justify his thinking; he actually presumes to define in a particular way the Latin terminology itself. He begins with the Aristotelian *species*, the status of which—either as a conceptual category or a material entity—was far from clear. He then proceeds, through the gesture of translation, into a linguistic argument that is designed to demonstrate the natural correlation of the Latin and German terms, effectively trumping what were, for some scientists, still-reasonable doubts about the definition of species according to the criterion of mating. Blumenbach presupposes with his argument that the category *species* is, in fact, real and generation-bound, because the verb *gatten*, which gives rise to the species-equivalent of *Gattung*, functions as part of the premise of the argument. Given the context in which Blumenbach's work was read, it is fair to say that his accomplishment here is not so much the defense of *Gattung* as the German equivalent of *species*, but rather an indirect assertion that *species* is real and genealogical, a product of *gatten* and thus equivalent to *Gattung*.

Despite his efforts to assure readers that language here faithfully represents nature—following the lines of the common metaphor of the time, that proper classification was a translation of "nature's own language"—nature seems to behave instead as language does. Or, perhaps both nature and language together, as elements to be known and to be wielded, comprise an effective, mutually mimetic system. Given the intellectual attention paid to understandings of linguistic referentiality and to the genealogical histories of language "families" during precisely these decades in Germany, Blumenbach's position might initially appear startlingly simplistic; one must bear in mind, however, that his concern was the credibility of scientific writing, a credibility that depended upon a reliable system of linguistic and visual representation through which the scientific community could share and build upon its knowledge. While mimetic powers of description might well have limits that rendered such a project difficult, they were not so compromised as to render it impossible. Or so Blumenbach hoped, and he proceeded accordingly.

That his attempt to fix a relationship between language and nature would be problematic is not surprising; it is not, however, our main point. To grasp the historical shift that occurred in the perception of species, it is important to study not only the flaws in the argument but also the structure of the attempt. Blumenbach's passage reveals the conviction that, in collecting evidence for an investigation of species, nature was the primary record to be read. This was not, however, in the tradition of the physico-theologists of the previous century who regarded nature ahistorically as God's own script, a Book that revealed to human beings fragments of a preconceived divine plan. For Blumenbach, visible nature was itself a chronicle of its own internal processes, recording the presence and passing of species in real generational lineages and in the material record of fossils.[37] Nature, from this perspective, is not itself merely a sign or semiotic system (of God's presence or design), but it *shows* signs of its processes. It is at once agent, sign, and referent. It is real, and it is legible at historical distance.

Blumenbach himself, however, seemed to signal that Nature, credited with showing the reality which language reflects, is actually not so reliable a communicator. Nature only points to the natural criterion marking the reality of a species, and even then only conditionally, "at least in the common course of things, *de regula*," according to the rule. There is tautology in the assertion that nature's "showing" follows a rule that itself is merely extracted from repeated observations of something that exists. In fact, the epistemological authority here is exercised not by nature *per se*, but by the rule, the cognitive construct produced by an observing intelligence.

Blumenbach made the argument cited above for the proper German translation of *species* as *Gattung* based upon natural facts in the 1791 edition of the *Handbook*; eight years later, in the edition of 1799, he still needed to persuade his reader of the following:

> The natural foundation for the German translation of the word "species" most naturally [*am allernatürlichsten*] into *Gattung* is the well-known and considered knowledge that in the free state of nature, every creature only mates with another from the same species.[38]

Struck as we must be by the urgency of his stress on the "natural" justification for a "natural" translation of a term representing a "natural" process, we shall return to the seemingly simple fact that a species is understood to be a product of biological reproduction, a natural category comprised of individuals identified *not* by any particular visually identifiable traits (those in fact get shifted to the category "race," and are discussed in the following chapter), but by their mating history. That is, the species is defined by breeding, like an individual family.

Let us return, then, to a consideration of Blumenbach's linkage of terms: the species, or *Gattung*, is also a *Menschengeschlecht*, a human family that includes all the collective *Völker* (that is, ethnically and geographically distinct groups) who have ever lived; and members of this species all have the same biological origin since they derive from a single *Stammraße*, in turn the product of a single pair of ancestors. Within a single statement in Blumenbach's *Handbook*, the categories of genus, species, race, and folk (equated with nation) are divested of the potential to denote exclusive entities, and instead are reinscribed as different modalities of the same generative process: that of a familial species. Such a leveling produces several effects: it associates familial loyalty with species membership, and, as we shall see now in the anthropological writings of Kant, it posits the historical physiological species as a reality that is the foundation for culture.

SPECIES AS CULTURE

More than some scientists of the day, Kant was prepared to conflate biological existence with cultural and moral conditions. Of course, he was not really a scientist, as his colleague and professor of medicine, Johann Daniel Metzger, was eager to point out.[39] Kant's anthropological writings demonstrate a slide from an engagement with the species concept in the terms of natural science to speculations upon the "nature" of its moral character. Kant employs the figure of a common "seed" or *Keim*, granting it both material and metaphorical power as that which determines the reality not only of species, but of national peoples and of individual lineages whose generation bares traces that evidence what he called the *Familienschlag*, or the "particular family stamp."[40] While he demurred when it came to identifying precisely the character of the human species because he claimed there was no available external term for comparison, it was nonetheless clear to him that both the human species and its separate races existed as something substantial as well as conceptual.[41] In his *Anthropology from a Pragmatic Point of View* [*Anthropologie in pragmatischer Hinsicht*, 1798], Kant theorized the species as something that moves conceptually—as well as naturally—toward the rational cosmopolitical: that is, toward a philosophical goal. In this writing, the material seems to take priority in determining both the physical and the moral/intellectual "character" of the concentric groupings of species, races, nations, and families.

In the *Anthropology*, Kant effectively connects the species and the family when he declares forcefully that "human beings belong not only to one and the same species [*Gattung*], but also to one family [*Familie*]."[42] It should be noted here that Kant, like most of his contemporaries, regularly substituted the German terms *Geschlecht*, *Gattung*, *Spezies*, *Rasse*, and

Familie interchangeably as synonyms for either species or race. His use here of "family" is ambiguous: if he is using the term as a scientific taxon, one possible referent is the classificatory category of "family" within which both genus and species are included. However, this use of *Familie* appears rarely if ever in the German scientific literature of the eighteenth century, and in any event Kant is certainly not attempting to widen the circle of human fraternity to include other species. We might also consider that he is using *Familie* as a synonym for the category *Geschlecht*; as we saw above, *Familie* is one of many commonly used synonyms. Certainly, the all-encompassing *Menschengeschlecht* was often enough called a *Menschheitsfamilie* (as well as a *Menschengattung*).

That we cannot identify exactly which type of collective Kant meant to signify with *Familie* is intriguing. He claims that all humans belong to a single species, and that they all belong to a single family. Since all humans exclusively constitute both the species and this "family," it is fair to say that the species and the family are materially the same thing. So why emphasize that human beings belong to both? The difference must lie in the connotative difference of the terms species and family. The very definition of species was still new and contested in Kant's time, and if anything it raised the issue of definitive borders between humans and non-human animals. Thus the claim that all humans belonged to a single species might more likely signal the exclusion of non-humans from the same rather than evoking a sense of human loyalty within the group (similar to the dynamic logic of Diderot's text). By contrast, mention of "belonging" to a "family" invariably evokes the individual family and summons forth (ideal) qualities of love, altruism, and loyalty. The family is also the unit of human community that was available to regulation in the interest of the greater human family, as the next chapter shall discuss.

We must also speculate as to why Kant at this juncture connects individuals by emotional bonds to a species-identification by suggesting it is equivalent to family ties.[43] He believes, and argues repeatedly that, unlike all other living beings, humans realize their potential only as a species, which is itself the product of gradual improvements and adaptations that occur along a genealogical, generational line:

> Above all, it must be noted that all other animals left to themselves reach as individuals their full destiny, but human beings reach their full destiny only as a species. Consequently, the human species can work itself up to its destiny only through continuous progress within an endless sequence of many generations.[44]

The ultimate goal of human development is the evolution of the collective family/race/species, not as a mere aggregate of individuals, but as a functioning "system" whose components are not only physiological but also cultural. In the final sentence of the *Anthropology*, Kant defines this ideal species-system as one characterized by cosmopolitan unity: "we cannot expect to reach our goal by the free consent of individuals, but only through progressive organization of the citizens of the earth within and toward the species as a system which is united by cosmopolitical bonds."[45] The adjective he chooses—*cosmopolitisch*—draws on a long history of linking the classical ideas of *cosmos* and *polis*, or the order of nature and the (rational) order of culture.[46] It is a term Kant used forcefully and to great effect in his political writings. Martha Nussbaum, in tracing Kant's use of the term to the Stoics (in particular, to Seneca, Marcus Aurelius, and Cicero), focuses on the figure of the "*kosmou politês*" or world citizen whose loyalties transcend the limits of familial and state allegiances to include all peoples everywhere. There is no doubt that such an ideal of ethical community binding all human beings was shared by Kant—even taking into account his thoughts on the cultural and moral inequality of various races (discussed in the following chapter). However, Nussbaum's reading seems to limit the meaning of "cosmos" to a universe that is already a rational, political artifact of human culture. While she argues that cosmopolitanism is not a call for allegiance to a world state, but rather "to the moral community made up by the humanity of all human beings," this reading does seem to exclude the larger sense of cosmos as encompassing all of nature.[47] The element of nature constitutive of "cosmopolitan" is crucial to Kant's use of the term in the *Anthropology*. In fact, its use suggests a particular relationship between nature and culture that is at once parallel and sequential. The order of nature is not simply the symbol for and promise of a possible societal order, as might have been the case a century prior to Kant; the relationship is, instead, genealogical. According to Kant's formulation, the social order—including its final, cosmopolitan, moral perfection—evolves in space and time from, and is a historical product of, the natural order.

While, in his *Critique of Judgment*, Kant posits a gulf between the laws of science and the moral law bridgeable only by reflective judgment,[48] here in the *Anthropology* (begun before publication of the critical works and published relatively unchanged late in his life) he bridges the two. That is, he offers them the species-existence of man as the only thing (a thing that is simultaneously an entity and a natural process) with the potential to form connection. While every individual's birth is, in his words, an "epigenesis," the species alone is the carrier of ethical culture. This marks a significant break from Stoic ideals of universal human community: Greek philosophers insisted that each individual owed respect and allegiance to all other people because they shared the capacity to reason as their "portion of the divine." Kant, by contrast, required that individuals treat other people as ends, and not as means, because of their fundamental existence as a part of the genealogical continuum of a biological species.

Kant's declaration that all humans belong both to a single species and to a single family potentially unites his scientific and ethical subjects. We shall see that between the categories of species and family—uniting them, effectively—lies race. In its intermediate position between the species and the family, race bridges the epistemological gap between the scientific assessment of species-man as animal, and a persistent understanding of the family as the model for and foundation of community. And so now it is to questions of race that we must turn.

4 Questions of Kind
(family) Race (species)

While the family is both an effective metaphor for community bonds and a dynamic model for the genealogical species, a problem arises when we examine the conceptual space between the individual family and the species. It is here that we must contend with the category of race, about which so much has been written over the past two hundred and some years. In order to unravel one particular thread of the tangled concept of race, we need to return first to its governing concept, the species.

Let us recall that, according to the genetic definition, a species can be said to "exist" only as the totality of all individuals comprising all generations, the entire genealogy of which one can only imagine. In other words, the (human) species that we identify and describe as real is always a hypothetical projection, and as such a representation. Because of the constant flux of death and birth, this representation of a projected whole continually requires emendation. The "real" genealogical species is, in fact, apprehensible only through (and constituted by) a combination of the genealogical species *concept* and continually changing information.

Each new member of the species provides this information. The significance of this point—the assertion that each individual human being's constitution directly determines the identity of the collective—cannot be overestimated, although it tends to be overlooked. If we adhere to the logic of the scientific species concept as it takes shape during the late Enlightenment, the human species can never be self-identical from one moment to the next, since its constituent membership is never static. Of course, the implications of this provoked consternation in some scientists and philosophers, who recognized that to control the shape (and color and culture) of the species, one had to radically limit its members; thus we might understand the desire to believe in multiple human species (polygenism) that found expression during the period. Within the parameters of a monogenetic species concept, however, there is no escaping the problem of a species' unrepresentability. Every individual member might serve as an equal representative, but no representative could function as a model from which to extrapolate and systematize a defining set of traits that make clear what the nature of the human being encompasses.[1]

According to the scientific construction of species, the whole is precisely the sum of its parts; however, the relationship of part to whole is asymmetric. That is, the part (the individual) is a proper part of the whole (the species group) but not equivalent with it, and the individual is a determining factor for the identity of the (continually changing) whole. However—and this is an important element of the definition—the species-whole does not determine or restrict the identity of the part. That is, one's species-identity can in no way limit one's individual identity.

This differs significantly from concurrent understandings of race. When race emerged as a scientific category, it was positioned along the already established line connecting individual and species. Significant complications become apparent when we consider the relationship of individual to race. Unlike species, race was not conceived as a category defined by the sum total of characteristics of all its natural members. On the contrary, race was identified as a group of people who exhibit a defined set of characteristics distilled from a finite sample group.

Having identified that sample, a particular race thereafter could include only those members who exhibited the defining traits that preserve its distinction as a subset. Because the category was set up this way and because scientists and anthropologists and ethnographers used race this way, the very structure of the race category placed a limiting function upon the individual identity of its members. Thus, while an individual was understood to contribute to the definition of a species, actually to shape its nature, he or she could—and potentially must—only illustrate limited aspects of the established race group (or a liminal hybrid, indeterminate group) to which he or she was already assigned.

Some scientists—Blumenbach and Ludwig notable among them—understood this limiting function of race as a collective description of a human subset that shared distinctive hereditary traits to be convenient for scientific discourse, but not significant for ascertaining permanent categories of human natural history. Adhering to the species-logic of hereditary continuity, they produced an idea of race as a tributary, marking lines of human flow from individual families and communities through ever-larger—but ever-changing—groupings toward the all-inclusive species. The logic of species compelled such scientists to regard different races as more or less fluctuating subsets of human beings that were marked by heritable differences (skin tone and skull shape being favorite examples), differences that were nonetheless mutable—blendable through processes of sexual procreation—and thus historically variable. It followed that race could not be considered a permanent category like species.

Consider: scientists and philosophers embraced the hereditary logic of the species concept for their development of natural history. This logic found its resonant parallel in the concurrent language of enlightened celebration of universal brotherhood, a language itself indebted to, if attempting to establish secular distance from, the long tradition of Christian representation of God the Father, Mary the Mother, and the brotherhood of priests and laity in the world. If anything, the species concept as a genealogical line coincided well with other dominant, metaphysical strains of hereditary thinking dominating both religious and emancipatory political discourse. And in its distancing from theoretical "original parents" and stress instead upon the continual re-constitution of species in the here and now (because species consists of all who are born into it, and must accommodate their idiosyncrasies), it was also harmonious with political rhetoric of brotherhood that sought to distance itself both from the governance of divine parentage and from the "self-imposed immaturity," in Kant's terms, of submission to entrenched political and institutional authorities.

What I described is a correspondence of rhetoric. By definition, the species included all humans born of humans born of humans. In theory, the brotherhood of man was also—potentially, suggestively—all-inclusive. Experience shows, however, that theoretical systems with an all-inclusive embrace are ultimately untenable. They either fail outright or are modified with sophisticated clauses that provide barriers between brothers who cannot bear to share the identity and obligations of "family" with each other. In the case of politics, the compromises are well rehearsed: enlightened universal brotherhood was, for the most part, limited to white, propertied men. The status of these "brothers" both claimed to supersede old patterns of paternalism and at the same time reinscribed these patterns as they assumed "fatherly" authority as factory-owners, slaveholders, masters of their domestic dependants, and governors of the colonized world.

What of the logic and the language of natural history? In the case of the all-inclusive species, two qualifying ideas in particular developed to inscribe natural and permanent boundaries between peoples, despite the countering efforts of some scientists. The first surfaced as the theory of polygenism, the notion that there were multiple species with discreet origins.[2] This theory, while advanced by some eighteenth-century thinkers, is only taken up and developed (before finally being dismissed) by mid-nineteenth century scientists. During the period around 1800, the monogenist theory of species dominated, and within that context theories of racial difference developed as the second counter movement against universal biological brotherhood. As we shall see, debates around the idea of "race" revolve around its fundamental conceptual problems: namely, a break with the logic of hereditary flow from family to species, allowing for a rejection of "familial" bonds linking different races; and at the same time an adherence to hereditary logic within racial divisions, particularly in an extension from the somatic to the psychological and spiritual character of genealogical communities, in order to justify claims about the fundamental differences of various peoples' capacity for good.

It behooves us now to pay some closer attention to how particular thinkers proposed that the line from the individual, procreating family to the all-inclusive genealogical species was mediated—and in some instances, diverted—by race. The idea of the species, modeled on generational lines that could be discerned upon bodies as a *Familienschlag* or "family stamp" (a metaphor that links natural generation to legitimate family minting or imprimatur), came to include under its umbrella the subdivision of "race" as a natural category. Writers developing a system of human classification described race a natural "kind" by which people(s) could be known and upon which social order could be founded. The language these writers used to try to fix meaning to the idea of race reflects a profound instability: in German alone, the disputed category was called interchangeably an *Art* or *Unterart*, a *Varietät*, a *Stamm* or *Menschenstamm*, a *Volk*, a *Völkerschaft*, a *Völkerstamm*, a *Geschlecht*, or a *Nation* (as well as the latin *gens*, a people or nation). To complicate things further, not only were many variously nuanced words used to refer to the category "race;" conversely, the term "race" itself was used (for the most part unscientifically) to represent a wide range of human groupings. The word *Rasse* (also spelled *Race*) or *Menschenrace* might represent a physiologically determined subset of the human species, but it was often as readily used to describe an individual family line (usually aristocratic), a regionally or politically defined group of people, or the human species as a whole.

If the species were to be understood as a large family, as the ultimate collective of reproductively related bodies, then it follows that any subset of the species must also be at once part of the universal genealogical family. Certainly the linguistic slippage evident in the early use of the term "race" suggests this presupposition, since it was used to denote a sweeping range of genealogically linked groupings of people. While the inclusion of all races within the species-family was a product of the logic of the concept itself and taken for granted by many engaged scientists and philosophers, some thinkers argued that different races should be considered fundamentally different in kind. Such thinkers (Voltaire and Kant among the more prominent) sustained—seemingly without qualm—the paradoxical view that different races might not all equally comprise a single tributary system that linked each real family to a humane, human species. Without exception, the difficulties seem to arise for thinkers who insist on conjoining a biological system of hereditary race and species with other aspects of human history, particularly the notion of cultural development.

THE DIFFERENT FATES OF KANT'S RACES

Kant has received the most attention in recent years for his highly influential, if scattered, writings on race. Much of this recent engagement has less to do with the particular structure of his thinking on race and more to do with the intrusion of such ideas into the Western philosophical canon, and thus careful analysis has been dedicated to questions of the impact that Kant's racialist (racist) writings ought to have on readings of his aesthetic theory or his critical epistemology.[3]

We cannot take Kant's writings on race as representative for the late eighteenth century. Indeed, contemporaries like Blumenbach, Herder, Ludwig, and Forster debated—even attacked—his theories. However, his influence was tremendous, simply by virtue of his authority as a philosopher. As Robert Bernasconi, Emmanuel Eze, and Charles Mills have pointed out, Kant produced the first developed, science-based theory of race.[4] And David Bindman has noted that, over the course of the eighteenth century, investigations into human diversity became, "increasingly the province of the university rather than the philosophical amateur."[5] Kant was in his lifetime revered as the great Philosopher at Königsberg, a university authority (howsoever ironic this might have been, given the tribulations of his career). Within the university, however, there was room for disagreement. Johann Daniel Metzger, a colleague and doctor in Königsberg, tartly prefaced a challenge to Kant's theories of four unchanging races with the revelation that he had been advised not to criticize "the new Prometheus who brought the pure fire of a critical thinking from heaven," because Kant was simply too important a philosopher to be challenged.[6] In 1804, the year Kant died, Metzger wrote a witty anti-eulogy, in which he attacked the great philosopher on grounds of rudeness, pomposity, and a willingness to write about subjects in which he had no expertise. At the end of a lively litany comes this dismissal of Kant's race theory: "It is clear from all that has been written since Kant engaged himself with this material, that the natural history of mankind was really not the subject in which he was destined to shine.... Blumenbach, Ludwig, and others have taught us better."[7]

While Blumenbach and Ludwig shall receive their due in this chapter, Kant's writings on race are interesting on their own terms, and we have to acknowledge their significant role in helping to shape scientific and popular opinion at the time. For this study, it is particularly fruitful to explore how Kant—never a lazy thinker—constructed a network of biological and cultural theories to support what would otherwise have been conflicting views of racial difference within a common human family.

In an essay of 1788, Kant defended race as a concept that still lacked terminological stability, but that nonetheless represented a real phenomenon of human natural history:

> What is a *race*? The word is not contained in any system of nature; presumably, therefore, the thing itself is not contained in nature? Yet it is known to every observer. For mere description, the term 'variety' is in use, but for the history of nature we need the term 'race.' The concept must of course be clearly defined, and this shall be attempted here.[8]

The extensive definitions of race that followed in Kant's numerous essays and lectures have been examined—not without conflicting interpretation—by philosophers and historians of science whose conclusions should not be condensed into facile summary. Here it suffices to focus upon a particular aspect of Kant's ideas that have bearing on the particular issue at hand, namely the position of race within a natural system modeled on lines of heredity.

Given his dictum to respect the innate dignity of all members of the human family, one might anticipate that Kant's belief in race as a natural and historically distinct subset of the human species would carry with it a regard for all such subdivisions as equally valuable in comprising the species, and as equally important to its ongoing process of improvement. On the contrary, however, Kant is quite clear about his belief in a fundamental *in*equality, insofar as the white race [*die Weisse*] has contributed most significantly to the species' cultural maturation process, in which the non-white races will never catch up.[9] While his derogatory pronouncements upon the various incapacities of Native Americans and Africans are often cited (one need look only to his essay on the "Races of Man" for ample evidence),[10] these remarks are by no means original. They simply echo a particularly bigoted perspective in circulation at the time. Far more provocative, I think, are Kant's unpublished notes on anthropology, particularly those to which Mark Larrimore and Robert Bernasconi have drawn attention: namely, those reflections in which Kant speculates on the likelihood that all races—with the exception of the white—would eventually die out, and that this represented a fulfillment of nature's grand purpose for the human species.

As noted in the previous chapter, Kant read the potential for human perfection through the "cultural progress" of the species, and he repeatedly referred to a natural tendency of humans to advance in cultural matters. How do we reconcile this with statements concerning the inability of certain races to advance at all? While many thinkers proposed that different races developed culturally at different times, Kant stated outright not only that certain races are culturally inferior to the white race (insofar as they fail to contribute to the ongoing process of species-perfection), but also that this discrepancy itself is an unchanging part of nature's design.

His argument here does adhere to a species-directed logic of hereditary development: Kant devised an explanatory system for racial division that involved a gradual, genealogically driven process of the elimination of particular traits within different discreet populations. He posited that the original *Stamm* or human grouping held within itself numerous capacities for climatic adaptability, among other things. For these capacities Kant selects the effective metaphor, "seeds" or *Keime*. This metaphor comes to the aide of his argument for diversification: as the original *Stamm* separated and migrated to various parts of the globe, the different conditions they encountered triggered the development of different "seeds," allowing for the development of particular traits enabling adaptation. These seeds and the traits that grew from them were heritable: ensuing generations continued to adapt and flourish by virtue of this organic adaptability.[11] However, Kant argues, while different seeds sprouted among diversified groups, helping them to adapt to different environments, the potency of other unused seeds each group carried was eventually extinguished, thus terminating future adaptability and fixing patterns of differences that now might productively be termed "racial." Kant writes in an essay, "On the Use of the Teleological Principle" the following:

> The race-differences must have been laid out potentially from the start, to adapt human beings to a few essential conditions, while the differences in what I call varieties predispose them for an infinity of different conditions. After the race-characteristics were developed (in the earliest times) no new types could develop, nor could the old ones become extinct. But the varieties seem inexhaustible in new characters, both external and internal.[12]

If one also accepts as part of this conceptual design the idea that different peoples extended their cultural productivity in different ways as a result of the particular combinations of seed, adaptation, and environment, then this explanatory system neatly provides an organic excuse for a qualitative difference among cultural development among races. As crude examples, Kant offered the observation that Native Americans and Blacks, particularly, were presumed to be incapable of change, because the "seeds" [*Keime*] that developed with their raciation involved the irreversible extinguishing of other potencies, such as a drive to activity. By the same token, because the same drive flourished in the white race, it is a permanent and characteristic element of its constitution.[13]

The argument does not stop here: Kant associated not only bodily traits and cultural inclinations, like "work," with all-determining, but variously germinating, implanted seeds. Significantly, he also used the same metaphor—the implanted seed or *Keim*—to defend the existence of moral good within the nature of human beings. In his posthumously published *Reflections on Anthropology*, Kant writes, "There must be a seed for each Good in the character of human beings, otherwise no one would express it; lacking these, one substitutes analogous drives like honor, etc."[14] While he does not expand here upon the link between seeds of raciation and seeds of moral capacity, the explicit inclusion of cultural values and behaviors in the former, and an individual's potential lack of sufficient seeds alluded to in the latter, provide ample invitation to conceptual blending.

It is a remarkable intellectual feat that Kant pulls off here, if ultimately unacceptable in its sweeping claims. He first works with the genealogical system to develop all peoples from an *Urstamm*, and then suggests that particular genealogical lines are destined, through their hereditary development, to cultural dead ends. That allows him a further gesture along this spurious logical line that ultimately provides a natural historical defense for considering the "white race" the equivalent of the species, when he theorizes about the unity and perfectibility of that species. As Emmanuel Eze has noted: "Strictly speaking, Kant's anthropology and geography offer the strongest, if not the only, sufficiently articulated *theoretical philosophical* justification of the superior/inferior classification of 'races of man' of any European writer before him."[15] And Mark Larrimore observes, with even more bluntness: "Kant's anthropology appears to disqualify non-whites from the work of civilization."[16] In his unpublished reflections on anthropology, Kant writes that "Whites possess all natural drives of affect and passion, all talents, all capacities for culture and civilization, and can obey as well as rule. They are the only [race], which always progresses toward perfection." By contrast, "The Negro can be disciplined and cultivated, but can never be truly civilized. He degenerates by his own fault [*von selbst*] into savageness [*Wildheit*]." Finally, it would seem that these disparities will not continue to plague humanity—not because various peoples will grow more similar over time, but because "all races will be exterminated [*ausgerottet*], with sole exception of the White race."[17] Larrimore argues that Kant "conceived of the (non-white) races as an unsalvageable waste, a mistake, meaningless in the grand teleological scheme of things."[18]

This is a hefty charge, by no means acceptable to all Kant scholars, and yet traceable through the private notes that Kant wrote but chose not to publish. One should also note that the idea of a gradual extinction of "lesser" races was not Kant's private fantasy: as Patrick Brantlinger's recent work vividly demonstrates, a discourse of the eventual extermination of savages beginning at the end of the eighteenth century and extending throughout the nineteenth, "acted on the world as well as described it," ultimately lending support to social Darwinism and eugenics research.[19] Of course, that does not excuse Kant from personal responsibility for his writings. One might note that we find a mechanism in the species logic to subvert the "sublime waste" argument; certainly, the defining condition of species as Kant himself accepted it is the potential capacity of all members to mate with each other. Does racial mixing not challenge Kant's absolute divisions?

Of course it does, and Kant acknowledged this ruefully, even as he looks for ways both to admit its physical possibility and to point to other means by which nature thwarts it, thus marking it as incompatible with human progress and the natural good. In the same series of notes that includes his pronouncement on the eventual extermination of non-white races, we read this simple declaration, devoid of elaboration: "It is not good that they mix together. Spaniards in Mexico." In the *Reflections on Anthropology*, he speculates at more length, and with rather extraordinary conclusions:

> It is Providence's intention that peoples [*Völker*] do not blend together, but rather through certain divisive power are in conflict with each other; thus national pride and national hatred [*Nationalhaß*] are necessary to separate nations. Therefore a people [*Volk*] loves its land over all others, either through religion, whereby a people believes that all

others are cursed (like Jews and Turks), or through the conceit of reason, that all others are incapable and ignorant, or [through the conceit of] courage, that one fears for one's people, or [through the conceit of freedom], that all others are slaves. Governments welcome this delusion. We have only this as the *mechanism* of the organization of the world that links and separates us instinctively.[20]

Kant could not argue that different races were physically incapable of interbreeding, though he noted often enough that the result of such mixing was the production of "half-breeds" who were "not worth much."[21] Lacking an anchor for his revulsion against miscegenation in the available evidence of natural history, Kant instead made an argument about the nature of culture. Since there did not seem to exist a natural antagonism among *races* sufficient to keep them apart, Kant shifted the terms of the discussion to the "instinctive" and thus natural hatred among "people" and "nations," as if such animosity existed to preserve discrete bio-cultural communities. Was he aware of the irony that resounds through this passage, as his own prejudicial arguments fashioned around a "conceit of reason" are effectively qualified as a delusion, albeit one that he claims is consistent with an overarching intention on the part of "providence" to maintain separation among *Völker*? As Susan Shell has observed, "Since human reason is itself, according to Kant, a hybrid [*Bastart*], whose laudable efforts toward self-union run the constant risk of straying into unproductive wastelands, it is no wonder that the phenomenon of race fascinated Kant was by as he perceived it, and that he was both attracted and—even more—repelled by the prospect of racial intermixture."[22]

As heirs to the eighteenth-century legacy, we are in the curious position of championing Kant's call for universal human respect while repudiating his particular account of the composition—via separation and eventual selective extermination—of universal humanity. The presence of racism in his writings suggests a belief that there is no inherent contradiction in upholding the value of all human life while simultaneously denying that all individuals or subsets of the greater human family share the same potential or responsibility for contributing to the ultimate perfection of the group.[23] In fact, this neatly replicates the logic of the contemporaneous political compromise between absolutism and "human rights" which we examined in the first chapter of this book: when Friedrich the Great championed the equal value of all people before God and the law, that ideal equality was in no way intended to undermine a harsh social hierarchy. Indeed, the rhetorical insistence upon a "familial" species might further contribute to this balancing act, insofar as the family model could communicate both natural belonging and a set of often-brutal inequities between genders and generations characteristic of family life as well as paternalist government.[24] But we might also consider, in trying to make sense of Kant's view of non-Caucasian races as "sublime waste," that, by suggesting the demise of the less accomplished (culturally and physically different) races, he foresaw an ultimate outcome by which his racial family does comprise the entire species. When Kant declared that we are all one species and one family, it might have logically followed that all races, belonging to the species, were also of one family; rather than embracing them as brothers, however, Kant devised his highly idiosyncratic theory by which the non-white races would eventually be exterminated [*ausgerottet*] by natural design—in fact, by an inherited destiny that evolved in their genealogical past in order to preclude a generative future. This is a particularly overt expression of what seems to inhabit eighteenth-century anthropological discourse: namely, a repressed emotional resistance to the philosophical ideal of universal humanity, masked as constructive scientific and aesthetic theories of natural, naturally meaningful separations. Such discourse theorized "inferior" peoples back out of the universal family.

RACE, VOLK, NATION

Many disputed Kant's not altogether clear views on racial-cultural difference, despite his authoritative weight. The naturalist, ethnologist and travel writer Georg Forster fought famously with Kant, rejecting race as a natural marker of human division and ridiculing the great philosopher for the elaborate systems that he concocted in his study, devoid of first-hand observation or evidence.[25] Herder, first Kant's student and later his intellectual opponent, reiterated a dismissal of racial division often, and generally with poetic flourish:

> In short, there are neither four or five races, nor exclusive varieties on the earth. The colors lose themselves in each other; forms serve the genetic character; and in the end, everything is no more that a shaded variation of one and the same great image, that extends itself through all places and times of the earth.[26]

Herder seems to have understood that scientific categories, regardless of their seeming objectivity, were invitations to and justifications for oppression, and responded accordingly. Thus he countered racialist theory with a discourse of brotherhood, inveighing upon his readers with full Biblical resonance: "Thou shalt not oppress, nor murder, nor steal from [the American or the Negro, the brother], because he is a human being, just as you are."[27]

While dismissing Kant's firm division of races, Herder did nevertheless identify and revere the *Volk* or the *Nation* as an organic, genealogically comprised unit. The question arises: was Herder's concept of an organic *Volk* a naturalization of racial difference by other means? Here I would submit that Herder's thought is better described by what David Bindman calls "biological nationalism," a phenomenon distinct from racism, although its manifestations "passed for racial theory in the nineteenth and twentieth centuries."[28]

Looking at the evolution of attempts to make sense of the various scales of community that organize the human family, it is clear that, before there is coherent talk either of "races" or of a German political "nation" per se, the words *Rasse* and *Nation* were both used to denote very nearly any group sharing ancestry and exhibiting hereditary traits. Nicholas Hudson has charted the parallel derivation of "race" and "nation" from a concept of lineage or stock, noting that, as a gradual result of linguistic practice, "race" ultimately was used for ethnographic scholarship, "nation" described political and social divisions of civilization, and "tribe" replaced nation in descriptions of "savage" non-European peoples.[29] The late eighteenth and early nineteenth centuries are squarely within the period of gradual change in linguistic practice that Hudson identifies. This change may be evidenced by the difficulties in pinning down terms by a writer like Herder, who is generally equated with the rise of nationalism in Germany. Recent studies tend to be more generously inclined toward Herder, focusing upon his genuine appreciation for the folk customs and literary expressions of all peoples, rendering him as a kind of proto-typical multi-culturalist.[30] Helmut Smith positions Herder as a medial figure between two concepts of nation, between a Renaissance-based "nation of the exterior senses, primarily sight, secondarily sound," and a later nation "conceived as an extension of the interiorized self," associated with the "late enlightenment search for the nation's center of gravity in its poetry and its language."[31]

Herder's understanding of different peoples occupies a position between the scientific writing of Blumenbach and the politically motivated nationalistic rhetoric of writers like Arndt, Fichte, and others—those "architects of nationalism" in the early nineteenth century who themselves deserve a more considered and nuanced reading than many modern historians of nation would grant.[32] Herder's rejection of biologically distinct races in favor of culturally distinct peoples rested upon a belief in a genealogical force that manifests itself sometimes physiologically (apparent as a "national stamp"), sometimes spiritually, and nearly always linguistically.

In his essay on the origins of language, Herder affirms: "Languages vary with every people, in every climate; but in all languages one and the same type of searching human reason is conspicuous."[33] Nevertheless, he retains a tie between language and the *Volk* or *Nation*, conceived as a group with common heritage (a mixture of blood and culture) that is both physically and linguistically evident. Both physical and cultural characteristics, their relationship unclear but asserted, are both transmitted along ancestral lines, from parent to child, constituting what Herder called the "flow of generations."[34]

Reading Herder's writing to the natural language and spirit that inhered in and was expressed by each *Volk*, we encounter the same constellation of figures to convey his understanding of the history of human groups that proliferated in scientific accounts of race: that is, the intersection of family, nature, and larger human communities. Herder championed the form of the tribal "nation," or "*Nationalstaat*," as something that maintains organic, ancestral culture, as opposed to the "state," a political construct that leads to despotism and cultural annihilation. The nation, he claimed, develops naturally from "the first form of government among human beings," namely, the "organization of the family".[35] Similarly, he wrote that states are lately evolved, along with their arts and sciences, but "families are the eternal work of nature, the ongoing domestic economy, insofar as they implant the seed [*Samen*] of humanity into the human species and then develop it."[36] The nation is thus a familial and organic unit growing naturally out of the relationships created by nature (manifest specifically within the family) and unified by common descent. This is contrasted with the purely political state, also called the "machine-state" [*Staatsmaschine*] which subjugates the individual to the role of an alienated part of the mechanized whole.

> Nature raises families; the most natural State is thus a people with a national character. For thousands of years this character preserves itself in the state, and it can be most naturally developed when its native prince concerns himself with it; for a people [*Volk*] is as much a plant of nature as a family, only with more branches.[37]

Herder's images here run typically riot: we encounter natural families that are plants with branches, and somehow we are to translate this into a political, cultural critique. As Sankar Muthu rightly observes in a consideration of Herder's political thought, the use of organic metaphors and genetic arguments "are, for good reason, sources of much confusion, and they indicate that there are tensions in his writings that no interpretation can or should overcome."[38] Certain images, however, are repeated with a consistency that suggests coherence, one of which is the "original family likeness" [*Stammbild*] each nation possesses. This identifying stamp, argues Herder, "extends all the way to families and its passage is as malleable as it is imperceptible."[39]

Though Herder dismissed racial difference *per se* as inconsequential, he nevertheless inveighed against the "unnatural growth of States, the wild intermixture of human races and nations under one scepter."[40] In an odd but revealing mixing of metaphors, he insisted that such "wild interbreeding" produces a "State-Machine . . . without an inner life or a sympathy among the various parts."[41] Peoples who retain their heredity exclusivity intact are able to maintain the spirit that inspires and individuates them; peoples who mingle lose the essential value of traditional culture and are left with nothing but the empty forms of sociality. This kind of interbreeding is not a problem on biological grounds, however, but specifically because it leads to a homogenization of the cultural legacies unique to each people [*Gattung*] and nation. This protection of difference, however, that he calls for does accommodate the value of more moderate cultural cross-exposure to nourish and inspire. As Brian Vick argues, in Herder's case, "recourse to the organic as a concept of cultural and historical analysis . . . under certain conditions welcomes the introduction of foreign matter. An organism, after all, must take into itself parts of its environment if it is to live and grow."[42]

Anthony J. La Vopa, in asking what led Herder to reach for the concept of national identity when working through problems of community, analyzes Herder's early writings on language politics. Herder, La Vopa reminds us, worried about a "linguistic and social bifurcation"[43] caused by the dominant presence of the French language in aristocratic society and its power to exclude other social orders from court life. As a result of the caste-bound German/French divide, people from different social realms lacked "a reliable common organ for their innermost feelings."[44] We are reminded here that, for Herder, every people has a language, and every language provides its own, expansive insights into the soul of that people.

Nationalism and modernity are generally understood to be linked phenomena; more to the point, Ute Planert has argued that the second half of the eighteenth century was the "beginning phase of 'modern' nationalism."[45] Liah Greenfeld goes so far as to assert that modernity is "defined by nationalism,"[46] and claims that, for German thinkers at the turn of the nineteenth century, "the spirit of the nation, and therefore its language, reflected the body; ultimately nationality was based on blood." As evidence for such sentiment, she offers Ernst Moritz Arndt, writing in 1815: "The Germans are not bastardized by alien peoples, they have not become mongrels; they have remained more than many other peoples in their original purity and have been able to develop slowly and quietly from this purity of their kind and nature according to the lasting laws of time; the fortunate Germans are an original people."[47] Reflecting upon Arndt's pronouncement, Greenberg both overestimates and underestimates the role of racialist thinking available to Arndt and his ilk. Overlooking the proliferating and profoundly influential speculations on race flowing from the human and natural sciences, Greenfeld falsely presumes that Arndt wrote at a time (1815) "long before the word 'race' acquired its specific meaning and . . . long before racism, bolstered by the authority of science, became an articulate and presumably objective view." By 1815, Europeans were debating the configuration and significance of racial difference without any doubt whatsoever in the legitimacy of the concept. Already in 1803, when Arndt published his first anti-French diatribe, *Germania and Europe* [*Germanien und Europa*], a vocabulary of racial divisions and character was available to the reading public through numerous literary, scientific, and philosophical weeklies. My point here is that Arndt was not "anticipating" race—to maintain that he did would be to suggest that he would have availed himself more explicitly of the concept, had it been available. The scientific concept of race was very much available, but Arndt, even in his most blood-bound moments, was not talking of race but of hereditary community, united by lineage and language and spirit and history. His notion of the familial nation had a conceptual foundation similar to that of race, but it is not the same thing. It is important to avoid the simplifying gesture that Greenfeld makes when she declares that, "the national identity of the Germans was essentially an identity of race."[48]

I would argue that Arndt is hardly a representative example of German nationalist rhetoric: as Helmut Smith notes of Arndt's major work, the *Spirit of the Time* [*Geist der Zeit*], "the book, and the ferocity of its rhetoric, stood alone."[49] It is also essential to read Arndt in the context of Prussian anxieties about Napoleonic conquest, and the conscious attempts by writers—encouraged by the Prussian Minister of State, the Freiherr von und zum Stein—to inspire and sustain a German national identity that could withstand French forces. The tensions of the period, particularly those between Prussian patriotism and rising German nationalism, triggered responses both rational and extreme, and influenced the language of German collective interest in provocative and inconsistent ways. For some, the German *Vaterland* meant Prussia; for others, it included various constellations of German-speaking regions. Arndt tackled this in his poem of 1813, entitled "What is the German's Fatherland?," insisting over several stanzas that Germany must not be limited to Prussia or Bavaria or Austria or any particular region, but instead "must be greater than that." In answer to the question, "what is the German's fatherland?" Arndt answers, "as far as the German tongue can be heard" adding also "wherever French means enemy and German means friend." The German *Vaterland* was far from being clearly identifiable, whether by geographic, political, philosophical, linguistic, or ethnic identity markers; people interested in a "German nation" approached contested territory. As Christopher Clark notes significantly about the decisive period of the Napoleonic battles and the restructuring of Prussia, "The word 'nation' was used for both Prussia and Germany," and the tension between the two was often unsettling.[50]

While statements invoking ideas of national purity unspoiled by "alien" peoples certainly can be found in political rhetoric around the beginning of the nineteenth century, they do not index an inherent "racism" in Germany's discourse of nationalism; they are, rather, evidence of a blend of rhetorical modes available for naturalizing particular group identities. The fact that both racialist and nationalist thinkers availed themselves of a common language of heredity, genealogical lines, and historical family ties does not imply necessarily that "race" was conceived as nationalist or that "nation" was conceived as racist. Only over time, as the concepts developed in concert with each other, were the notions of race and nation mined for proleptic evidence of a belief system that was yet to form. If we heed Karl Deutsch's remark, that a nation is "a group of people united by a common delusion regarding their ancestry and a common hostility toward their neighbors,"[51] it is no doubt interesting to consider nationalism as a potent mixture of political enmity and an interest in hereditary identity that scientific inquiries into racial variation newly legitimized. Conversely, we might easily speculate that theorizers of "race" borrowed from the parallel concept of nation the license to hate the other as a cultural threat. In any case, it may be said that figures like Blumenbach and Christian Friedrich Ludwig—those theorizers of race primarily interested in the production of scientific knowledge—were uninterested by the phenomenon of interracial enmity, while thinkers like Kant or Herder, whose concerns shifted back and forth across the conceptual bridge of race-culture-nation, faced it head-on. Kant, as we have seen, accepted this enmity and gave it an historical and organic narrative. Herder, on the other hand, chose to celebrate the challenge of difference.

Herder's beliefs in the individual family as a natural core of community and in the single, inclusive human species are linked by his belief in the value of distinct peoples and by his rejection of race as a natural kind. His formulation of the organically generated people or nation is not a scientific subset of species, nor is it defined strictly as an unbroken genealogical lineage through conjoined family lines. A people is conceived less as a product of the family than as a similar product of the same greater natural design.

Herder's effort was focused upon the preservation of rich cultural difference and specificity, behind which lies a belief in a quasi-mystical dynamic of the transmission of original linguistic culture through ancestral lineage. He theorized a murky realm—part biological, part conceptual, where the material natural state ends and reason, patterned on nature, takes over. He presumed that the powers of abstraction and organization that underscore human social structures exist subsequent to the manifest force of real, material nature. The transition from nature to natural human culture is, according to such conception, something that is itself determined by nature, which initially engineers society's foundation via the family, and then hands over its agency to the "human understanding, or the need to build greater structures upon it."[52] Although this description is an allegorical drama rather than a scientific account of the process, readers of subsequent eras understood—or misunderstood—his words to support claims of the priority of processes that were at once historical and organic.

THE INSIGNIFICANCE OF RACE (AN UNPOPULAR ARGUMENT)

Herder disagreed with Kant's racial thinking primarily because it offended his understanding of species unity and it was incompatible with his own ideas of the flow of multiple, different, and equally valued cultures through time. A very different kind of criticism of race theory *à la* Kant came from Christian Friedrich Ludwig, a professor of medicine who tried to keep the notion of culture out of the debate altogether.

74   *Heredity, Race, and the Birth of the Modern*

Ludwig, in his 1795 *Outline for a Natural History of the Human Species* [*Grundriss der Naturgeschichte der Menschenspecies*], told his targeted readers—identified in his introduction as medical professionals, philosophers, and legal scholars—in no uncertain terms that, despite manifold variations, "the human being exists within the system [of natural science] as a single kind, a single species."[53] Ludwig presented a full spectrum of scholarly perspectives on the terms "species" and "race," noting wryly that "the term 'race' [*Menschenrace*] is defined very differently among numerous discerning philosophers."[54] Following the leading anthropologist of the day, Johann Friedrich Blumenbach, Ludwig took an increasingly unpopular position in arguing the insignificance of racial differences for a rigorous understanding of human nature. He honed in on a critical relationship between race and species, when he wrote:

> If I regard other animal species or even plant species that branch off into countless variations, I am inclined to increase the number of races or varieties, in order to lend weight to the evidence of the unity of the original stock [*Urstamm*]. But who will ever decipher all of the races that are subdivisions of the primary races, and all the varieties of varieties of these subordinate races, etc.?
>
> More important than any racial differences is, without a doubt, the evidence of the unity of the stock [*Stamm*].[55]

This text reveals an awareness that the theorizing of species and race continue to influence each other, and that the notion of universal relatedness is at stake in the relationship theorized between them. Concerned for the unity of man, Ludwig argued for a multiplication of racial divisions, as if hoping to destabilize the race concept by overwhelming it with data. To emphasize that racial variation is arbitrary, he linked his voice to Blumenbach, citing that, "only arbitrary or haphazard borders exist between the varieties of the human species."[56]

While granting that Blumenbach's division of peoples into the "five major races" was useful as a scientific shorthand, Ludwig insisted that a more comprehensive list of significant, hereditary, and relatively consistent patterns of physical difference among the world's peoples would necessarily require far more distinctions than a mere five. As a kind of rebellious demonstration posing as science (in this natural-history "handbook," as he called it), Ludwig provided an extraordinary, poetic list of skin tones and specific peoples that render absurd the reduction of human beings into five "natural" groups.[57] He lists peoples according to thirteen different color variations. Particularly provocative is his inclusion among "the white color" only "most Europeans," along with Greeks, peoples around the Black Sea, certain Persians, Tibetans, Chinese, and Japanese. He provides seven categories of dark skin: simple brown, "a brown that tends to red," "more or less dark brown," "black-brown," "especially black-brown," simple black, "less black," and "blacker." For each color, he lists peoples with a specificity that defies the European tendency to create crude groupings, insisting for example on identifying individually as separate peoples the "Californians," "Canadians," and "Floridians" where many of his contemporaries simply noted "Americans"; likewise, Ludwig distinguished an impressive array of particular African and Pacific Island peoples, effectively foreclosing an attempt to group such non-Europeans into coherent racial collectives.

Ludwig goes so far as to ask, "Which among these colors is the original?—the white—or the yellow?" and wonders, "Couldn't the Negro just as well insist that he is the original man [*Urmensch*]?"[58] And perhaps most provocatively, he suggests that racial difference is entirely the product of what we today would loosely call sexual selection: he notes that, "the propagation of our species is based upon an impulse that is particularly lively and active during a given period of life and that is connected with sexual diversity [*Sexualdiversitaet*]."[59] This "sexual diversity" is not merely a sexual drive prompted by gender difference; he specifies that "the most potent cause of the play of color across the skin of our species is the mating and mixing of genders and peoples [*Stämme*]."[60]

At work here is a lively mind, intrigued by the multiple perspectives on race in circulation, and utterly unconvinced by attempts to naturalize simple hierarchies. Ludwig campaigns against the exploitation of visible differences to construct systems of racial classification that are at once declared "natural" and that also pass judgment upon qualities of soul and the moral good. Ultimately, he rehearses the unoriginal but clearly called-for declaration of the equal capabilities and worthiness among all peoples: "I come to the fundamental sameness of all human beings with regard to their capacity for thought, and the power of their souls, and their similar tendency toward the moral good. Moral good is not a privilege of any single human variety. From time immemorial there have been found wiser and the nobler people among every *Volk*."[61]

The back-and-forth arguing among intelligent men about the reality and the significance of "race" is surprising both in its predictability and in its longevity. It is important to note that serious doubts about the validity of race as an intellectual construct existed as soon as such constructs were ventured. I wish to suggest here that the persistent role of visible difference as the primary marker of the distinct races should be understood as an after-effect of the still-new (and still-disputed) species concept. As scientists no longer defined the species according to morphological similarities, but rather along imperceptible lines of generational continuity,[62] the visible traits (skin color, hair texture) by which folk taxonomy identified facts of affiliation and difference were shifted: not out of the scientific system altogether, but into the category that is, in theory, the species' smaller tributary. If race, as a particular extension of species, remained scientifically vague for most of the century, it nevertheless was the subject of vast speculation. Eyewitness accounts of the visible distinctions of the various non-European peoples of the world remained an essential component of the popular understanding of racial difference.[63]

Particular physical similarities were identified as racial traits, despite scientific skepticism regarding their nature, stability, or relation to other physical and intellectual traits; they functioned effectively as the "visible bands" necessary for a united community. Although the universalism of a human species—a family of man—made for effective rhetoric, it failed to compel emotional loyalties; particular families were too individuated to unite people. Race, on the contrary, functioned as a primary visible cue of group identity, despite the strenuous efforts of people like Blumenbach, Herder, Ludwig, and others to disengage the science of race from racism. And thus it was Christian Meiners, a prolific advocate of the natural inferiority of non-European races and a second-class scientist at best, whose writings were so popular that a colleague called him "the beloved philosopher of our fatherland."[64] This much-admired man proliferated views of frightful, animal-like Africans, describing them as cannibals with "a frightful, tiger-like, hardly human look" and with jagged teeth "that lock together like the bite of a fox." These Negro cannibals, he claimed, are so "greedy for human flesh, that they bite huge chunks of flesh from the arms or legs of their neighbors and fellow slaves, and swallow them down."[65] With such prose, Meiners entranced a reading public with synthesized and sensationalized presentations of travel accounts, presented as the accumulated evidence of a natural racial hierarchy.[66]

BLUMENBACH'S AMBIVALENCE

Johann Friedrich Blumenbach's position on the significance of a race category is complex and often under-appreciated by intellectual historians, somewhat surprising in view of the dominant role he played in a lengthy (and continuing) scientific debate over whether or not "race" actually represented a real and distinct group existing in nature. While defending the reality of species and the inclusion of all humans into a single species produced and governed by laws of physical generation, Blumenbach considered the further subdivision of species into races to be conceptually useful but scientifically unfounded. In his *Handbook* he insisted:

> All of the national differences in the form and color of the human body are not a whit more significant or mysterious as those among other species of organized bodies, for example domestic pets, that change [*ausarten*] under our very eyes. All of these differences flow imperceptibly together through so many nuances, that there cannot be any boundaries between them other than the purely arbitrary: nevertheless I have decided for the sake of convenience to arrange the entirety of the human kind under the following five varieties.[67]

Here, as with Herder, "national" signified something other than political or even geographical affinity. Blumenbach used it without apparent need for qualification as an acceptable synonym for race or tribe. He thus identified observable national/racial differences in physiological structure and color as products of breeding (comparable to domestic animals that "degenerate" before our eyes), though these patterns should be understood as being neither consistent nor exclusive. As Herder also observed, an individual's hair color or skull shape may approximate traits characteristic of more than one nation or race, thus failing to identify its bearer as belonging to one or the other. On such grounds, a category like race can never be precise or have any but arbitrary [*willkürliche*] boundaries between its various instances. Species, by contrast, was a real division in nature because the barrier preventing the intermixing of species was a natural (if occasionally breachable) fact.

Troubled by what already appeared to be a misapplications of the race idea, Blumenbach reiterated in numerous publications that races did not have the status of small species, but were functionally similar to other types of impermanent (if historically significant) variation: "Only this is certain: all of humankind's differences that are so striking at first glance prove, under closer examination, to flow together through imperceptible transitions and nuances, and thus only the most arbitrary borders between these types may be drawn."[68] While reminding his readers often of the "imperceptible transitions" and the "arbitrary borders" that prevented race from being a historically stable category, Blumenbach adopted the terminology of race—with caveats—as a useful scientific convention by which to organize perceived patterns of difference. To this day, he is associated with "identifying" five dominant races, although disputes remain as to whether Blumenbach or Kant should receive the dubious honor of being credited as the "inventor" of the modern race concept per se. As Robert Bernasconi, John Zammito, Phillip Sloan and others have demonstrated in recent years, attributing the invention of race to Blumenbach may have been a standard gesture of nineteenth- and twentieth-century histories of science, but it is nonetheless a misleading simplification.[69] It took Blumenbach many years to accept the use of "race" as a classificatory term, and once he did, he consistently stressed that the concept had limited use as a descriptive heuristic for science. While historians of race thinking dutifully cite this qualification in critical literature, generations of subsequent scientists cite with far more resonance Blumenbach's identification of five races.[70]

Among Blumenbach's many public positions on the race question, one of the most interesting occurs with the publication of an atlas designed to accompany and illustrate his *Handbook of Natural History*. In 1796, he produced a scientific atlas entitled *Images of Natural-Historical Artifacts* [*Abbildungen Naturhistorischer Gegenstände*].[71] Seven of the book's one hundred illustrations provide instruction in the natural history of the human species; the subset of five with which the book opens are identified as "characteristic model heads of men from the five primary races [*Hauptrassen*] of the human kind [*im Menschengeschlechte*].[72] This book includes a remarkable textual negotiation of conflicting epistemologies: present throughout Blumenbach's collective work and highlighted by the *Images* is the certainty, on the one hand, that race can function as an always-temporary category of physical classification, and on the other hand, that race must be rejected entirely as an analytic category of culture.

The textbook was a medium Blumenbach knew well; by the time he designed the atlas, his *Handbook* was in its fifth edition, already a standard reference for current knowledge of the process of human generation, the nature and history of the species, and the causes and significance of human diversity. Of this work, a colleague would remark in 1840: "If it can be said of any scientific work of modern times, that its utility has been incalculable, such a sentence must be pronounced on Blumenbach's *Handbook of Natural History*. Few cultivated circles or countries are ignorant of it."[73] Once the *Images* was published, all subsequent editions of the *Handbook* included direct references to the atlas, indicating an assumption that a reader would have access to, and make use of, both books. And the atlas itself appeared in four editions between 1796 and 1810—critical years for debates concerning the race question.[74]

I have written elsewhere at length on the extraordinarily unconventional presentation of the "five primary races" identified in the *Images*, on the strain that Blumenbach put onto the conventional form of the atlas, and on its relation to contemporaneous theories of portraiture.[75] Blumenbach, I argue, defied the very logic of type the atlas presupposed in order to reframe his examples of racial types as historical subjects who are as much creative participants in the possible forms of their own racial and cultural identities as the (presumably) European reader. In so doing, Blumenbach effectively removed race from playing a role in the continuity between individuals and the species: it is clear that, while each of the five men portrayed might well be used to represent typical racial traits, the significance of their presentation is the stress upon their individual accomplishments which are, if anything, typical of human potential available to the entire species. Race, in fact, plays almost no role in the presentation of race, and the lack of the very term suggests that Blumenbach tried to perform for his readers a necessary erasure of its prevalent but misplaced signifying power.

Blumenbach spent his illustrious and long career researching and writing about the physical processes of human generation and the generation of the human species. In his writings on race, he remained committed to theorizing the dynamic changes of dominant heritable traits. It is thus all the more significant that, in his textbook atlas, he removed all references to generation or heredity, and instead staged a visual argument for the united species. However, in what amounts to a non-presentation of race within the *Images*, there is one notable exception to his evasion of the "race" idea, on the page devoted to the Caucasian.

This exception is of interest in part because other writers of the period tended to de-emphasize the racialization of the white Europeans, thereby underscoring an implicit association of "race" with "otherness." Blumenbach's discursive gesture in the atlas is a provocative refutation of this mode of thinking: whereas with his four non-Caucasian portraits he deemphasizes the signifying range of the facts of race, with this portrait he explicitly and provocatively racializes the Caucasian.

Blumenbach's Caucasian subject is Jusuf Aguiah Efendi (alternatively, Yusuf Agah Efendi), the first Ottoman ambassador appointed to England in 1793. In commenting upon his choice of Efendi as the typical Caucasian (the race, as Blumenbach notes pointedly, "to which—according to *our* notions of beauty—the best-formed humans belong"), Blumenbach stresses that he could as easily have chosen "a Milton or a Raphael."[76] The creation of such a cohort of alternatives—Milton, Raphael, and Efendi—implies that the three men are potentially exchangeable in terms of their racial identity. They also share professions that mediate representations, be they literary, visual, or diplomatic. Milton and Raphael signal the heights of European cultural achievement. Blumenbach explains that he selected Efendi, however, as most appropriately representative of the race not based upon cultural attributes or physical traits that the picture might convey, but specifically because his home [*Heimat*] is closer to the Caucasus, where the race itself was originally "at home" [*zu Hause*] and from which it derives its name. This information refers to the priority of origins, a concern at the core of race and species theories; in Blumenbach's brief text, it serves to reassign the topic of race to its appropriate realm, that of scientific speculation into the natural history, rather than the current or future cultural expressivity, of various peoples.

This identification of Efendi with the Caucasian race and its original "home" also distances the Western European Old World from its purported racial origins by selecting an image of the "Caucasian" with whom a (Western-European, Christian, Caucasian) reader might not readily identify, be it physically, culturally, religiously, or politically. With his other portraits and descriptions, Blumenbach combats the tendency toward primitivist fantasy by actively conveying the selfhood of his subjects, all of whom represent for a typical European reader of the time some combination of racial and cultural otherness. Yet in presenting an exemplary Caucasian, Blumenbach requires of his reader what Hal Foster identifies as "a recognition of an alterity in the self."[77] Efendi, depicted as a turbaned, Muslim, Ottoman ambassador to Britain, serves not only as a diplomatic translator of multiple cultural languages on the European stage; Blumenbach's use of his image compounds Efendi's role as a go-between to mediate (and thereby render visible) tensions between various forms of difference. By pointing to a potential discrepancy between racial categorization and personal, cultural, or national identity, Blumenbach encourages his readers to recognize this discrepancy in other peoples categorized within other races.

THE CAUCASUS: ORIGIN OF THE SPECIES

European scientists posited a system of racial identity that generally explained the current state of each group as the product of two forces: a process of degeneration and separation from a (no longer extant) original stock, and a process of development—ideally, improvement—of both cultural and physical attributes, along paths distinctly different for each race. Distilled to simple form, this suggests a separation of history into two periods of time, each marked by progressive change: the first phase of human history witnesses a proliferation of kinds from an original purity; the second phase is marked by the gradual refinement of these chaotic kinds into limited and discreet races, each progressing toward its own, new pure form. We have seen how several prominent writers formulated theories of refinement and distinction among the races. But what of their beginnings?

In an era obsessed with origins, German theorists of race collectively located the origin of the "white" race—and often, the origin of all races—in the Caucasus. Why, we should ask, were the European "whites" named "Caucasian," and why was the white race, the purported *Urstamm* of the various human kinds, supposed to have originated there, as Blumenbach's use of Efendi—"at home" near the Caucasus—reinforced? It is important to keep in mind that the Caucasus Mountains were (and still are) a highly fraught dividing line between Asia and Europe, and territories in Caucasia are variably considered to be in one or both continents. The region was less a border than a blending zone between Christian Europe and Muslim Asia. Further, the Caucasus was (and is) one of the most linguistically and culturally diverse regions on earth. It would seem that, with the designation "Caucasian," the origins of the European were not so European after all; the line was rooted instead in a liminal zone, with its babel of languages, ethnic loyalties, religions, and cultural practices. It was not the Europeans *per se* but the people of the Caucasus who were identified as the source—a hybrid hereditary source—of the newly racialized European present.

This does not fit intuitively with most historical accounts of racial thinking; Vanessa Agnew repeats what has come to be a truism when she asserts that, "for all eighteenth-century theorists race was an oppositional category: the European was the yardstick against which others were compared and contrasted."[78] It is all the more startling, then, to realize that the racial schematization of the European Caucasian is one of the least stable—and least investigated—of the identity categories produced at the end of the eighteenth century. Rather than marking a fixed identity, "Caucasian" is better described by Homi Bhabha's metaphor of a "third space," a discursive condition in which signs and symbols of culture remain in flux, continually subject to translation.[79] This flux is evident from the initial gestures toward locating European racial identity within this unstable territory: we see a tangle of justifications that include Biblical tradition, historical geography, and conclusions drawn from the physical beauty of the inhabitants themselves, especially the women. Georg Forster scoffed: "Most of the old divisions of the human species have long been rejected anyhow. Noah's sons, the four parts of the world, the four colors, white, black, yellow, copper red—who still thinks of these outdated fashions today?"[80] Despite Forster's scorn, however, none of these "old divisions" had been rejected entirely; there existed, for example, a conceptual residue of old beliefs in the population of the earth by Noah's three sons, and the location of his Ark's landing in the Caucasus atop Mount Ararat was generally accepted as an historical fact.

Historical narratives, whether Biblical or folkloric, sufficed as valid grounds for the arguments put forth by Christoph Meiners, the professor of *Weltweisheit*. It was Meiners who divided the human kind into two races, the Caucasian and Mongolian, in his *Sketch for a History of Mankind* [*Grundriß der Geschichte der Menschheit*, 1786]. He only needed two primary categories; as Susanne Zantop observes, "Meiners makes clear that the world is, in fact, constituted by only two kinds of humans: the culturally superior, 'beautiful' ones—the Europeans—and all others who are 'mongolized' [*mongolisiert*] to varying degrees and hence 'ugly' and inferior—Asians, Africans, Americans."[81] As Zantop points out, Meiners did proceed, in voluminous later writings, to subdivide his races, a task that included the division of Europeans into an elaborate hierarchy, elevating the German "nation" over "ugly, effeminate Latin races."[82] But as long as Meiners treated the "beautiful" Europeans as a collective, he justified their identification with the Caucasus thusly: "Almost all of the Sagas and tales of ancient nations indicate that the human race originated on the Caucasus [mountain range] and the plains to the south of it. From here, the humans spread to all ends of the world."[83] Meiners further notes:

> The Caucasians are no longer very pure and unmixed in the Caucasus. The Caucasians, however, especially their women, are the most beautiful in the world. These nations and their offspring differ from the Mongolian nations through their height and the structure of their bodies, through a more beautiful facial formation and other body parts, through stronger hair growth and through nobility of spirit and heart.[84]

This beauty of body and implied nobility of spirit provided the justification beyond myth and legend for the location of racial origins in the Caucasus. These traits also compensated for the apparent lack of (racial) "purity" among the contemporary Caucasians, as if the kernel of Caucasian descent transcended any admixture, or, more intriguingly, as if the admixture itself produced the beautiful alloy that were Caucasians.

Those interested in racial difference had long noted the beauty of the Caucasians. In fact, in the earliest texts identified as engaging a "racial" division of peoples, descriptions included references to the particular beauty (and the white skin) of the women of the Caucasus, particularly the

Circassians and Georgians, although the observations on Circassian and Georgian beauty appears in texts to be a digression—the men writing seem to get carried away, distracted by their own descriptions.

When Francois Bernier—a century before Blumenbach, Forster, and Meiners—wrote his "New Division of the Earth According to the Different Species or Races of Men" [*Nouvelle division de la terre par les différentes espèces ou races qui l'habitent*, 1684], it was the first text in which "race" functioned as a dominant classification scheme for the patterns of difference among human peoples and in it the beauty of those from the Caucasus region stood out. In fact, this text is one of the earliest sources to feed what will later develop and circulate throughout Europe as the legendary figure of the "Circassian beauty":

> It cannot be said that the native and aboriginal women of Persia are beautiful, but this does not prevent the city of Isfahan from being filled with an infinity of very handsome women, as well as very handsome men, in consequence of the great number of handsome slaves who are brought there from Georgia and Circassia.
>
> The Turks have also a great number of very handsome women; besides those of the country, who are by no means ugly, they have . . . an immense quantity of slaves who come to them from Mingrelia, Georgia, and Circassia, where, according to all the Levantines and all the travellers, the handsomest women of the world are to be found.[85]

We have seen already that beauty—in the form of female slaves from the northern Caucasus—is valued, although Bernier does not reflect on its importance. Beauty is not theorized; Bernier just reacts to it on a visceral level. Here, as in other texts, the irrationality of desire trumps the rational attempt to systematize and organize. And yet the expression of that desire—the writing of it into these texts that make a tradition—becomes absorbed into the tradition of thinking about the nature of these various peoples.

Bernier notes, after asserting that "the handsomest women of the world" are found in the Caucasus: "Thus the Christians and Jews are not allowed to buy a Circassian slave at Constantinople. They are reserved for the Turks alone."[86] The whitest and the most beautiful of women are at once identified with—and offered tantalizingly by the text as sexually off-limits to—any men but Muslims, which include the Europeans. At about the same time, Bernier's compatriot, Jean Chardin, wrote, in his *Travels in Persia*:

> The Complexion of the Georgians is the most beautiful in all the East; and I can safely say, That I never saw an ill-favour'd Countenance in all that Country, either of the one or other Sex: but I have seen those that have had Angels Faces; Nature having bestow'd upon the Women of that Country Graces and Geatures, which are not other where to be seen: So that 'tis impossible to behold 'em without falling in Love.[87]

Later race theorists cited this passage as evidence of how deserving these women were of preeminence in human racial history. When Blumenbach quoted this rich and subjective travel narrative to validate his claim for the superior beauty of the Circassian, we are witnessing the fate of a text that, as one part of its legacy, was adopted and blended with geographical, philosophical, popular, and natural scientific conceptual systems and writing traditions that together are distilled to produce a normative scientific discourse of race.

The official naming of the white European's race as "Caucasian" is credited to Blumenbach, who first used the term in the 1795 edition of *De generis humani varietate nativa*. Blumenbach defended his nomenclature thus:

> I have taken the name of this variety from Mount Caucasus, both because its neighbourhood, and especially its southern slope, produces the most beautiful race of men, I mean the Georgian; and because all physiological reasons converge to this, that in that region, if anywhere, it seems we ought with the greatest probability to place the autochthones of mankind. [....] It is white in color, which we may fairly assume to have been the primitive colour of mankind, since ... it is very easy for that to degenerate into brown, but very much more difficult for dark to become white.[88]

While Blumenbach referred here generically to the Georgian "race of men," most narratives that were constructed and condensed and repeated by writers of all ilk attest specifically to the beauty of the women—these women who belonged to "wild, barbarian, heathen" tribes before their capture and conversion into Muslim harems. Even Blumenbach, when arguing that the "racial face" is mingled in instances of mixed-race breeding, offered as a typical example the blending of extremes, "the offspring of the Nogay Tartars is rendered more beautiful through unions with the Georgians." Similarly, in demonstrating that all humans belong to a single species based upon their ability to produce fertile offspring, he writes: "Take ... a man and a woman most widely different from each other; let the one be a most beautiful Circassian woman and the other an African born in Guinea, as black and ugly as possible." The point that he draws in each case—and that many other writers, including Chardin, also note with a striking matter-of-factness—is that the Caucasian women (specifically, the Circassians and Georgians) may be used (both actually and rhetorically) to "improve" less beautiful peoples.

I write elsewhere of the extraordinary role that the fantasy of Circassian beauty played in the construction of Caucasian racial identity, and in particular of how that racial identity absorbed and reflected fears of (and fascination with) the Ottoman Empire.[89] Here, I wish only to stress that regular references to the use of Caucasian females for the improvement of lines makes of them the ultimate medium for racial assimilation. If everyone were to mate with Caucasian women, we might conclude, then all peoples would become more beautiful and more nearly European.

These ideas complicate how we might understand the intersection of race and gender at the end of the eighteenth century. Felicity Nussbaum, writing on the development of racial conceptualization in this era, has argued that "white women's sexuality becomes the carefully guarded line between the infected and uninfected spaces of racial and cultural contagion, as an intact normative femininity and a bolstered masculinity free of defect serve as signs of successfully fending off contaminating forms."[90] While a fear of racial contagion and miscegenative degeneration certainly did dominate racialist discourse, there were precursors—lines of discourse on the composition of the Causasian, as one example (and medical arguments for racial blending, explored in chapter six, as another)—that implied radically hybrid genealogies for the category of race.

5 Genealogical Purification

While eighteenth-century investigations into hereditary racial identity struggled with purifying impulses to categorize and regulate hybrid lines, more practical investigations into heredity and what might be done with genealogical transmission produced a discourse of judicious improvement of the human kind, with various ideals of "purity," both moral and physiological, posited as goals. During the second half of the eighteenth century, heritability was subjected to the microscope and dissected by science to expose its real, material content. A range of essayistic engagements with the problem of hereditary transmission raised concerns that extended to its consequences for urbanism, hygiene, and moral philosophy. As even the science writing of the era attests, knowledge of a blood-bond between people was assumed to be a guarantor of a higher affinity, with claims—for better or worse—upon the emotions, spirit, and reason. This chapter identifies a struggle by eighteenth-century writers to represent a socially organized, ethically inclined human kind based upon "natural" principles of affiliation and transmission, relying upon the blood-bond's presumed function as a mediator between the real, physical world and a metaphysical realm of beholdenness and mutual care. When hereditary lines are presumed to transmit characteristics (physical, emotional, and intellectual) with some reliability, then the consequential logic easily becomes—to use a term anachronistically but precisely—eugenic: in theory, at least, family lines, and then ever increasing population groups including villages, nations, and ultimately the entire species, can be improved by controlling breeding.

Programs for perfectibility characterize the Enlightenment; they include philosophical, pedagogical, legal, theatrical, psychological, and scientific theory and practice. The human being was celebrated as unique in part because it strove for, and was capable of, continual improvement: as Christian Ludwig declared confidently, the mind and spirit of the *Mensch* "strives unceasingly toward perfectibility. He is therefore more than animal." Elaborating, Ludwig argued:

> The soul of the human being is capable of the greatest possible perfectibility; the soul of the animal is not matured for reason. Human

reason, however, consists of a relationship, a sum and a direction of ideas that belong to his organization, that exist in relation to his way of life; he alone has the advantage to hearken to and to preserve this relationship.[1]

This relationship—among soul, reason, organization, and way of life—is presented in such sweeping and vague terms that it is hard to imagine a field of inquiry that would *not* have some potential impact upon it. Isaak Iselin, who asserted in his very popular book, *Philosophical Speculations: On the History of Humankind* [*Philosophische Muthmaßungen. Ueber die Geschichte der Menschheit*, 1764], that the process of perfectibility was the sole condition of human happiness, separated historical human kind into two classes: the "*Wilde*" or wild peoples, and the "*Policierte*," those peoples for whom a process of civilizing refinement—policing—led to contemporary European culture. This policing, he believed, was crucial to the movement of mankind's continual improvement, toward a future of unlimited enlightenment.[2] At the end of the eighteenth century, the policing of morals and manners was specifically extended—for the most part, only in theory—to the policing of reproduction for the improvement of the bodies and minds of future members of the species. Such theories about the potential use of the "facts" of heredity to improve the human race (or parts thereof) have a history that we now identify as eugenic.

The eighteenth century is rarely included in considerations of the history of eugenic thinking: more typical are statements like Carolyn Burdett's, who writes in her introduction to an excellent collection of essays on the topic that "The modern notion of eugenics first began to emerge around the 1860's, when the meaning of heredity made a decisive shift to include, along with the familiar forms of succession to status, land, wealth and office, the properties of organic beings."[3] While it is certainly true that the systematic study of heredity and the terminology of eugenics are nineteenth-century products, it can hardly be disputed that the heritability of "properties of organic beings" was of central concern to scientists, philosophers, and policy-makers far earlier. The term "eugenics," coined by Francis Galton in 1883, is now associated with early theories of heredity and often concurrent fears of cultural and biological degeneration. It has come to connote almost exclusively the last century's responses to such fears, culminating in programs of euthanasia, genocide, and now genetic engineering.[4]

The idea of eugenics, though, is more complex than current usage would allow. The word comes from the Greek *eugenes* meaning "well-born," which includes ideas of "highly born," the production of a beautiful body, and nobility of mind; *eugenes* also denotes a refined or good style, and—simply—the birth of the good. This multivalent "good," from the Greek *eus*, introduces a productively imprecise evaluative element into the discussion. In its basic articulation, eugenics promises the birth of the good on the biological, the societal, the discursive, and the metaphysical level.

Eighteenth-century suggestions for breeding the good were principally concerned with the production of a biological good that was defined to great extent by the elimination of heritable illness and deformity. Medical and scientific discourse attempted to trace the facts of transmission, along with the appropriate responsive measures, in objective terms.[5] However, the biological good for which scientific writers strove was marked and measured by standards of health, physiological proportion, and temperamental balance that are already products of social and aesthetic evaluation. Further, the rhetorical point of origin for such a project was the higher moral call to use whatever knowledge is at hand to improve the lives of individuals and the citizenry as a whole, based upon principles determined by political and ethical philosophy as well as by religion. And finally—as we shall see in several examples—the discourse that developed to theorize and implement an augmentation of the species through breeding relied heavily upon figures of the family, embedding the process within an encompassing context of the bonds of love and loyalty that family (and categories like fatherly, motherly, brotherly, sisterly) are presumed to guarantee.

This heterogeneity of discursive sources and references becomes apparent in the rhetorical complexity, and not infrequent confusion, that accompanies (perhaps inevitably) the "objective" and "scientific" accounts of eugenic ambitions for human individuals and the human race.

ARRANGING MARRIAGE

In 1714, decades before attempts to scientifically identify (much less improve) races and species began in earnest, a story by Richard Steele appeared in the *Tatler* that made liberal use of the desire to produce an improved "Race." In this instance, the "Race" in question was a particular family, and the method of improvement was the careful control of marriage with an eye to breeding progeny freed of the flaws that had too long compromised the family physiognomy. The story, entitled simply "From my own Apartment, September 30," is written in the form of a letter to the readership and chronicles the evolution of the Bickerstaff family through deliberate sexual selection.[6] Focusing first upon certain unfortunate physical traits that had come to characterize his particular aristocratic line, the narrator explains that the only remedy available was a series of strategic marriages that sacrificed the integrity of the family's genealogical history in the interest of a stronger chin. These marriages culminated in an outright misalliance with Maud the Milk-Maid, whose absorption into the family line fully "spoil'd our Blood, but mended our Constitutions."[7]

The absurd humor of the tale results from a reconfiguration of that august convention, the arranged aristocratic marriage. Instead of the age-old process of familial alliances by which children were married to each other in order to preserve a nexus of family names and social power, the arranged marriage advocated by Steele's narrator is made only according to physical criteria, with the intention of reinvigorating the blood of a family that has suffered the consequences of the former pattern of inbreeding. The first kind of marriage ensures a social isolation; the second is designed to end a physiological isolation, both of which are characteristic of old family lines. Of course, the second also serves *de facto* to end the social isolation of the family in question, as the old line is "spoil'd" with common blood. Certainly this contributes to the political resonance of the story, which insinuates that only a legalized union of the social classes might bring health to the general "Constitution" of a family—or a state.[8]

The humor of the piece, as well as the edge of its critique, is sharpened by the narrator's characteristic imprecision in setting up "blood" and "constitution" in opposition to one another. He uses blood, the more particular of the physical terms (considered in Steele's day to be one of the fluids comprising the general constitution), metonymically for the social family line (as in, "spoil'd our Blood"); the constitution, on the other hand, is used to represent the physical condition that flows through and identifies the entire family. Usually this, too, would be referred to as the family's "blood," but the narrator needed two terms to oppose the social and the physiological identity of the family. Of course, he might have written "spoil'd our social Blood, but mended our physical Blood"—but that is awkward and pedantic, and Steele is a better writer than that; additionally, he would have lost the political impact of the term "Constitution." In any case, the story locates and advocates a separation of biological "fact" from customary forms of social signification with regard to the identification of individuals and the groups to which they belong. "Blood," which in its function as metaphor could represent both a physical and a social continuity through generations, is suddenly divided into two components that are potentially—or perhaps necessarily—at odds with each other.

Following the narrator's assertion that attention to the well-being of the physical bloodline—achieved through marrying outside of appropriate circles—results in social degeneracy (a "spoiling" of the blood), it would seem that socially "good" blood and physiologically "good" blood occupy an individual (as well as social) body in inverse proportions. The nature of the two "goods" is complex: for social blood to be good, it must be pure, singular, isolated, genealogically consistent, identifiable and identical throughout the "Race." Bodily blood, on the other hand, is good if it is healthy, robust, the product of mixtures and impurities, a blending of extremes. Thus the narrator, in the interest of health, advocates an interbreeding across socially demarcated (and also biologically "real") groups, families, or "Races," advocating a kind of cosmopolitan miscegenation.

Significantly, the beneficial impact of such mixed breeding is not limited to the range of physical traits, which are visibly heritable, but include "Men's Minds and Humours":

> After this Account of the Effect our prudent Choice of Matches has had upon our Persons and Features, I cannot but observe, that there are daily Instances of as great Changes made by Marriage upon Men's Minds and Humours. One might wear any Passion out of a Family by Culture, as skillful Gardeners blot a Colour out of a Tulip that hurts its Beauty.

Body and mind coexist here in strong connection; both are reduced to functioning as aesthetically graded attributes of a family, which is now more concerned with its own tulip-like (expensive, delicate, elite) "Beauty" than with aristocratic lineage.[9] Extending his gardening metaphor, the narrator remarks: "One might produce an affable Temper out of a Shrew, by grafting the Mild upon the Cholerick; or raise a Jackpudding from a Prude, by inoculating Mirth and Melancholy."[10] The verbs of ordinary horticulture (grafting and inoculating) make the generative process—a baffling scientific mystery at the beginning of the century—something familiar and technically manageable. By a process represented as a kind of engrafting, two influences combine and mitigate each other's extremes to produce the temperament of a child.

With this in mind, the narrator confesses that he is plagued by the worrisome task of determining a suitable match for his sister, a notable wit. What types of children might such a woman bring forth? Resolved to employ the same methods used to improve the family's physical stock, the narrator concludes that it is "absolutely necessary to cross the Strain"—that is, she must at all costs marry a sober man of business. Were she to marry a "fine gentleman" who shared her spirit, they would not only be eternally "Rivals in Discourse," and "in continual Contention for the Superiority of Understanding," but, in terms of the family line, the disastrous combination would be certain to bring forth nothing but "Criticks, Pedants, or pretty good Poets."[11] After musing at length over his dilemma concerning his sister's reproductive future, the narrator returns to more generalized comments, pointing out that the ultimate object of everyone's concern should be the relationship between individuals and the constitution of their "Race." This leads him finally to admonish his reader to "study your Race, or the Soil of your Family will dwindle into Cits or 'Squires, or run up into Wits or Madmen."[12]

Steele's amusing story destabilizes the traditional genealogical family monopoly. By constructing an internal either/or of the potential nature and strength of a bloodline—either it can maintain a line of social power or a line of physiological health—he does establish a potentially serious challenge to traditional forms of aristocratic power. Roxann Wheeler reminds us of this period that social rank (along with civility and religious confession) was "more explicitly important to Britons' assessment of themselves and other people that physical attributes such as skin color, shape of the nose, or texture of the hair." If concepts like social class or rank "constituted visible distinctions that are difficult for us to recover today," then Steele's maneuver in shifting value from rank to bodily character should perhaps be seen as a rendering visible of the absurdities of such categorization at all.[13] The challenge resounds precisely as it is diffused by the ridiculous posturing and mixed metaphors of Steele's narrator, which, along with his unshakable sense of the importance of his own family line or race, undermine any possibility of taking his suggestions of breeding too seriously.

But if Steele can lampoon the entire notion of faith in the reality, the continuity, and the control of a familial "Race," yet these ideas of physiological continuity (including both body and mind or character) over generations and of the potential human control over that continuity are soon taken seriously, not just in service of a familial race, but with an eye to the cumulative effect on the national and human race.

FAMILY PECULIARITIES

Neither cultural nor discursive histories tend to develop in a clear line, and so it should not be surprising that the do-it-yourself eugenics program lampooned by Steele in the *Tatler* could serve as an object of satire half a century before its institutional potential was seriously considered. It was only after mid-century, concurrent with the classification and historical account of the human species discussed in the prior chapter, that there emerged in Europe and America an interest in the possibility of manipulating human breeding to control both character and constitution, both for the good of the individual and for the good of the state.

For ambitious scientists eager to use emerging knowledge of heritability and biological generation to facilitate the generation of a new and better world, the species as a whole functioned effectively as a rallying point toward which efforts could be focused. However, in terms of developing any practical plan for improvement, the species was far too large and abstract an entity to be useful. Instead, attention was turned to the reproducing individual, who was both a direct producer and a product of genetic history, and one who occupied the present as a mid-point along a progressive line extending toward the future.[14] By this thinking, in order to improve the collective human species (or a single race, or a national "*Volk*," depending on the scale of concern), one need simply control the genealogy of families.

Not everyone believed such control was advisable or possible. Kant exemplified one position when he maintained that, since the gradual improvement of the species and its races was directed by Nature, the task of science was to comprehend and respect this natural process. There existed already, however, a well-entrenched and more ambitious position with regard to the ongoing improvement of the species, one which profited from a rhetorical tradition that identified Nature as a garden in need of human cultivation. With this figure as a conceptual basis, scientists (as well as satirists) could advocate as responsible stewardship the tending to the progress of the species. The Scottish philosopher and professor of medicine John Gregory took a common-sense view of the links connecting the reproduction of individuals, the condition of the species, and the state of society, utilizing yet another rhetorical (as well as practical) model which proved invaluable to discussion of human improvement: the practice of breeding domestic animals. Animal husbandry was an activity clearly within the proper expanse of human endeavor, consecrated by the Biblical subjugation of animals to man's dominion within the original garden. Once science classified the human species with the rest of the animals, it was easy enough to argue for a logical extension of animal husbandry to the human population.[15]

In his essay published in 1764 entitled *A Comparative View of the State and Faculties of Man with those of the Animal World*, Gregory identified a natural character or "stamp" passing genealogically through families. Its impression upon both the body and the character of each individual might appear weaker or stronger in certain generations, and its impact upon the individual might be altered by education, but its traces, he maintained, are discernible, are real, and are a permanent part of the individual marking him as belonging to a particular line. However, just as physical and temperamental characteristics of dogs or horses are enhanced or eliminated over time by careful breeding, so too might the "original stamp" of human nature be refined by the careful regulation of marriage. Gregory writes:

> How a certain character or constitution of Mind can be transmitted from a Parent to a Child, is a question of more difficulty than importance. It is indeed equally difficult to account for the external resemblance of features, or for bodily diseases being transmitted from a Parent to a Child. . . . A proper attention to this subject would enable us to improve not only the constitutions, *but the characters of our posterity*. Yet we every day see very sensible people, who are anxiously attentive to preserve or improve the breed of their Horses, tainting the blood of their Children and entailing on them not only the most loathsome diseases of Body, but Madness, Folly, and the most unworthy dispositions . . .[16]

Gregory's call for "proper attention" to the legacy of constitution and character was clearly prompted by something more than the promotion of scientific knowledge; in fact, the biological mystery of transmission, a question "of more difficulty than importance," was of less interest to him than making practical and responsible use of the fact that traits are carried.

Practically speaking, one need not know why the traits of one's mate will very likely appear as part of the complex character of one's child, but knowing *that* it is so ought to influence one's choice of a mate in the first place. And while such insights might beneficially inform individual selection, the implications were weightier: since the quality of the citizenry determined to some extent the well-being of the state, it was, in fact, of community interest to develop a politically and morally weighted technology for the improvement of "the characters of our [collective] posterity."

Reinforcing a belief in the heritability of not only physical but also moral traits, the American doctor and statesman Benjamin Rush wrote in his *Inquiry into the Influence of Physical Causes upon the Moral Faculty* of 1786 the following:

> Do we observe certain degrees of the intellectual faculties to be hereditary in certain families?. . . . The same observation has frequently extended to moral qualities—Hence we often find certain virtues and vices as peculiar to families, through all their degrees of consanguinity, and duration, as a peculiarity of voice—complexion—or shape.

Sound (voice), color (complexion), and form (shape) are signs by which an invisible bloodline erupts to the surface of the body and becomes legible (or audible); similarly, claims Rush, virtues and vices are transmitted in some (unspecified) traceable way through generations.

There was no paucity of speculation to this effect. In 1756, Charles Augustin Vandermonde wrote in his *Essay on the Manner of Perfecting the Human Species* [*Essai sur la manière de perfectionner l'espece humain*] the following: "If chance is responsible for the degeneration of the human species, art can just as well perfect it."[17] While nature brought forth variety, Vandermonde continued, human industry would profit by learning to combine "with intelligence the different products of nature."[18] Maupertuis, in his *Venus Physique* of 1744, had already advanced a theory of breeding a superior stock of human beings marked by "understanding, diligence, and probity" through a process of controlling births. (This emphasis on "probity" was somewhat offset by his amused speculation on the production of entirely new varieties of humans within the hypothetical context of a bored sultan and his diverse, languishing harem.)[19] Kant, unamused, remarked in his 1777 essay on race that, while Maupertuis's theory was "certainly practicable," it nevertheless had to be dismissed because it was not in accord with Nature, insofar as it attempted to direct, rather than to follow Nature's plan.[20] Condorcet added his voice to those asserting that far more than physical characteristics were in all likelihood heritable—and thus, in theory, manageable. Writing on the "improvement of the human spirit," in a chapter entitled "Future Progress of Mankind," Condorcet pointed to analogies between human populations and the "diverse races of domestic animals" in order to frame scientific propositions that might then be confirmed by direct observation of the human species. Condorcet offered the following:

> May not our physical faculties, the force, the sagacity, the acuteness of the senses, be numbered among the qualities transmitted in the process of individual improvement? [. . . .] Lastly, may we not include in the same circle the intellectual and moral faculties? And our parents, who transmit to us the advantages or defects of their conformation, and from whom we receive our features and shape, as well as our propensities to certain physical affections—may they not transmit to us also that part of physical organization upon which intellect, strength of understanding, energy of soul or moral sensibility depend? Is it not probable that education, by improving these qualities, will at the same time have an influence upon, will modify and improve this organization itself?[21]

Of course, the terms here are still speculative, and the implied analogy is admittedly shaky: Condorcet asks whether we might not have the same aspirations toward breeding human moral traits that we do in refining the physical lines of domestic animals. And he reveals a basic presumption characteristic of French mechanistic philosophy underlying that ambition: while he refers to a soul, he locates the energy of that soul and its moral sensibility in an unspecified part of physiological organization.

While this "part" of human physical nature in which intellectual and spiritual attributes presumably developed remained unidentified, there was an increasing presumption of a direct correspondence between optimal physiological and mental conditions, both of which were the products of the "real" developmental process of human nature. In England in 1802, Erasmus Darwin would write in the appendix to his lavish poem, "The Temple of Nature," the following confident assertion:

> [Because] many families become gradually extinct by hereditary diseases, as by scrofula, consumption, epilepsy, mania, it is often hazardous to marry an heiress, as she is not unfrequently the last of a diseased family. . . . [Thus] the art to improve the sexual progeny of either vegetables or animals must consist in choosing the most perfect of both sexes, that is the most beautiful in respect to the body, and the most ingenious in respect to mind.[22]

This pronouncement is as amusing as it is informative, though it is somewhat difficult to imagine how to determine the "ingenious" quality of mind in a vegetable. There is a revealing gender bias overlaying this theory of biological degeneracy: if an heiress is "not unfrequently the last of a diseased family," the implication is that a healthy family produces male heirs—or at least, perhaps, a sufficient abundance of daughters with claims to the family money that none might count as an "heiress."

Nonetheless, Darwin's statement, similar to ideas expressed by a broad array of European thinkers over the course of the eighteenth century, reveals an increasing tendency to regard the potential improvement of the species as a product of a particular kind of knowledge and its technology: that is, the identification and deliberate combination of specific qualities of both individual bodies and minds that together might harness nature to overcome nature.

TRANSMISSION: *ERBSCHAFT* AND *FORTPFLANZUNG*

By the mid-eighteenth century, scientific attention to the physical processes of heritability bolstered these speculative positions. Scientific societies increasingly focused their investigations upon what in German was vividly called the *Fortpflanzung* of traits: a "planting-forth" that has a very different resonance than *Erbschaft* (inheritance) or its many variations stressing something received from the past. As *Fortpflanzung* implies, heritability was not only a historical process explaining the present as a result of the past, but it was a dynamic process occurring in the present in order to affect the future.

Biological *Fortpflanzung* was no longer merely an idea that belonged to folk wisdom, according to which common observation of plant and animal husbandry, family lines, and travel accounts of different cultures had long provided reason enough, if not outright evidence, to believe in the transmission of traits through generations.[23] In conjunction with investigations into the processes of generation, as well as the natural history of species and racial lines, the transmission of specific traits, proclivities, and identifying weaknesses was now increasingly defended in scientific terms. That these terms were really not conclusions so much as interpretations by scientists of tentative initial experiments and observations did not diminish their authority.[24] The scientific speculations—backed by appeals to common sense and general observation—carried sufficient weight that they ultimately provided the basis for policies to control the development and improvement of the human species through regulated breeding.

Hoping to stabilize their knowledge of these phenomena, scientific and social engineers during the last third of the century paid very serious attention to developments in the investigation of generation and transmission. The hereditary forces that propelled an individual embryo along its path of development were increasingly the focus of discussion in the natural science journals and in the prize essays of the various European scientific societies. The historical development of the science of embryology and the emergence of a theory of epigenetic development, as well as the establishment of theories of hereditary diseases as separate from infectious diseases, have been treated elsewhere, and they are not our real concern.[25] Important to this study is the constant intrusion of social values and terminology into presentations of this physiological science of heritability.

When Joseph Claudius Rougemont, Professor of Anatomy and Surgery at Bonn University, defended heritability in an essay contest sponsored by the French Academy in 1790, his winning essay was widely circulated and quickly translated into German.[26] Significantly, Rougemont found it appropriate in such a context to explicitly defend the issue of paternal contribution to the mental as well as the physical composition of offspring. Reinforcing the efforts of Ploucquet and others, Rougemont strove to defend the significance of paternity and paternal inheritance by marshalling what physical scientific "evidence" already existed. Rougemont made a case for the real and significant hereditary contribution a father made to his child of physical *and* moral traits: "Fathers share with their children their children not only their form and inner structure, but also their idiosyncracies, their virtues, their vices, and their qualities of understanding and emotion."[27] These inherited qualities—accounting for physical, moral, intellectual, and emotional capacities—provide the basis of the identity of a new individual in addition to providing new life.

But what of the power of education? Certainly, in the late eighteenth century such a protest might be anticipated, given the unprecedented flourishing of pedagogical philosophy and the establishment of institutes claiming that education alone could produce the sorts of citizens a model state required. Rougemont acknowledged that education could well influence a child's moral sense and behavioral patterns significantly; that influence, however, was simply a process of responding to and developing an inherent capacity to learn, which was physiological and thus inherited. "Who can deny," he asked, challenging his reader, "that a particular disposition of our brain, or the nervous system, or the entirety of our organs taken together, are capable of bringing forth this or that particular characteristic?"[28] Moreover, while the generic ability to learn might well be considered a defining human trait that all individuals inherited along species lines, the degree to which any single person possessed intellectual and moral gifts was determined to great extent by his or her parental legacy.

While intellectual and emotional qualities were understood to be the product of one's complex physiology, Rougemont added another complex turn to his account of the human system by observing that moral experiences may in turn give rise to changes in temperament. A defense of the psychosomatic in itself was not radical or new: mid-century psychological theories developed by Georg Ernst Stahl and medical writings by figures like Samuel Schaarschmidt and Ernst Anton Nicolai argued persuasively for the mutual influence of mind and body.[29] Schaarschmidt went so far as to insist that the mind or spirit [*Seele*], "insofar as it catalyzes changes in the human body and can likewise be affected by it, belongs unequivocally to medical science."[30] In other words, the relation between mind and body with regard to human behavior was not strictly unidirectional. However, while admitting that the powers of mind and body influence and effect change upon each other, Rougemont did insist, if somewhat unsteadily, on the priority of the physiological as the conditioning factor for the development of the moral capacity: "one can observe that, when the moral capacity manifests its power sometimes earlier or later, sometimes with stronger or weaker force, that this is contingent upon the bodily constitution [*Beschaffenheit*].[31] Rougemont filled his essay with anecdotes, examples, and citations from contemporary scientists and medical essayists, as he attempted to persuade his readers of the scientific legitimacy of heritability. He did not expand beyond the descriptive mode, however; he made no attempt to surmise or suggest what might be done with this knowledge.

As Carlos López-Beltrán has noted in his analysis of developing medical understandings of heredity in the early modern period, the essay contest Rougemont won garnered responses that together reveal much about the uncertainty of heredity as a category. However dissatisfied the Royal French Society of Medicine may have been, there was sufficient demonstration of consensus on the existence of transmission of traits from parents to children that heredity as a (howsoever sketchily understood) medical fact was *de facto* acceptable. In López-Beltrán's terms, it was in a "depathologized sense [that] the whole system could be synthetically referred to as heredity."[32] In any event, the next several decades saw the adoption of heredity as a focus for the medical communities of Europe. If no stable explanation of how transmission functioned was at hand, medical professionals could nevertheless attempt to conjoin what knowledge they had with practical application. In this, they united forces with governmental bodies increasingly interested in public health and hygiene.

HEREDITY AND PUBLIC HEALTH

The practical application of theories of heredity at the end of the eighteenth and the turn of the nineteenth century was primarily the domain of a peculiar—and in some ways, particularly German—institution, the *medicinische Policey*, or medical police.[33] The medical police was a branch of eighteenth-century cameralism that took account of disease, hygiene, death, and birth, and was charged, among other things, with developing policy to improve the all-around health of populations, including their physical well-being, strength, beauty, moral sensibility, and civic discipline.[34] Isabel Hull has described German cameralism as "literally utopian, or 'eudaemonistic,' . . . aimed at the continuous improvement of government, society, and individual, until each had helped the other to achieve perfection."[35] The medical police understood its unique power precisely as a synthesizing discourse. Joseph Bernt, a doctor and professor of forensic medicine in Vienna, wrote that the medical police, in its central role as the propagator of a "popular medical Enlightenment, counted among its resources the following disciplines: "anthropology, psychology (*"Seelenlehre"*), ethics, strategy, pedagogy, natural state and common law, knowledge of civil and criminal law, state and religious constitutions, the mathematical and physical descriptions of the earth, regional statistics, economics, physics, and technology."[36]

While advocates of the medical police theorized and suggested new policies far more often than they actually drafted it, nevertheless their writing, devoted to the common weal, provides surprising evidence for the degree to which a proto-eugenic program was advanced in the eighteenth century. Essays and textbooks by medical bureaucrats reveal, in their structural and rhetorical complexity, an indication of the political profits to be gained by uniting an analysis of the biological and the moral good—writers infused their accounts of the new biological science and its relevance for hygienic policy with a moral metaphysics based in a language of family, heritability, and race. Such texts consistently clouded any boundaries that might be drawn between the biological, the social, the aesthetic, and the metaphysical good.

It is worth keeping in mind that German medical professionals engaged in programs of hygiene and education believed themselves to be the vanguard of the enlightened reform.[37] Johann Karl Osterhausen devoted a particularly well-written book to the issue of "medical enlightenment," modifying Kant's phrase to define such a project as "man's emergence from his immaturity in matters that involve his physical well-being."[38] Typical of such vision is a conviction that books were as necessary as legislation in bringing about the sweeping changes necessary for the common good. Osterhausen devoted most of his text to an analysis of misconceptions, superstitions, and folk beliefs that, by his reckoning, seriously impeded the progress of public health. Johann August Unzer, in the preface to his enormously influential journal, *Der Arzt* ("The Doctor"), asserted that the importance of his weekly magazine was to teach readers to "think medically" [*selbst medicinisch denken lernen*], given that the "general awareness of the fundamentals of health" was second only to moral conduct in its necessity and value.[39]

Popular medical journals provide some insight into the infractions of "moral conduct" the practicing medical police might confront within its jurisdiction. Bucholtz's "Contributions to the study of forensic medicine and the medical police," published in 1782 and 1783, and again in 1790 and 1793, chronicle investigations into murder and cannibalism, the regulation of meals at the local orphanage, countless cases of infanticide and infant abandonment, epilepsy, poisoning, insanity, dog bites, death by duel, charges of impotence, sudden deaths, and suicide.[40] All of these are approached as issues of public health. We find in such practical compendia discussions of infectious diseases, and occasionally there are reflections on hereditary ailments. In Ernst Gottfried Baldinger's journal, the *New Magazine for Medical Professionals* [*Neues Magazin für Aerzte*], a contribution by "N. N." in 1785 takes up the problem of inherited mental deficiency, defending its status as a medical phenomenon and thereby suggesting that some action should be taken; no practical suggestion follows, however.[41]

Certainly, the medical police understood its mandate to include disease management, but contributions like those found in enlightening journals stress more a reactive, rather than proactive, approach to problems. The statesman and jurist Günther Heinrich von Berg, the first to present *Policeyrecht*, or laws concerning public administration, in a systematic fashion, conveyed the broad parameters of the practical side of hygiene.[42] In addressing health policy specifically, Berg outlined the initial duties of regional officials: foremost among such responsibilities was "the draft and elaboration of a medical topography of the region; that is, a purposeful representation of all local factors that have either an immediate or an eventual impact upon the health of the residents." In addition to such factors as climate, winds, available food sources, consumption of luxury items, animals, local flora, and the "customs, practices, moral standards, life- and clothing styles" present in the area, Berg stressed the importance of an account of "how many insane, disturbed, blind, epileptic, deaf-mute, fragile, elderly poor, and other such types in need of aide are to be found in the region."[43] What could be done with such an account, however?

The translation of such statistics into both public policy and private conviction was a larger task that required the writers of the "medical enlightenment." If we do not find developed policies of reproductive control in police reports, allusions to the topic abound in the textbooks and "handbooks" written to develop the profession. Berg himself, in his multi-volume *Handbook of German "Policeyrecht"* [*Handbuch des Teutschen Policeyrechts*, 1804], suggests that a *Landesvater* (the governing authority, literally "father of the land") try not to alienate citizens by intruding too far into every private circumstance or marriage; nevertheless, he advocates measures like excluding the very poor from marriage (that is, from reproduction) altogether, since they breed weak and crippled children, and become burdens upon the state.[44]

Without question, the most ambitious engagement with the subject was the work of Johann Peter Frank, one of the most influential physicians and medical professors of the late eighteenth century, with a career that included positions of authority in Göttingen, Pavia, St. Petersburg, and Vienna. His great publication in the field of health policy is the six-volume *System for a Complete Medical Police* [*System einer vollständigen medicinischen Policey*], which began appearing in 1779. During ensuing decades, this work was read, translated, adapted, and adopted piecemeal throughout German-speaking lands and beyond.[45] A prominent contemporary reviewed it as "an inordinately important book, replete with extensive knowledge of carefully considered positions, written with courage and philosophical precision—to date, the only one of its kind."[46]

Frank's work had an unprecedented scope, providing scientific explanations, social analysis, and policy recommendations for a range of issues including pre-natal and infant care, the structure of schools and charitable organizations, the containment and prevention of illness, the regulation of food, drink and housing, the prevention of accidents, and the education of the poor in basic hygiene. Also treated were such varied issues as gambling, noise pollution, superstition, theater censorship, the regulation of dancing, military conscription, and proper clothing. Frank drew upon an extraordinary range of medical, legal, philosophical, and anthropological sources to support, and often complicate, his proposals. He addressed his arguments to an audience of doctors and policy makers, as well as the typical *Familienvater* (the household patriarch) and mothers who were particularly encouraged to cultivate new habits of pre- and post-natal infant care.[47] His arguments reflect an eighteenth-century attention to statistics, to new ways of assessing population and productivity; they reflect broader goals that include the promotion of a stronger tax-base, increased yields in domestic productivity, a reduction in crime, and a reduction in the number of destitute requiring public support.

For our purposes, the focus of the initial two volumes is of primary importance. There Frank set out his radical, proto-eugenic plan for a state-sponsored program of restricted breeding practices. In brief, he outlined a policy for the regulation of marriage and the production of offspring specifically in order to eliminate targeted diseases, mitigate individual suffering, lessen the public burden of the orphaned and infirm, and proactively generate a healthier and generally more productive population. He insisted there was no issue more central to political interest than the study of heredity and the translation of its consequences into practical legislation.

Frank was critically positioned with respect to the emerging understanding of genealogy as something primarily organic and historical. He identified as his first task a theoretical and practical explanation of how the scientific knowledge of generation—the emerging and exciting "facts" of individual heritability and transmission of traits—could be translated into a social policy of human perfectibility. By taking control of breeding in this way, to ensure the increasing perfection of the population and the flourishing of the empire, Frank proposed that the medical police assume control of the genealogy of the state. While Frank did not claim to be the first to conceive of such an idea—he cites contemporaries throughout his work who had already advanced related notions—he did know that his was the first comprehensive book on the subject to be written and that he would have to create an appropriate tone for what would amount to a new discourse.

Any treatment of the mechanics and consequences of regulated breeding was both novel and bold; it was also open to charges of immorality and of heresy. Speaking in the first person to his readership, Frank adopted a tone of confessional honesty and full disclosure, presenting his work as a contribution to the collective responsibility to "our descendants."[48] In order to preempt any protest over the sexual subject matter, Frank opened his book with an admission of his own fear of the controversies that might be aroused by his treatment. Convinced, however, of the book's potential social value, he describes how he subordinated his fears to a sense of duty, determining to deliver to the public the first-ever systematic and explicit presentation of *"menschliche Fortpflanzung"*—literally, a "human planting-forth," or human propagation—which he described as an increasingly significant science.[49]

The scientific basis for Frank's program was comprised of two theories, both of which were ultimately accepted as standards by the scientific community but which, in the 1770s, were still vigorously contested. These were the theories of epigenesis and heritability. Frank devoted a significant early portion of his book to both these theories, necessary to establish the foundation of his program. Arguing against a dominant view of development that human beings develop along pre-determined lines from a single, pre-formed seed or egg (the theory of preformation), Frank assured his reader that all evidence supported instead an epigenetic theory of development: this involved an initial combination of two distinct seeds (sperm and egg) that combined and catalyzed the development of a unique individual.[50] Once this model of generation was accepted, one could then argue that each seed—including both the maternal and the paternal contribution—imparted various traits to the embryo, consisting of physiological and dispositional traits, as well as the susceptibility to specific diseases, each of which becomes a constitutive part of the new person.

Nature's law was clearly genealogy, progressing through generations ad infinitum. Citing Haller, Frank acknowledged that scientists had not yet identified all of the patterns of heritability that contributed to human propagation (for example, Haller was unsure whether dwarves always bred more dwarves); nonetheless, it was certain that with each new generation, nature worked from the model of the parents to fashion the child.[51] Ultimately, the scientific fine points of the epigenesis debate and the transmission of illness were not Frank's primary concern, nor are they ours. Frank's unique contribution lay not in any impact he had upon the development of these theories, but rather in his instrumentalization of the science of heredity to create a discourse and a policy structure of social improvement through a proposed network of genealogical controls. The potential social rewards for guiding this pattern of production were tantalizing:

> Would it not be wonderful if only a portion of the care devoted to the development of good animal breeds—which involves identifying precisely which animals one will use for reproduction and excluding badly formed or poorly developed fathers or mothers—would be applied to humans, thus prohibiting marriage among those who are entirely degenerate, dwarfish, crippled, and misshapen; if, on the contrary, we saw to it that beautiful people blessed with a strong, well formed and healthy body, even if they were robbed of all other resources, were supported in marriage with their equals in health and bodily perfection, and further supported in the raising of large

families just like themselves, so that the number of strong, well-endowed citizens would eventually be increased?[52]

All human suffering, Frank maintains, should be understood "as damage wrought by the degeneration that is linked to civilization, which itself however is the product of the existing social order."[53] This seems at first to resemble an anti-civilization rhetoric common enough at the end of the eighteenth century and used particularly in the wake of Rousseau to bemoan the physical and moral weaknesses which characterized city-dwellers and the overly refined. Similar issues arise vividly in the "philosophical physician" Johann August Unzer's *Medical Handbook* [*Medicinisches Handbuch*, 1791]. Unzer utilizes elaborate narratives to stress intertwined problems of conditioned upbringing and hereditary strengths and weaknesses: in a section of the book entitled, "More Mistakes of Upbringing," he recounts within an anecdote that hard-working country children die less often than urban weaklings, in no small part because "they bring the strength of their parents with them into the world."[54] John Gregory, with a nod to Rousseau, had declared in 1765 that, if it weren't for a constant supply of new blood from the country, city-inhabitants would "perish in a few generations" and even so are, due to a lack of exercise and a pursuit of debauchery, able only to produce a "puny and diseased race of Children."[55] Frank himself cites fellow "experts" writing about the ills produced by civilization: he refers to the work of both Johann Georg Zimmermann and Samuel Auguste Tissot on the increasing frequency of hypochondria and nervous disorders [*Nervenkrankheiten*], resulting from a general decline in physical robustness and an increase in mental and emotional stimulation characteristic of urban life; he also points to the writings of Thomas Withers on problems that arise as urban populations get less and less exercise.[56] For the most part, Frank's attack on the urban degeneracy was not attributed to civilization as such, but to specific elements of the social order that could be changed. While hypochondria and lack of exercise were culturally specific ailments, a far more serious set of problems derived from unregulated individual procreation, which itself was the product of constantly developing, complex cultural values. If misguided reproduction was responsible for spreading illness and weakness among entire lines and peoples, intervention was to be found in the authority of medical police, acting on behalf of the *Vaterland*.[57]

In presenting his program, Frank mobilizes the "facts" of genealogy, such as they are, to produce an explanatory discourse of social well-being and to justify a systematic policy program to support public well-being, all the while utilizing the emotional and morally charged rhetoric of the family to persuade the reader of the greater metaphysical promises of his program. It is the emotionally and morally inflected language of kinship that provides the basis for—and the cognitive limits of—Frank's project for individual and collective (political as well as physical) betterment, as he develops a program for the institutional mobilization of the science of heredity.

Frank's discursive strategy rests on a limited set of interdependent metaphors and examples that work together to convey the moral, physical, and political urgency of his project. At the outset of his project, Frank joins the science of heredity to a political program and to a moral program, both of which are based upon the conceptual model of the family—as something with both absolute value and individual malleability—and which rely upon the family as a primary trope. The personification of the State as *Vater* is as unsurprising as it is extensive. Readers confront the well-rehearsed image of a land governed by a concerned father and populated by citizens who simultaneously share a collective identity as children, and who bear individual responsibilities as fathers (and mothers) in their own right. The enduring threat to the stability of the *Vaterland*, the scourge that Frank targets immediately as a priority for the intervention of the medical police, was a collection of *Familienkrankheiten*, or "family diseases," which threatened not only the physical but the moral well-being of individual families and the familial state. As he repeatedly stressed, the transmission through generations of such a *Familienkrankheit* was not merely a medical problem for an individual or for a suffering family; it produced a host of social ills, threatening the collective social family. Christian Ludwig went so far as to speculate that heritable illnesses were so significant in shaping populations that they might well ultimately be responsible for creating "particular strains and racial differences"; he also wondered to what degree the history of heritable disease within closed communities like social ranks [*Stände und Casten*] was responsible for shaping those communities.[58]

An obvious source of community corruption was venereal ailments believed to infect a hereditary line after being contracted through nonprocreative, extramarital sex. These diseases accompanied a sexuality that violated the claims of marriage, thereby undermining not only the health but also the institutional stability of the fatherland. Marriage was, as Frank declared, "the primary basis (or first principle) of human propagation."[59] In his discussion of venereal diseases, their causes, and their effects, Frank did not limit his opprobrium to the sexuality that transmits them, but instead suggested that the physical and moral conditions of their being are inextricably intertwined. Thus it followed that moral and medical resources should be united in an effort to expurgate them.

A sexually transmitted disease associated with debauchery provided the ideal example through which Frank could establish the connection between heritable disease and public moral health. In discussing the *geile Seuche* or syphilis, Frank identified children born daily with the disease as "sacrificial victims" of a process of contamination that began when the mother's blood was infected by the father's semen; such infection then poisoned the blood throughout subsequent generations "even without new transgression."[60] Such children were free of any personal guilt, and yet they literally carried the sins of the father in their blood. This sign of paternal sin could,

Genealogical Purification 103

however, could be eradicated: over time and as a result of attentive breeding between the heirs of tainted lines and individuals with "good blood" from healthy lines, Frank argued that the poison might be cleansed and the traits disappear. The fact that a tainted bloodline could be cleansed by crossbreeding, he maintained, was sufficient proof of the need to regulate marriage, not only to cure but also to prevent such diseases. The cleansing process was both technological and spiritual, as good blood washed clean the bad and the sin was eradicated from the social body.

It is important to note that the term *Familienkrankheit* applies not only to diseases affecting individual (biological) families, but also to those carried by the collective social family. Frank defended a complex understanding of the symbiotic nature of individual bodies and minds and the social and environmental conditions in which they live. He made a broad, ecological argument that illness should be understood not merely as a result of imbalances within the individual body but rather the "consequences of a disruption of social balance" and as the "inevitable component of social inequality."[61] Individual bodies were affected by the body politic and affected it in turn. And indeed, the state itself was a body with a condition of health that must be maintained: "The overall health of a state suffers its accidents and its particularly stubborn illnesses just like the single body of a citizen."[62]

In this program devoted to the physical generation of the social and individual good, each point of reference was articulated within the conceptual, representational domain of the family. These include the diseases targeted by Frank's program (*Familienkrankheiten*), the mode by which social health is transmitted and propagated (breeding), potential harms to society (through "inappropriate" marriages), the family-centered morality behind Frank's proposed regulations, the beneficiaries (individual families as well as the *Menschheitsfamilie*), and even the political powers (the *Landesväter*) called upon to implement the plan. Problematic cases were identified with their exclusion from healthy family structures: these included orphans, illegitimate children, widows, sterile or celibate men (non-fathers), debauched and diseased men (sick fathers of sick and neglected children), and mismatched couples who produced sickly children if they reproduced at all. A widely accepted, if necessarily imprecise ideal of the patriarchal family was both the source for and the product of Frank's project. Only a healthy family could serve as the embodiment and source of the good; such a family generated both new members and extended the social good in service to the *Vaterland*.

As Frank's *System* tirelessly attempted to demonstrate, the harms that the human race and its various races have suffered are not simply part of an inevitable teleological force; rather, these harms were the product of social determinants that could be controlled. Frank was not alone in elevating illness to a category within human taxonomy: when Johann Karl Illiger, in his *Systematic and Complete Terminology for the Animal* and Plant Kingdoms [*Versuch einer Systematischen Vollständigen Terminologie für das Thierreich und Pflanzenreich*], delineated the variously identified types of *Abartungen*, or lines of degeneration from species, he discussed not only race [*Rasse*] and type [*Spielart*], but varieties [*Varietät*] that included heritable diseases.[63] Just as racial traits per se were identified by the science of the day as manifestations of degeneration, so too should diseases injurious to humankind be understood as marks of *Entartung*, comparable to (and subsets of) racial traits. Simply put, heritable disease should be understood as the manifestation of a gradual process of falling away from the integral "Art" or species of human being; however, unlike those theorists of race who believed in the permanence of the differences that had developed, the impact of disease as a degenerative force could be controlled and even reversed.

Placing such disease within a classificatory schema had several advantages. First, it meant that hereditary disease accrued the prestige granted to those subjects of theoretical and experimental scientific inquiry that had their own ontological status and that were identified as fundamental forces or entities shaping natural history. The study of heritable disease, when configured in this way, was transferred out of the uncertain, idiosyncratic realm of medicine and into the increasingly prestigious domain of science.[64] Second, by placing disease within the taxonomic order of the genealogical species and of its subsets, Frank (along with Illiger and others) identified hereditary disease as a producer, as well as a product, of variation. Thus, instead of feeling compelled to justify claims regarding the heritable nature of and control for each particular heritable malady that he believed threatening to the human race, Frank could advocate for a broad policy overseeing the process of a singular, degenerative (and effectively racializing) phenomenon. And so he maintained that, with a policy of controlled breeding developed by the medical police—one that combined medical and scientific expertise with political authority and resources—numerous *Abartungen* could be expunged from the body and blood of the human kind, thereby allowing a healthier, more beautiful race its birth.

We shall see in the next chapter that the resolve to eliminate physical variation identified with disease and disability required the production of other physical variations. The most interesting of these were various crossbreedings that would produce a healthy stock rather like that produced by Maud the Milk-Maid: that is, a race with "good blood," but—if evaluated against current standards of racial and social norms—illegitimate and anything but pure.

6 Medical Police and Hybridization

In his 1801 introduction to a book on *Medicine, Surgery, Midwifery and Forensic Medicine* [*Arzneykunst, Wundarzneykunst, Geburtshülfe und Gerichtlichen Arzneykunde*], Samuel Gottlieb Vogel seized the opportunity to identify and to promote in glowing terms the medical police and its policies, through which "poisonous, dying, unlivable, barren places" could be transformed into "healthy paradises":

> In a State [with an active medical police], there rules in every regard the spirit of order, of lawfulness, of morality, of tranquility and of peace. There blooms not only the rosy color of health and good cheer; there bloom also fertile fields, arts, and sciences. People more willingly and competently meet their obligations, and they love more righteously their *Landesvater* [lit. "father of the land," i.e., the sovereign] who cares for them so benevolently.[1]

This is, of course, pure fantasy. Where in Europe in 1801 was there a land in which there reigned the spirit of "order, lawfulness, morality, tranquility, and peace"? A population characterized by rosy cheeks, good cheer, an abundance of nourishment for body and mind, and an eager, loving willingness to serve the father of the land could at best be found in sentimental fiction. Vogel's lavish rhetoric is not a description, but rather a prescription for what he hoped would develop if society were to adopt measures its medical police offered: from lawful order would come legitimate well-being, a perfect union of health and discipline, a fully realized instance of Foucauldian bio-politics. The language of this articulated ideal includes the familiar, potent pairing of an aestheticized organicism with a familial social order. Vogel identifies the medically regulated State as a garden, the site of beauty, abundance, and civic virtue. In such a state, organic cultivation—metaphorically, the blooming of health and virtue and knowledge; literally, the eradication of disease, the promotion of education, and the production of strong and healthy new citizens—leads to culture, a culture that is identified not only by its arts and sciences, but also by its physical well-being, its general embrace of duty, and its love of the *Landesvater*.

We might speculate on the value of the displacement that occurs when a writer, in a discussion of medical police policies, refers to a garden. These agriculture metaphors do what metaphors should: they complicate the set of associations accompanying the object of representation. The struggle to keep the association of oppression out of an image of a patriarchal state made metaphors of garden cultivation and agriculture particularly useful. In the case of controlled reproduction, the full implications of the suggested restrictions upon individuals are deflected by a set of agricultural images offering a familiar and acceptable model of human control over natural generation. This language conveyed responsible stewardship (which brings with it Christian overtones affirming a moral imperative) and a nurturing of human "seeds" and "plants"—hardly a picture of the raw exercise of power. Furthermore, agricultural tropes were common to the pedagogic discourse of the era, where the representation of children as plants or seedlings proliferated, and where educational institutions were referred to officially as garden nurseries [*Baumschulen, Pflanzschulen*]. Ludwig Joseph Schmidtmann, in a book dedicated to the practical implementation of a medical police, certainly regarded this task in great part to be educational, acknowledging that the best, and perhaps sole driver of medical policy was its respectful acceptance by the citizenry ["*buergerliche Hinsicht*"].[2] At the same time, he, too, adopted a language of cultivation when approaching the topic of human *Fortpflanzung*, or propagation, and similarly extended his planting metaphors to warn of the danger in allowing "uncultivated individuals" to persist unchecked and unchanged.[3]

Even Frank, the most forthright spokesman for regulated reproduction, often adopted agricultural imagery. Beyond the use of *Fortpflanzung* for propagation in general, he described attempts to increase the population as "sowing the land" and "harvesting the land." And the primary function of the medical police was, in his words, the guarantee that all procreating couples, "under the auspices of good laws," would produce "the best, healthiest, and most resilient of fruits."[4]

Within Frank's text, these metaphors of fruits and harvests, speaking to a culture that was still primarily agricultural, functioned as an effective circumlocution for sexual practices and outcomes that did not have at the time a more direct public language. However, this particular set of organic figures also serve to cover or counter the blunt instrumentalization of sexual practice and reproduction that could be distilled from his proposals. The garden imagery also inserts itself effectively as a mediator between the real families the book targeted—some judged worthy, others diseased or debauched—and the "family" ideal that shapes his program. Real families, as his text makes clear, are in need of the regulations his program proposed to be properly "family-like"—that is, to approach and ultimately embody the qualities possessed by the idealized, rhetorical figures of "father," "mother," and "child." To preserve the power of those idealizations, however, he had to protect them from too much contamination from their real-life counterparts. Thus, when writing about the state, or about community bonds, Frank wrote of families; but in writing about actual families, Frank wrote of seeds and harvests.

In a program devoted to the literal generation of both the social and individual good, the idea of family is both the source for and the product of his project. Science, politics, and morality converge via the language of the family and the "facts" of heritability: that is, the representation of "real" genealogy. The metaphors of family roles and kinship bonds Frank uses throughout his text are based on cultural ideals believed to pre-exist the social order under examination. They function principally as a textual layer that affirms and activates a set of collective values. And as we shall see, the values this set of metaphors conveys—governed by the deep belief in the structuring power of hereditary kinship in configuring any understanding, including scientific, of community—shape to a great degree Frank's program, revealing just how central he believes the "truth" of family ties to be for a program of generating the good.

Let us return to the problematic figure with which we began this chapter, the figure of the *Landesvater* overseeing his blooming subjects. There were, to be sure, readers unwilling to be lulled by the image of benevolent stewardship that the garden-state rhetoric offered. Johann Albert Heinrich Raimerus charged that the medical police led to abusive restrictions upon rights and freedoms; he compared the vision of a well-ordered state to a marionette theater. Rather than associating the medical police with enlightenment, Raimerus claimed that the institution reproduced precisely those chains of traditional social order that the *Aufklärung* had struggled to eliminate.[5] Frank confronted this criticism head-on in the preface to the 1783 edition of his *System*, reformulating common reservations with the following query:

> [We must ask] whether, as a result of the expanding purview of the police (as perceived since the initial publication of this work), the increasingly limited natural freedom of human beings will be unimaginably shrunken; the rights of household patriarchs, married men, and parents compromised; and these then appropriated and placed in the despotic hands of the authorities?[6]

Could it be possible that, instead of healing social ills through a strengthening of the family, the medical police actually weakened the rights of the household fathers, husbands, parents—actually made them sicker [*gekränket*]? Was the real power behind the figure of the *Landesvater* more aptly conveyed as a despotic authority, or *Obrigkeit*?

In formulating this question, Frank named a tension between two locations of the "fatherly": the realm of individual fathers presiding over households, wives, and children; and the arena of higher political figures, the *Landesväter*, whose potential abuse of power Frank acknowledged. The rhetoric of his textual address itself attempted to balance the tension, aimed as it is at both the aristocratic and bureaucratic "fathers" (addressed in one preface as "*ihr gelehrten Väter*"[7]) and at the individual citizens whose identity as good fathers rests on their willingness to conform to certain collective values and behaviors. One might well ask which rights and responsibilities accord with each iteration of fatherhood. Frank's text implies that, in a discussion of political rights and responsibilities, the appellation "father" might rightfully apply only to one group. Here, discussing the rights of the citizen-father, he acknowledges that, under certain adverse conditions, a ruling authority might cease to be a *Landesvater* and instead figure as the *Obrigkeit* with despotic hands. And yet, he declares:

> In all of these and other actions of the medical police, I do not see anything that too closely encroaches upon the freedom that is possible in a social collective, nothing that could make a reasonable and responsible citizen appear to be the slave of the law-giving authority, apart from those things that strive merely to guarantee the well-being of those citizens, and simply takes from its children the knife, with which they could injure themselves.[8]

Frank deftly implies that the enlightened figure of the "reasonable and responsible citizen," who is not and should not be a slave to the state, is instead the non-slave and is granted all the "freedom that is possible." Where restrictions apply, they may be seen as measures a parent takes on the part of the citizen-child who is thereby protected from his own (natural, not self-incurred) immaturity.

Nevertheless, Frank argues, the notion of living in society with unlimited natural freedom was impossible and overly philosophized "à la Rousseau."[9] Frank's understanding of enlightened freedom was far more closely aligned with Kant, for whom, as Robert Bartlett phrases it, the "emergence from self-incurred immaturity presupposes an understanding of maturity, of the proper development of the human mind and character; it is on such a conception of human maturity that Kant grounds his powerful appeals to human dignity."[10] It was only through limits placed upon individual behavior (whether by reasoned will, by moral inclination, or by law) that human beings developed culture at all and thereby distinguished themselves as human; foregoing those limits would be tantamount to returning to the woods to our "half-brothers, the remaining animals."[11] Registering a certain trepidation with the precarious gap between freedom as license and freedom as responsible choice, Frank offered the Enlightenment's middle-of-the-road solution: moral education through reading. His text itself was offered as evidence of—and as an active part of—the freedom to read, to learn, and to decide according to reasoned principles that had as their ultimate referent the "common good." In this vein, Frank styled himself as an advocate for the political responsibility of all citizens to improve the genealogical human (national) species through control of its breeding.

How does this work when one is proposing to limit certain people's right to procreate? As Isabel Hull writes, by the end of the eighteenth century, the sexual drive was considered "the motor of society and the mark of the independent, adult, productive citizen."[12] Frank was quite forthright in his affirmation of sexual desire (in both men and women), as well as the "natural" desire to propagate one's line or *Race*. At the same time, he described at length the necessity of preventing reproduction among the unhealthy of any social rank. That involved the discouragement or outright official prevention of marriage for people suffering from epilepsy, syphilis, or consumption; or for those who were physically deformed; or for those suffering from any of the "diseases of the spirit," including "idiocy, insanity, severe melancholy, sleepwalking" and the like.[13]

It may well be the case that Frank was instrumental in formulating and promulgating theories that, in Foucault's terms, present "the 'body'—the body of individuals and the body of populations—[. . .] as the bearer of new variables . . . as between the more or less utilisable, more or less amenable to profitable investment, those with greater or lesser prospects of survival, death and illness, and with more or less capacity for being usefully trained."[14] Distilling his writing in this way, while it would conform to a dominant interpretation of the function of police at the end of the Enlightenment, would require a dismissal of the often ambivalent, ultimately undisciplined aspects of his work that I think is far more interesting for what it suggests about the cognitive possibilities of the era.

Despite his conviction that curtailing reproductive rights would benefit the greater population over time, Frank was unable to dismiss the ethical problems the elimination of the freedom to reproduce raised. His language betrays a fear of the threat to human dignity that would arise if policy decisions were based entirely upon the logical extension of the scientific "facts" of heredity. To justify the restrictions that he advocated—and they were radical—he clearly felt compelled not merely to argue, but to persuade his reader (and perhaps himself) of the legitimacy of the proposed demands upon the individual citizen.

Frank devotes extensive text to the invocation of his reader's—the citizen's—virtue, linking it to a capacity for self-discipline. He asks for voluntary renunciation on the part of those whose breeding would more harm than benefit the state: just as one must renounce one's freedom to murder or pillage, so must the unhealthy renounce their freedom to mate if the greater virtues of a civil society are to flourish. Arguing at length, drawing on relevant scientific as well as political literature, Frank devises guidelines for a kind of Schillerean renunciation on the part of the individual, whose decision not to reproduce would free him from suffering the force of legislation, and would also free the state from charges of oppression and abuse. Even this strategy, however, does not seem to satisfy Frank entirely.

While statements and summaries of the long-term benefits are unambiguous in the *System*, there are moments when the structure of his argument provides an invitation for questioning by the reader. The writing seems to acknowledge the inadequacies of a purely objective or argumentative mode of writing when the implementation of a science of heritability and perfectibility are discussed. A systematic understanding of human life as a product of hereditary lines—whether that system be designed by scientific, philosophical, or hygienic discourse—proves to be a difficult basis from which to render a complete account of the complexity of human life, and Frank is not able to dismiss that rich complexity. Amid a carefully reasoned presentation, Frank abruptly inserts the following narrative anecdote:

> A consumptive, long withdrawn from the common responsibilities of citizenship, feels desire to propagate his race.... What will you do, poor man!—Is it not enough, that so many hands have to work for you, and can you truly provide for a family, when your fatherland is already burdened by you?.... Apply yourself, if it is still possible, to your health; occupy once again the position in which your fellow citizens now must work for you, and then go ahead and say: "I wish to give my fatherland yet one more citizen, who will work toward the common good"—If you cannot do this, unfortunate man! then relinquish your claims; spare the society, in which you live, a new burden, by restraining your desires, and, at least provide the service, since you have become useless, of not increasing the number of the poor and suffering.[15]

This excerpt is effectively a translation of the argument of its surrounding text, not into another language but into a different narrative mode. This imaginative intermission, in which a fatherly authority figure makes the same argument that the text has made, continues at some length, providing a dramatic script of personal renunciation for the good of the *Vaterland*. It is difficult to say just what this bit of text is: it is *like* a sermon, it is *like* a catechism, it is *like* a piece of sentimental bourgeois theater. It is like all three in that it attempts to persuade by an emotionally charged rhetoric, by creating identification (in this case, a double identification with both the threatened wretch and the sermonizing voice), by the modeling of "correct" responses to questions within a fictional situation.

This fictional insertion represents a violation of the strictures more rigorous scientists placed on scientific writing during the era. Here, in the very punctuation (in the marks of exclamation and ellipsis), we have examples of what Blumenbach dismissed as typographical "ornament" designed to communicate the emotional (and therefore suspect) pitch of the text.[16] Medical writing, however, still relied upon a conjunction of scientific argument and evidence, with anecdote, narrated case histories, and fictional stories. Certainly, the punctuation works here *deliberately* to interfere with the presumed objectivity of the work. The first sentence seems to introduce an example, common enough in a scientific text. It is followed, however, by an ellipsis that marks a transition from an explanatory to an outright theatrical mode—a transition that reconfigures the consumptive (someone suffering physical illness) into the addressee of the sermon to come; he is now no longer merely sick, but a "poor man," an *Armseliger*—literally, someone less blessed, whose soul is in peril.

As readers, we witness here the performance of moral coercion that induces a subject to internalize laws yet to be legislated. Deliberately evoking pity and fear, the text performs the delivery of a moral lesson from a fatherly voice to a diseased, burdensome son; further, it models the reception that can redeem the wretch, transforming him despite—or rather, because of—his childlessness into an acceptable "fellow citizen." The *Armseliger*, cut off from physical procreation, can nonetheless make an appropriate and admirable personal sacrifice for the good of *Vaterland* and the Family of Man—he can, in fact, become a kind of social father if he is adequately catechized by the moralizing script at hand. Notable in either case is that the script that Frank constructs to supplement his scientific argument draws upon links between biological reproduction, social responsibility, and morality, all of which is united in his various figurations of "fatherhood."

The tyranny of the dramatic voice dictating the path of free will is hardly subtle, and it is made visible as a fictional device for all to read. What is the function of this device? Perhaps this passage is simply a script or catechism that Frank provides his readers, many of whom, after all, were in positions of authority and who required the tools, including rhetorical ones, to implement Frank's suggestions. Perhaps Frank's prior discussion of freedom, human rights, and duty left him uncertain of the moral valence of a eugenic program, and the simplicity of the sermon was necessary to convince not only his readers but also himself that the impositions of a breeding program upon the individual were legitimate. Perhaps Frank, influenced by the psychological and dramatic theories of the period, consciously chose to utilize the aesthetic power of a dramatic text to affect his reader emotionally, thereby conditioning that reader to be more receptive to the rational argument.

Whatever its ostensible function might be, this particular text produces an alienating impact. Frank's use of this fiction makes the coercive power of authoritative moral reasoning all too apparent. The reader, rather than being discreetly coerced, is given an extra opportunity to become conscious of and to evaluate the web of political, moral, and physical concerns that together shape the book's presentation of the biological "facts" that are its ostensible subject.

THE GERM OF VIRTUE

For many eighteenth-century thinkers attracted by the potential benefits of public hygiene and the medical police, the effects of directed breeding were not limited to physical health and to social order. Many believed as Herder did when he asserted: "It is known the world over that illnesses and characteristics of physical form, as well as inclinations and dispositions are transmitted and inherited."[17] For those who were convinced of the heritability of an intellectual and a moral sensibility, the potential good that directed breeding could yield was all the more promising. In his *Essay on the Manner of Perfecting the Human Species*, Charles Vandermonde pressed upon his readers already in 1756 the importance of reinvigorating the "corrupt source of their humours and their vitality" by attending to hereditary lines, and therewith strengthening the "germ of virtue" by which the beauty and health of the species might be restored to its full force.[18] He described in detail the mechanisms of physiological transmission, linking his presentation of "science" with the argument that newborns inherit not only the wit and the stupidity of both father and mother, but "they also inherit their sentiments, their inclinations, the same vices, the same virtues." For this reason, he continued, one nearly always observes that "children who come from virtuous parents carry at birth the germ of virtue, and debauched fathers inevitably bequeath to their children the inclination to libertinage."[19] The "germ" of vice or virtue was, in Vandermonde's mind, inborn and inherited, and subsequent education and experience would serve to either cultivate or discourage its qualities.

Frank also acknowledged a line of spiritual inheritance that accompanied observable physical paths of transmission. He did not develop (or borrow) any theory to explain or elaborate the phenomenon; nor is there much concern apparent in his text to distinguish, for example, between the process of transmission of character traits in the process of begetting and the transmission through breast milk, whether from a biological mother or from a nurse-maid. Instead he focused upon the hereditary processes of physical refinement, and for these issues he took great pains to marshal arguments and evidence from medical, scientific, and philosophical fields. One related issue that did interest him, however, was the impact of love upon the act of procreation and the children thereby conceived. In addition to prohibitions against "unproductive" unions—those between partners of vastly unequal age, or between partners both very young—Frank urged that new legislation be drafted to ensure that no one could be forced to marry against his or her will. Specifically, he wrote that a union should not contradict the inclination of either the heart or the imagination of either party, for both a lack of love and a lack of erotic excitement (linked to the imagination) were causes of impotence, infertility, and poor progeny.[20] It would seem that qualities of the spirit were generated by and transmitted through the sexual act itself, although there was neither scientific evidence to support it, nor did Frank see fit to utilize a scientific tone for its mention:

> Whenever I see a sluggish, peevish temperament, I feel inclined to think that the mother thereof, enjoyed—at an inopportune moment, and that the father must have thanked her half asleep. [. . . .]

Medical Police and Hybridization   113

> Children of love, who sadly! are for the most part illegitimately born, have distinguished themselves since time immemorial through their lively appearance and natural affect, which is well-neigh unknown among dutifully conceived heirs; and every friend of human society must wish that the business of propagation between married pairs would not degenerate to mere mechanics.[21]

It is hard to avoid thinking here of the opening pages of *Tristram Shandy*, in which the entire course of Tristram's life and circumstances are generated by the material and emotional circumstances of his conception: "I tremble to think what a foundation had been laid for a thousand weaknesses both of body and mind, which no skill of the physician or the philosopher could ever afterwards have set thoroughly to rights."[22] Laurence Sterne provoked laughter with his satiric treatment of a belief in such transmission; but for Frank and his colleagues, it was a serious matter.

In this bit of Frank's text, punctuation highlights what is far from an objective passage. Abandoning an objective tone, Frank relates associations that observation catalyzed ("whenever I see ... I feel inclined to think ..."). And it is here in this rumination on the begetting of peevish children, a rumination that is a result of a feeling mixed with thought, that Frank suddenly appears shy of his subject. In a work full of explicit references to breeding, he chooses to insert an ellipsis when speculating that the mother of poor specimens must have "enjoyed—at an inopportune moment." Why use an ellipsis rather than write of sex? This choice marks a delicacy that is not representative of the book as a whole. I would suggest that the ellipsis functions to suggest, rather theatrically, that delicacy *ought* to be marked here. Why here, exactly? In this passage, Frank presents sex not merely as a technology for the production of a healthy species; instead, he stresses the significance of the affective and metaphysical aspects of the act. These aspects are reinscribed onto the representation of sex (which, over the course of his *System*, is treated quite pragmatically). Frank makes meaningful sex (as opposed to purely technical propagation) something indescribable, something that certainly escapes the parameters of either scientific, medical, or bureaucratic discourse—perhaps the better to assert its difference from eminently observable and representable "mechanics."

There are two modes of reproduction that are at issue in this excerpt: one is emotional and the other is mechanical. There are also two types of children opposed here, types that differ in kind: bastard children of loving unions, and legitimate children of indifferent couplings. Babies made in love, Frank claims, are better, more lively, more appealing to any "friend of human society" than sluggish babies made mechanically or dispassionately.[23] In this particular example, the emotionally-charged, metaphysical quality of love is responsible for transmitting, by way of the generative act, a capacity for the good. Otherwise phrased, biological reproduction creates a person, but only a loving, indescribable act between two parents (even if unwed) makes a good person. Children, according to Frank, should be begotten and not made.[24]

Ultimately, the passage in its entirety calls for what we might refer to as a "reproducing family unit" that unites the optimal biological, legal, and emotional components: good blood, social legitimacy, and love. The various "goods" that are the core of eugenics are communicated here, but only in a passage that interrupts Frank's argumentative text to reveal rather than state its claims.

But what is Frank saying here about bastards? As we do well to recall from the early chapters of this book, early modern social convention and legal tradition prohibited and punished bastardy. Illegitimate children, *spurii*, the traces of illegal fornication, were excluded from family name and lineage. The legal system denied them a place within a family's hereditary line. The social genealogy that was maintained this way, based upon gestures of deference to the "natural" bonds of blood-kinship, was a legal fiction, an artifact generating artifacts called "families." Bastards could not inherit social status associated with a hereditary line, and the law thereby closed them out of public community with a kind of finality. However, with increasing attention paid to what they might inherit "naturally" (biologically), the "natural" child's inheritance from both parents attained a scientific status that brought it into direct conflict with the legal system.

Frank's text makes a claim for a radical transposition of authority over the meaning and value of heredity from the social to the scientific realm. According to a logic that places the health of the social body at the pinnacle of a state's priorities, society can no longer afford to exclude bastards. Previous notions of legitimacy are effectively dismissed in favor of "health" as a criterion for productive, and even morally desirable citizenship.

This is a mark of modernity, this prioritizing of what styles itself a scientific perspective. This position opposes itself to a position that is identified as being less knowledgeable, and thus more susceptible to error, superstition, and myth-bound tradition. In a moment of contested authority, heredity is reconfigured, ascribed to the domain of scientific knowledge and from there to social institutions. This coup had dramatic consequences, but we must recognize that it continued to rely upon the cognitive structures of kin relations and their metaphysical bonds that provided the foundation for the "older," ousted system of social order. In fact, heredity in the domain of the biological ultimately proves less flexible that it was within the law, with its flexible narratives and fictions. For a writer like Frank, however, still relatively undisciplined and able to maneuver between scientific "fact" and moral, social fictions, the biological take-over of heredity made possible a logical progression of challenges to social structures, from poverty or aristocratic privilege to racial difference itself.

THE LEGITIMACY OF (MEDICALIZED) ANCESTRY

As Frank traces the impact of heritability from individuals through graduated scales of genealogically produced groups, including family, region, race, state, and species, other entrenched categories of social organization, like those of estate or class, are challenged. Social differences based upon geographical, political, or religious orientation are all subordinated to the new overriding criterion of identity: a shared medical ancestry and its corollary, the shared potential for shaping the future members of the race.

In addition to his use of family terms to convey moral imperatives (like loyalty to the *Landesvater*, or the parental love that catalyses care of children), Frank liberally deploys the term "race" to designate, and thereby link together, all of the social groups from family to species that can be included under the jurisdiction of his program. Critical here is the way that Frank makes productive use of a discursive slippage to convince his reader of the direct links between individuals propagating (to carry on their "race") and the development of the human race, or the species. He uses the term as an indeterminate category that shifts between a propagating pair and the species. I would argue that part of the appeal of the broad and vague notion of race for writers of the era—not just for Frank—was its function as a bridge between these two extremes, the individual reproducing unit and the species, the part and the whole. In Frank's text, we are struck by the flexibility of the term to refer to any group—family line, village, nation—that is less than, but contributes to, the entirety of humankind.

He begins with an obvious, logical claim for his program: if a community can optimize breeding between pairs of citizens to produce stronger children, that community will benefit from the healthier population that develops. And if this claim is valid, then the target communities can range from extended families to social castes (a race of farmers, a race of aristocrats), nation-races, and the entire species—all of which, he maintains, are produced by, identifiable by, and thus improvable by controlling their ongoing history of reproduction. He does not claim outright that all of these human groupings should be regarded explicitly as kinship groups; he did not state outright that they are all extended biological families or branches of the species-family. Instead, by cycling back and forth between vocabularies of family and race, he deftly and repeatedly implies both. When he identifies the populace as a large "family," he uses the term as a metaphor primarily to assign a "natural" allegiance and hierarchical structure to the political collective. When, on the other hand, he expressly wants to identify differently scaled groups as genealogically produced (and reproducing), he tends to refer to them as "races," making productive use of the word's diffuse and imprecise signifying power. Even as he uses the term loosely (not subjecting any group to a scientific standard of "race," but using race to signify any group defined by common ancestry), he effectively "racializes" the entire spectrum of community groupings.

While tradition (the heredity of public identity) was responsible for the division of people into different social strata, Frank asserted that the various classes or *Stände* had developed particular characteristics largely as a result of their generative practices. Pointing to the ill health and poverty characteristic of the farming class, he argued that their misery was a manifestation of gradual degeneration [he uses the scientific term *Abartung*] caused by lack of good breeding stock. As strong young men were conscripted, the reproductive work in the countryside was left to a remaining "small and ill formed race of men"—a group who, upon being deemed unfit for military service, found their health further compromised by strenuous labor and poverty. Frank identified this social problem—namely, the loss of the strongest sons of the farming class to the military—not only as the "origin of human degeneration among the peasantry," but also as that which catalyzed (as the origin or *Ursprung*) a subsequent natural, historical, genealogical process [*Abartung*] resulting in the physical and social character of an entire estate [*Bauernstand*]."[25]

Such problems were, however, correctable; degeneration affecting the peasant "race" could be remedied by making adjustments in marriage practices. First of all, no man blessed with robust health and beauty should be permitted to waste his physical gifts "in an ambiguous bachelor life, to the detriment of our posterity."[26] Citing references ranging from Plato to laws in the American colonies, he argued that healthy men resolutely opposed to marriage should be made to function as social fathers (that is, as male supporters of the social family) by taxing them to support widows and orphans. More dramatically, however, changes in military practice that would require, rather than prevent, the marriage of soldiers would bring about dramatic changes in the population, since soldiers were generally the healthiest, strongest and largest men recruited from different regions.[27] To bolster his argument, Frank referred to the Swiss military system, in which all citizens (by implication male, married, potent, and already fathers) went to war and then returned home as "hardened fathers of strong children."[28] In Switzerland, he seems to say, the race is strong simply because the men are strong fathers who produce strong children.

Such policies that take seriously the supply and quality of potential fathers could not help but gradually redress the problem of degeneration among peasants. Of course, changes would have to be made to the myriad legal prohibitions restricting marriage among the lowest classes. Hence to challenge such prohibitions, and to pave the way for healthy pairings without regard to social or economic position, Frank again casts his argument in racial terminology. In the case of healthy young people too poor to qualify by law for marriage, he proposes that the state financially support their union, and that the state then consider as its property the union's offspring, who will be relocated to areas where "human perfection appears to have suffered the most."[17] This policy would guarantee a necessary infusion of better blood into degenerate communities; without such intervention, Frank warns, the "good race of human beings" itself is threatened with extinction.[18]

Frank did not limit his proposed reforms and restrictions to the less privileged. He argued repeatedly that, if "rights" had anything to do with the social good, then members of the decadent aristocracy often have far less right to propagate than the healthy poor. His health-based meritocracy requires that the diseased members of bourgeois or aristocratic classes be legally excluded from corrupting future generations and from contributing to the deterioration of the body politic's health. Only healthy people ought to reproduce themselves; to protect them and society in general, he advocates in great detail the organized support of the healthy poor in their procreative efforts and at the same time insists without hesitation that the diseased members of middle or aristocratic classes should be excluded from contributing to future generations. Frank's health-based meritocracy makes possible the rejection, at least in principle, of the potential progeny of a diseased aristocrat in favor of the flourishing child of a robust, "beautiful" farm laborer, on the grounds that only the latter is useful to the state and therefore deserving of its protection.[29]

Frank also deployed a "racial" argument to challenge the myriad legal prohibitions against marriage among the lowest classes and to pave the way for "mixed marriages" between classes or estates. In the case of healthy young people too poor to marry, Frank proposed that the state financially support their union and consider the offspring property of the state, to be relocated to areas where "human perfection appears to have suffered most grievously."[30] Without the infusion of better blood into degenerate communities, "the good race of human beings" would ultimately vanish.[31]

This use of race to establish hereditary health as the dominant criterion of differentiation for state purposes brings with it the displacement of the long-entrenched category of class or social position, assuming the power to legitimate in its stead the physically privileged. Such a complex reconfiguration dismisses conventional social difference as traditional, myth-bound, ephemeral. By contrast, the real biological differences that class behaviors and breeding patterns cause are remedied. Under Frank's program, birth still largely determines the status of an individual, but that "birth" is legitimated not by the purity of one's social lineage but by the purity of one's medicalized ancestry.

MIXING THE *"MENSCHEN-RACEN"*

One distinct social problem Frank identified as a threat to the development of the "good race" of human beings in a region was the often murderous animosity between neighboring villages, where hatred and fear felt toward the respective other were expressed in part by violent attempts to prevent intermarriage. Men who came courting from a neighboring town did so at the risk of their lives, noted Frank, "whereby it is not uncommon that the results lead to numerous death-blows."[32] The results were predictable and disastrous: many healthy young women remained unmarried because there were not enough men within their own village to go around and those villages that had enough of a population to marry their young people amongst themselves weakened over generations due to inbreeding. Identifying this trend as a significant problem across all of Europe, Frank cited a French ordinance from 1718 severely penalizing anyone causing disruption and violence when a village youth brought in a "foreign" girl—that is, from another village—as his bride.[33] Frank attributes the adoption of this law both to the wise recognition of the benefits of intermarriage and the need to combat destructive xenophobic tendencies throughout the lands. In fact, the actual document that Frank praises seems more concerned with public order and the potential disruption of local business than with the hereditary health of the villages, but Frank is clearly eager to use it for the advantage of his agenda. Extending the argument, he discusses at length the necessity of reducing hatred and jealousy among neighboring clusters of villages, "in particular, the overall jealousy that the young men of different communities feel toward each other."[34] Frank speculates that irrational and intense sexual rivalry between adolescent boys is the root cause and the continuing fuel for these conflicts. Hence if villages could somehow be brought together and sexual energy be rechanneled (which ought to be easy, since the erotic excitement that is dulled at home by "daily exposure" to local girls would be ignited by exposure to those from another village), not only would public order gain, but everyone in a given village would—in what amounts to equal or greater benefit—also be prevented from eventually being related to each other.

After asserting that diseases that pass from parent to child may be eliminated by regulating propagation and by carefully crossing bloodlines, Frank widens his net yet further with the claim that the well-being of the state requires "that the human races are refreshed from time to time with foreign blood, whereby the propensity to particular heritable diseases [*Familienkrankheiten*] will be mitigated and the excellence of the lines [*Geschlechter*] can be fostered."[35] Just as individuals pass traits from parent to child that eventually become identifiable within certain family lines, Frank observes that entire peoples often bear physical characteristics that are intensified when transmitted over generations, particularly among peoples who avoid intermarriage with others:

> We know that entire peoples, as long as they infrequently or never mixed with foreign nations, carried particular identifying characteristics upon their faces which, like a personal legacy from father to son, always and in a predictable manner were transmitted. The lovely blue eyes and the golden hair of the German made him recognizable among all peoples, as long as the blood of German fathers exclusively engendered children of German mothers.[36]

It is tempting to identify via Frank's use of value-laden adjectives (the blue eye that is beautiful) and of the potentially nostalgic tone that colors his final comment a cultural prejudice, and to suspect him of advocating that peoples—and particularly the Germans—maintain (or attempt to reclaim) their racial purity through the proper alliance of (German) *Vaterblut*, literally "father-blood," with (German) mothers. If we read on, however, noting Frank's comparison of the German appreciation of (its own) golden hair with the Chinese preference for (its own) small feet,[37] we might grant that Frank acknowledges the cultural relativity of the "beauty" attributed by a people to its own peculiarities.[38] In fact, we might reasonably enough presume that Frank believed, along with Herder, that all peoples should be respected equally for their various and unique characteristics, but that it was at the same time advisable to preserve the boundaries between those peoples; thus Herder admonished against the "wild intermixing" of peoples and races, urging: "Wheresoever and whosoever you were born to be, oh Man, that is where and who you ought to be; do not let go of the chain, nor place yourself outside of it, but rather fasten yourself to it!"[39]

However, while Frank might dwell upon the "beautiful blue eyes" of the genealogically pure German (located only in an indistinct past), such an example functions merely as evidence for the heritability of traits over time. The significance of the example is its function as part of a larger argument against, and not for, sexual insularity. On the contrary, Frank ventures farther than most of his contemporaries in his thinking about the consequences and the benefits of what he calls racial mixing. And while we cannot overlook the evidence of his personal belief in a European cultural superiority, Frank devotes a significant amount of text to his advocacy, on biological grounds, for intermarriage among all cultures and races. Frank's project does not at any point advocate for the preservation of a biological distinction among various peoples—unlike Herder, for example, or Kant. Rather, he considered intermarriage among variously defined 'peoples' to improve the health of each, believing that such mixing would eliminate problems born by each, rather than any "valuable" differences. In this case, he is historically minded but forward looking, whereas the thinking of most of his contemporaries is historical and nostalgic.

Frank begins with an authoritative declaration that the perfection of the various human races [*Racen*] clearly suffers when they don't mix with foreigners [*Fremden*], but instead always marry among themselves "and continue to sow the same fruit upon the same acre."[40] Frank is not the first to make this argument. Vandermonde, like Frank, explained to his readers the "natural" law against incest: "It may be presumed that the first men would have observed that these alliances within the same families caused their races to degenerate, and that the true way to rejuvenate them would be to mix with foreign races."[41] The connection of the two clauses within the one sentence effectively equates "family" with "race," implying that any weakness in the family line signals degeneracy for the entire race, and that only breeding with "foreign races" can ameliorate the problem and "elevate" the family/race to its appropriate heights.

Vandermonde expands at length upon the ongoing necessity of interbreeding the human races (*"les races humaines"*) to prevent them from degenerating, and he argued that the assimilation of foreigners into any native population resulted in enhanced physical beauty, military strength, and culture:

> The most politically savvy sovereigns must have attracted foreigners with promise of recompense; by gratifying them, sovereigns enriched themselves, and in depopulating other countries of the most attractive men and the greatest geniuses, they repopulated their own states with subjects capable of defending them and of causing the arts to flourish there.[42]

We might note that the science of breeding is here, as in Frank's text, invoked not to define and preserve exclusive groups, but rather to introduce inclusively, intentionally blurring physiological differences and thereby—at least potentially—keeping notions of "race" (in the historical-biological sense) separated from what is, comparatively, a strictly maintained, discrete political identity. There is in the above passage the sense that good blood is a finite resource, such that if some states attract the best breeding material, other states will be depopulated directly. This is, in effect, a science-based appeal for a cosmopolitanism that is particularly interesting in its welcome of strangers into the city of Paris. In fact, it is precisely the interbreeding that produces greatness: "The great geniuses, the men of wit, the people with talent who find themselves there probably owe their existence to the fortunate marriages of their fathers with Parisian women"—that is, with women of complicated and mixed descent.[43] Further: the *"grand génie,"* the exceptional man of talent who affects the civic body and raises Paris to a position of rivalry with ancient Rome is the progeny of a local, urban mother (the *"Parisienne"*) and of a stranger-father from a foreign place. This is striking in its inversion of the classical (Greek) identification of bastardy. The two figures—the Greek bastard and Vandermonde's cosmopolitan genius—are at once opposed and quite similar: both embody a relationship to the city in which they live that is determined by the foreign status of one parent. However, the gender assignments of the alien and the native parent are reversed, as is the positive or negative value placed on the exceptional (marginal) progeny. The son born in Athens of a native father and an alien mother is a bastard and a non-citizen, excluded from making official contributions to civic life; the son born in Paris of a native mother and an alien father is a genius, responsible for the city's glory. Vandermonde champions a kind of hybridity as an essential characteristic of modern cosmopolitanism. He reconfigures the illegitimate, the suspect, the alien as the (still idiosyncratic and potentially suspect) genius. Vandermonde continues: "The groups were repeatedly crossed; chance and sometimes necessity united people from very different climates and produced very good races. The more foreigners there are in a city, the more it becomes famous."[44] Specifically, it is successive intermarriage over time that leads to the success and renown of a populace—it is a historical, progressive process. Vandermonde initially identifies the strangers entering Paris as people from "the provinces," and thus probably still "French," so that their unions are not what we initially would consider the mingling of races. But then his scope widens as he specifies the crossbreeding of people of different climates (one of the tenaciously maintained sources of racial difference) and how that mixing specifically produces the most beautiful races (*de trés-bonnes races*). It is because of such interbreeding, he argues, that cities on the seacoast have always flourished: their high population of "strangers" produced an unusually high percentage of men of genius.[45] To this point, he notes that there are more great men in London than in the rest of England,[46] not merely because the city attracts adventurous and talented men born elsewhere, but because those men reproduce once they arrive.

Vandermonde identifies this breeding practice as the dominant influence upon the bloodlines of entire peoples. Praising Turkey as one of the most flourishing states in the world (an interesting position politically, and one that Frank also takes), Vandermonde connects its thriving to the fact that among its people "the blood is most beautiful."[47] This "beautiful blood"— which is the opposite of pure blood—is, he argues, not surprising:

> This vast empire is only a composite of different peoples who have become its tributaries. The Armenians, the Arabs, the Egyptians, even the Europeans themselves during the time of the Crusades contributed much to the beauty that is a characteristic of the natives of the region. Among others, the prodigious quantity of female Georgian, Mingrelian and Circassian slaves that were transported every year into that region, managed to perfect the positive traits that these people had received from nature.[48]

Various peoples are regarded as tributaries flowing politically, economically, and biologically into and comprising the vast empire, thus reversing the anxiety-producing image of a species or collective group degenerating outward into numerous racial varieties. The individual peoples (nations, races) flow toward each other, the parts not diffusing or threatening a whole but strengthening it, precisely because of the mingling of their collective "racial" differences.

When Frank declares that each of the human races must mix with foreigners, he uses highly-charged language: by the end of the century, the references to *Racen* that proliferated in travel and anthropological writing generally signaled physical and cultural differences that ought not be violated. Further, referring to someone as a "foreigner" or "stranger" carried an anxious, if not outright pejorative, connotation. Thus Frank's statement would, in 1780, initially bring to mind an improper, if not frightful, mixing of peoples who ought to remain separate. As if aware of the minefield he has entered, Frank does not continue with a direct defense of his statement, but instead—with what feels like defensive tactics—briefly shifts his description to nature and the animal kingdom, arguing that "the history of procreation among all animals gives perfect evidence of this."[49]

Pointing out that the law against incest is regarded by "us" (his European readership) as a law of God, he argues that it should be understood more expansively as a law of nature, designed to protect all creatures from degeneracy.[50] One need merely heed the lessons offered by various animal species: the members of many strong groups, when they are ready to breed, leave their established habitat and "emigrate from their fatherland." It is this migration alone—this *Wanderung*, a term used for itinerant journeymen—that, according to Frank, allows for their flourishing over time.[51] A contrary example presents itself in the condition of many domesticated animals, and even more so in the condition of those found in zoos: such animals that are not free to wander and to mix with "foreign races" inevitably weaken and gradually die off.

The terms "fatherland," "emigrate," "migration," and even "foreign races" anchor the reader's attention to the fundamental concern motivating Frank's argument: that is, the identification of optimal behaviors for a flourishing humanity. These behaviors, Frank is well aware, run counter to the inclination of many. His word choice is provocative, even inserted as it is within a discussion of animal breeds: we read "fatherland," a term signaling familial roots, belonging, and insularity; we read "foreign races," words announcing a confrontation with alien bodies and with cultures. Frank's animal analogy translates into an order: "emigrate, leave your fatherland, wander into the regions of foreign races and there select your mate—for the good of the human race." He employs culturally fraught terms in such a way that he reverses the negative/positive valuations placed upon them. While fatherland becomes something no doubt desired but nonetheless debilitating, foreign races are understood to be initially daunting but ultimately the source of positive partnership in propagating one's own healthy race (family) and so reshaping—indeed strengthening—the human race. Frank does not try to soften his program with circumlocutions, with softer language (he might have written about "neighbors" rather than about "foreign races," for example), or with admonitions against insularity left vague. On the contrary, his argument demands that the reader first confront entrenched binary values of home and foreign, same and other, and then choose consciously what he (or possibly she) has hitherto been socially conditioned to reject. Frank does not propose or even imply that such a mixing of the races might ultimately eradicate these crude and difficult binaries. One has the sense that, though his program would certainly eradicate all fixed biological boundaries between groups, human social behavior would still produce self-understandings that include simultaneously an inclusive human race and potentially divisive, separate human races. This is not a problem, however, that Frank has set out to solve. Important for him is not those fictional identity-boundaries between groups that appear to be a human cognitive necessity; he simply seeks the elimination of the static physiological and genealogically produced identities separating the same groups.

Stressing that human races have suffered whenever they have failed to intermarry, Frank cites as results of inbreeding arguments ubiquitous in contemporary anthropological literature, including references to both the constitutional weakness of the Native American and the particular physiognomy of the Jews.[52] While praising Jews for their migratory practices—for the fact that they as a people were detached from any particular *Acker* or geographical area—he observes that they nevertheless suffered physiologically as a result of vigilant, religiously regulated inbreeding. In the case of Native Americans, Frank observes that tribal insularity has resulted in the transmission of debilitating diseases through generations until the seed of each disease is spread throughout an entire community—thus rendering the community [*Gemeinde*] an extended consanguineous family. There is no end to the misery, writes Frank, "when the evil is not defeated through the influx of pure sources and through certain reciprocal effects."[53] "Reciprocal effects" are in all probability a tacit answer to the challenge that, by mixing good and bad blood, the strong lines might be corrupted by the sickly foreign influence; and this argument is more along the lines of Frank's advocacy for the exclusion of sickly individuals from the social-breeding program. Frank, though distinguishes importantly between individuals and populations: individuals who carry particular diseases must not reproduce; a population that exhibits weakness or degeneration, meanwhile, must aggressively pursue remedy through intermarriage with vigorous individuals from outside its self-identified boundaries.

Frank emphasizes that all creatures must move and must marry outside their own lines. This form of racial deterritorialization is a kind of ideal for the production of the "good race of human kind." By advocating the state-supported mixing of *Menschenracen* (be it on a local or an international scale), Frank directly challenged a legal status-quo that carefully restricted the movement of people and that defined citizens as "native born." In other words, he challenged a status-quo that, by virtue of *ius sanguinus*, emphasized the restricted kinship nature of political affiliation and a hostility to any foreign element and reinforced geographic conceptions of race. Frank's advocacy of intermarriage for the good of the "race" or "races" could, therefore, be understood to deploy the notion of race and of its reproductive mechanism so as to counter what he identified as a human inclination to cling to—and perpetuate—small, exclusive, and incestuous (racial) units. To combat this inclination and to rectify or prevent altogether the weaknesses undermining the well-being of any group of people, Frank stressed the necessity of careful attention to interbreeding: "It is entirely proper, that mutually opposed constitutions (even including visible flaws) perfect themselves in their children, and that the races [*Geschlechter*] improve through the mixing of foreign blood."[54]

As a sign of the positive effects of mixing the human races—specifically, as a sign that intermarriage between ethnic groups is blessed by nature—such unions (so claims Frank) produce offspring with more ideally regular features. That is, it is within these unions that the more extreme signs of physical difference—the signs of degeneration that determine the existence of racial boundaries—are blended and thus made more beautiful. Drawing heavily from Peter Simon Pallas's writings on Russia, Frank observes:

> The half-Tartar Persian mitigates his natural ugliness through mixing his blood with the blood of a beautiful slave from Tiflis; among the Calmuck, [certain tribes] distinguish themselves through their height and through the better formation of their faces, 'which they possess thanks to the strong influx of Tartar blood via captive women'; and we daily see the influence that the natural difference of parents expresses upon the formation of their children, as when a white blonde woman, through the mixing of her fluids with those of a coal black Negro, so reforms the fruit that she receives from him, that only half of the paternal ugliness is retained[55]

Writing in greater detail of another racial combination, that between Europeans and Mongols, Frank writes that, "such marriages produce a race of mulattos called the 'Karymki'; these appear somewhat Mongolian in the face, have black or very dark hair, and usually have the most regular and pleasing features."[56]

Frank's unqualified attributions of ugliness to those features most different from northern-European norms do provide evidence of a connection between racial prejudice and European aesthetics. However, his suggestion that "regularity" (a classic European requirement) should characterize beauty is a bit complicated, since he believes regularity is produced by the gradual elimination of extreme racial traits—including those of northern Europeans. It is as unusual as it is significant that, when discussing marriages between people of different races and their typical offspring, Frank identifies as a positive gain for the species the eradication of what amounts to all race-determining traits. Certainly, the traits he is happiest to see go are those characterizing non-Europeans. But he never expresses concern that the characteristic traits of the "white blonde woman" who marries a black man will be lost to subsequent generations as a result; he never suggests that certain races or peoples—even those with particularly robust health or beauty—should isolate themselves to protect their better blood from contamination or compromise. On the contrary, he advocates a mixing of all types, advocating controlling breeding not to defend and preserve racial difference (and an accompanying hierarchical value system), but to eliminate all physiological group identities, to effectively eliminate the physical patterns of sameness and difference that were fueling the invention of race. And this he proposed all in the name of the health of the human race.

DESIRE

Is it possible that male desire, following its natural course, would take care of the physical perfection of the species? Frank seems to suggest this to be the case, if two conditions could be met: first, male desire for (and competition for) mates who are foreign (visibly other, racially different) should be unimpeded by counterproductive social regulations and traditions that stigmatize or outright prohibit mobility and intermarriage; and second, the potentially disruptive force of male sexual aggression that accompanies this desire should be properly channeled. In other words, if certain "illegitimate" behaviors were allowed, men would naturally reproduce with optimal results. Here Frank has no practical suggestion to offer, but he argues that an acknowledgement of sexual competition must be included within effective social analysis and subsequent policy.

Frank elaborates on successful mixed marriages between Europeans and Mongols, noting in particular that Mongol men are happy to baptize their daughters so that they might marry Europeans (for the girls, a step up a ladder that is simultaneously and indistinguishably social and racial). European men, for their part, wish to marry Mongol girls because they are "hot-blooded." At the same time, rich Mongol men often marry Russian (Caucasian, European) young women who are, by implication, not of wealthy families and glad to acquire a rich husband. The role that gender plays throughout these and other examples is critical. In each case, women are identified as the object of male sexual desire, whereas men offer women increased social, racial, or financial status. In most of Frank's examples (culled from other travel and anthropological sources), the women are of lighter races. By virtue of their racial beauty, they dilute by half the ugliness passed from their mates to their offspring. In every instance of beneficial mixing of the *Menschenracen*, women are the crucial factors in the process of physical improvement. The beneficial role he imputes to racially attractive women in improving all the races exists in fascinating parallel to the idea that women, by virtue of their natural spiritual beauty and virtue, act as civilizing agents upon their mates so as to transform the latter into milder, better citizens. Never does Frank write about the mitigating influence of a racially beautiful man upon the progeny of an ugly woman.

In the example of European men marrying Mongol women, Frank identifies a "natural" desire for the racially exotic other also described in his discussion of village rivalries and relations. A natural attraction between different ethnic peoples, which results in marriages yielding strong and particularly beautiful progeny (as in the case of the European/Mongol mix), is, Frank contends, evidence of nature's guiding the species. There is at work here an anticipation of sexual selection theory, in the insinuation of a universal male sexual desire for a beauty in women that specifically balances a man's racial traits in the production of progeny.[57]

In short, men desire different women (while wanting to compete with different men) and to that desire Frank attributes a natural, unconscious impetus, which, because it seeks to produce children approaching some ideal of "balance" in their color, stature, and features, might prevent genetic weaknesses that result from inbreeding. Nature, evidently, works through male desire. Meanwhile beauty, it seems—and we speak here of physical female beauty—functions as the driver of successful sexual selection. This beauty is, by Frank's account, crucially associated with a physical difference that he identifies as hereditary, as historical, and as "racial." At the same time, a more general and non-gender-specific human beauty marked by "regularity" is the legible result of the natural eradication (that is, the correction) of degeneracy-related (that is, racial) differences. According to Frank's program, an effective medical police can restrain the psychological and social behaviors that prevent the flourishing of such beauty and it is under this program that controlled breeding potentially becomes a global technology.

While Frank's writing on the subject of radically hybridizing the human race(s) has no equivalent during the eighteenth century, it is worth noting, if only briefly, an earlier figure who shared certain core ideas. Anne Vila has written about the French "philosophical physicians" of the eighteenth century and their thesis that, "under the right physiological conditions, man's sensibility and everything connected to it could quite literally be cultivated."[58] As examples of such physicians convinced that medical expertise was necessary to guide programs for improvement, Vila discusses the writings of both Antoine Le Camus and Charles Augustin Vandermonde—both of whom, during the mid-century, ventured to speculate on regulated breeding for the betterment of the species. As Vila notes, "according to the organicist cosmology of sensibility that framed all of [various Enlightenment] discourses, the significance of the individual could only truly be conceived in terms of his or her relation to the greater, resonating whole of which he or she was a part."[59]

Such writing seriously complicates the concept of a people or *Volk* associated with the end of the eighteenth century, a concept that carries the implication of shared kinship-origins of community—origins that served as a basis for regional, national, and racial self-understanding. To combat this kind of *völkisch* thinking, Frank offered a striking critique of xenophobia insofar as he linked ideas about the nature of human sexuality to the cultural and physiological phenomenon of biological community. Contrary to the goals of eugenics research that were identified and pursued during the late nineteenth and early twentieth centuries, Frank theorized a program of state-controlled breeding, not to defend and to preserve racial difference with its entrenched hierarchies of better and worse, but ultimately to eliminate altogether those physically generated and physically manifested patterns of sameness and of difference that were fueling the scientific invention of race. If a group of people could be identified as a "race" of some sort (be it a family or a country), then by definition that group was the product of potentially detrimental inbreeding. For the good of the human race, urged Frank, such a group's racial identity (distinguished from its familial or national identity) should be sexually blended out of existence.

Frank did not imagine that human society would forego delineations of sameness and of difference; he did not advocate the end of community sensibility that requires a sense of the common if it is to devote energy toward the common good. He did, however, insist upon the value of every community's constant variation through sexual migration. The sprawling sweep of Frank's *System* represents a movement toward ideals of purity and a new regime of legitimacy in terms of physical qualities that were included under the rubric of health. Among the hygienic mechanisms he advocated, those involving controls over reproduction are certainly designed as processes of moral and biological purification, whether by elimination or construction. However, this process also necessarily generates a proliferation of precisely the kinds of beings marked by cultural standards as illegitimates. If Frank's various proposals and thought experiments were carried out, if standards of normalcy were to be primarily biological and only secondarily social, it would catalyze a radical reconfiguration of the previous norms to include bastards of all kinds previously outcast from the panoptic, legitimizing view. The future health and moral well-being of the commonwealth would best be found within the bodies and spirits of bastard love children, the progeny of the (robust) poor, mixed-race offspring, and the subsequent communities they would comprise. With such visions, we can think of Frank either as radically modern or as hopelessly out of sync with his time: it is fair to say that he finds the "lack of reality in reality" (to borrow Lyotard's phrase), opening the idea of heredity and the language of family and race to create an alternative reality that violated the limits of what his present age found conceivable.

7 Literary Insight
Brotherhood, the End of Tolerance

We concluded the last chapter with the image of proliferating bastards and hybrids, whose identity as "illegitimates" was explored in earlier chapters as an essential legal fiction. Here, I propose more directly that lineage itself is an essential cognitive fiction. This chapter, engaged with a single canonical literary text, approaches the conceptual complex of heredity in ways very different from the preceding pages of this book. This kind of disciplinary and discursive shift is necessary—if initially somewhat jarring—in order to follow the full Gordion tangle of possibilities provoked by the heredity problem at the beginning of what we now call the modern era.

Gotthold Ephraim Lessing's play, *Nathan the Wise* (1779), offers a philosophically resonant meditation upon the ambiguous knowledge of parentage. I shall read this play specifically as a tapestry of the interwoven themes engaged by the previous chapters of this book. A variety of legal, philosophical, and scientific texts grappled head-on—and in many different ways—with issues of heredity. Lessing's *Nathan*, produced during the same period, does not argue these ideas; it does not strive to create knowledge, or policy, or systematic understanding. This play is rather a poetic palimpsest which tells its story based upon—and in response to—the full range of concerns about the significance of heredity at the end of the eighteenth century.

Nathan the Wise is a drama catalyzed by the desire to ascertain family ties; a mother is central to the conflict but missing from the text; children are of uncertain origin; numerous religious and legal codes are in conflict. Here we shall focus upon *Nathan*'s presentation of a nuanced tangle of issues surrounding what critics have long thought to be one of the play's central assertions: that hereditary ties are real and knowable, and that knowing them is not only useful but necessary. *Nathan*, I believe, tests the epistemological limits of lineage to yield an ultimate if uneasy acknowledgment that the blood-tie is primarily a social fiction—one that is dangerously available as the ground for intolerance, but that is at the same time necessary for social cohesion. In dramatizing the capacity among people and cultures to sustain simultaneous and yet conflicting beliefs articulated in the language of kinship, and in presenting the blood-bond as a fact as well as a fiction, as something equally able to unite people in loyalty and to divide them murderously, Lessing paves the way for a particular kind of ethical practice that fills a space between reasoned skepticism and emotional need, between intellectually and emotionally driven responses to the knowledge of lineage. In reading the play this way, we shall raise questions about the significance of kinship for human cognition and for the fate of "tolerance" as a mode of negotiation between groups of people.

For those readers unfamiliar with the twists and turns of *Nathan*'s plot, here follows a brief summary:

Nathan, a rich Jewish merchant, returns to Jerusalem after a business trip to learn that his daughter, Recha, was saved from a fire by a German Templar who is in Jerusalem on the Third Crusade (1189–1192). When Nathan tries to thank the Templar, the young man scorns both Nathan and his daughter because they are Jews. Eventually, however, he allows Recha to thank him in person. The two young people fall in love. The Templar struggles against loving a Jewess; when he finally accepts his feelings and asks Nathan for her hand, he is stunned by Nathan's hesitation.

The Templar learns from Nathan's housekeeper that Recha was born a Christian child whom Nathan adopted as an infant. Hurt by Nathan's apparent refusal of his proposal, the Templar assumes the posture of sacred duty and approaches the Christian Patriarch of Jerusalem with a tale of Recha's conversion. Frightened by the Patriarch's virulent anti-Jewish sentiment and self-righteousness, the Templar then turns to the Sultan, Saladin. Earlier, the Sultan had spared the Templar's life because the young man looked like a lost brother whom Saladin had not seen for decades. When the Templar complains of Nathan, however, he is chastized by Saladin; nonetheless, the Sultan promises to try and unite the lovers. Saladin, meanwhile, has learned to value Nathan's wisdom. In need of money, the Sultan had tried to trick Nathan with a question that could only lead to punishment: namely, Nathan was asked to identify the one true religion. Realizing that if he answered, "Judaism," he would offend the Sultan, and incapable of lying, Nathan tells a story: the parable of the three rings. A father has a ring which guarantees the love of his subjects and the flourishing of his kingdom. As he is dying, he cannot choose which among his three beloved sons shall inherit the ring, so he has two counterfeits made. To each son he gives a ring, guaranteeing that it is genuine. After the father's death, the three quarrel over the identity of the true ring and come before a judge, who tells each simply to live as if his ring were genuine. Saladin recognizes the value of the story as an allegory of the three historical religions, and instead of punishing Nathan, makes him an offer of friendship.

When Saladin calls Nathan, the Templar, and Recha together (along with Sittah, Saladin's sister), Nathan makes a stunning revelation: he has discovered that the Templar and Recha are siblings, both children of a Christian woman and the Sultan's long lost (and long dead) brother—a friend of Nathan's. The play ends with all characters involved in an embrace.

It is perhaps easiest to begin an investigation of the claims of blood by looking at the end of the play: a final, silent embrace uniting the Muslim ruler Saladin and his sister, Sittah with the European Templar on crusade and the Jewish merchant Nathan, along with his adopted daughter, Recha. There is a long history of reading this ending as a (more or less problematic) unification of a newly recovered, "universal" family. The apparent mysteries of identity are resolved at least sufficiently to establish blood ties among the siblings, Saladin and Sittah, and their newly discovered nephew and niece, the Templar and Recha. Nathan, remaining Recha's father of sorts and embracing the Templar as his son, represents another, interlocking family circle.[1] Only Nathan's parable has received more critical celebration for its lesson of enlightened humanity. Together, or so critics to date would have us believe, the three historical religions—Judaism, Islam, and Christianity—are allegorically united; the ultimate tableau offers the audience a glimpse of a more or less utopian *Menschheitsfamilie*.[2]

These statements are, of necessity, generalizations, and cannot do justice to the subtle variations and sophistication of particular readings. In reminding the reader that Lessing's play has figured predominantly as the canonical work of enlightened tolerance, I do not discount a more recent set of dissenting voices, which focus variously on the implications of Nathan's exclusion from the blood-family;[3] on the exclusion of certain characters from the final tableau;[4] even on the lack of maternal figures comprising the "family."[5] There is even formal criticism of the ending: one critic argues that in order to provide the utopian harmony of the final tableau, Lessing was forced to manipulate his material in ways that are all too evident, resulting in a conclusion described as "a famous example of a patchwork resolution verging on the ludicrously improbable."[6] Finally, one critic has written off the so-called harmony of the ending as nothing more than a "kitschy finale."[7]

Critical dissatisfaction with dramatic endings is hardly unusual: endings are famously the sites of poetic compromise, impatience, or outright failure, if not, in the words of Gerhart Hauptmann, "a criminal assault upon the plot."[8] But in this case, the criticism is misplaced: I do not think Lessing's conclusion can be described fairly as "patchwork," nor do I think it opens itself to judgments of probability or improbability. In fact, I believe its troubling dissonance is a deliberate challenge to the audience. We can begin to identify some of the questions the ending raises if—allowing our thematic search for origins to influence our interrogatory procedure—we look at the origins of the play itself, focusing on the difference between what we will call the original (though incomplete) version and the final (published) version of *Nathan*.

Following a pattern used so effectively by Shakespeare, in which long-lost siblings are reunited and both are paired off to willing partners, the ending in Lessing's first version satisfies traditional comic genre expectations. In the final scene, Rahel (Recha) and the Templar learn of their "real" relationship; but, unlike in the final version of the play, that bond of kinship does not include Saladin. On the contrary, the audience is made to understand that there will be a dynastic connection forged by marriages between Saladin and Rahel, and between the Templar (who has been given a territory to rule by Saladin) and Sittah.[9]

Thus, the principle relationships the drama cements—relationships which promise to bring an end to the conflicts of war, of religious difference, and of conflicting self-interest—are, in this early version, legal and political, and not biological as in the later version. One might read this resolution, if such it is, as the state-building solution to problems of difference and dissent.[10] And if we understand the impending marriages in the context of genre conventions, we can regard them as a promise of future issue continuing the peace and prosperity that the marriages inaugurate.[11]

In the final, published version of *Nathan*, differences from the earlier version, in part signaled by the play's unexpected generic label, abound: Nathan, as a "dramatic poem," locates itself free of the limits of comedy or tragedy (or *Trauerspiel*, or even tragi-comedy), and it therefore fails to signal a generically predictable ending.[12] Marriage is no longer part of the resolution; instead of the earlier redirection of sexual desire from inappropriate objects (siblings) to appropriate objects (socially and politically advantageous marriage partners), the various affinities felt between characters—whether sexual, as between Recha and the Templar, or non-sexual, as between the Templar and Saladin—are internally reconfigured and explained by ties of kinship. Instead of a procreative finale, the ending is, according to one critic, philosophically utopian but sterile,[13] ironically marking not only the inaugural unity of kinship, but in the same moment (to borrow a phrase from Marc Shell) an "end of kinship."

The political alliance established in the early version is replaced with a highly unstable family hierarchy headed by Saladin as the ersatz *pater*, whose break in his relationship with his brother Assad undermines any sense that "family" ties are necessarily reliable. Moreover, the change in the final line of the play, in both versions given to Saladin, is an indication of the ultimate instability represented in the later version: originally, the final embrace follows Saladin's tribute to Nathan as a man who should be celebrated not only as "the Wise," but as "the Good." The published version replaces this with an ambiguous threat. Saladin pulls the prostrate Templar to his feet, raising him up (*"ihn aufhebend"*) and thereby transforming (with the full implication of *aufheben*, destroying the old to create a new) the young man he has aggressively claimed as "my son." The adoption is not merely a gesture of love, but also an assertion of newfound authority, an authority over not only the body, but also the emotional allegiance of the Templar (and of Recha); this assertion is clear when Saladin declares to the former, "Now you have to love me, you have to, you stubborn boy!" And to Recha, "Now am I not what I asked your permission to be? [That is, her new father.] Whether you like it or not!" And his final word, upon raising up the Templar, is the threatening imperative, "Just you wait!"[14]

132   *Heredity, Race, and the Birth of the Modern*

The early version of the play, with its marriage alliances promising to restore both emotional and political order, could be understood to offer one possible model of a rationally constructed "human family"—certainly more so than the revised ending. The final version does not merely eliminate the political element in conjoining people at the end; elsewhere in this version, the law itself as a literal bearer of truth is undermined.[15] And while, in the transition from early to published version, the legal and political realm is rejected as the arena for defining the human bonds that reliably support an ongoing community, the new version does not simply suggest that the blood-bonds of family are the more reliable cornerstones of community. These bonds are sought, both by characters and apparently by critics, as the truth behind the law, as it were; but Lessing's project is too subtle and perhaps too ambivalent to satisfy this antinomian quest. Saladin's position alone precludes our accepting the final family constellation as a satisfying allegory for a *Menschheitsfamilie* (whether biologically determined or not).

Thus, as we shall read it, the much-vaunted finale of the published version is not an "ending" with any closure *per se*.[16] The curtain descends over a moment of silence, a silence that just manages to hold many questions at bay. These questions become audible only when we begin to consider each of the characters, not as elements of a collective philosophical allegory, but rather, to borrow terms from *Ernst und Falk*, as "*bloße*" rather than "*solche Menschen*." Given Lessing's declarations elsewhere that spectators ought to be engaged with the future of the characters beyond the end of the play, it is fair to assume that unanswered questions should not be glossed over, but are instead a deliberate provocation to readers. So what are those questions?

First, since the critical tradition has it that the three historical religions are merged in one familial embrace, we might ask: how are the characters to be religiously identified after the curtain goes down? Saladin remains without doubt a Muslim, but what of the Templar? He himself expresses doubt with regard to his religious identity: is he a Christian or a Muslim? And what is Recha, raised (apparently unconventionally, and therefore questionably) as a Jew, with a rumored but unverifiable Christian baptism? Even Nathan's own Judaism is unclear.[17] What will become of Recha's religious identity? Is it tied, as it was throughout the play, to her family allegiance? And in that case, what will be the influence of her father Nathan, of her brother Curd, of her father Saladin? Will Recha remain a Jew (if she ever was one), true to the father she swears she will not renounce? Will she become the Christian that Daja insisted she always was? Will she become a Muslim once her new father Saladin claims her?[18] Or is she a figure of eighteenth-century assimilation, renouncing specific religious dogma for the general enlightened views in which Nathan has instructed her?[19]

Another set of questions surrounds the Templar. Saladin has warned that the Knights in the region are stirred up, and another outbreak of war is imminent. Will the Templar, who is not by accident identified throughout the text by this title even after we know his given name(s), face a personal conflict of allegiance in such a war? Perhaps his earlier monologic confession—that his release from a death sentence at the Sultan's hands constituted a rebirth—makes his political allegiance to Saladin (as opposed to the Knights Templar) an easy decision, but what about his religious conviction and identity? Will he continue to be the Christian he was raised to be, the aggressive Christian ready to destroy his friend Nathan when he believed the salvation of Recha's soul was at stake? Or will his status as the son (nephew) of Saladin require a conversion to the Muslim faith that was his father Assad's?[20] Do Recha, the Templar, and Saladin have to share a religious creed to constitute a family? And if they are, in fact, a family, does Nathan—defended vehemently by Recha, less vehemently by Saladin and the Templar, as ever her father—also belong? If Nathan and Saladin are both fathers to the orphan siblings, are they brothers?

WHAT IS "FAMILY"?

To address these questions, we might begin with a (seemingly) far simpler one. Since the dramatic plot revolves around the question of who belongs to whose family, we might begin by trying to identify just what a family is. I should note at the outset that the term "family" does not appear in the play, which is otherwise filled with references to father, daughter, son, sister, brother, and mother; as a collective term, only *Haus* is used, both in the context of the parable (the ring is passed down through generations within the *Haus*) and with regard to Saladin (whose *Haus* is both a personal and a political entity, subject to both personal and political influences). This is not, however, necessarily important, since the term *Familie* was, during Lessing's lifetime, a fairly new moniker for the social unit traditionally called (within specific class parameters, of course) a *Haus*.[21] While "family" as a term is not an articulated subject within the play, Lessing has structured the drama so that the characters focus upon the specific iterations of kinship. It is fairly evident that, given the collection of problems which the knowledge of blood-ties is intended to resolve, "family" is understood by most of the characters to determine one's identity within the social world and to determine one's personal network of emotional and moral bonds. The drama's concern with the legitimacy of Nathan's fatherhood of Recha is only one obvious example.

But this concern is an indication of how family as a social category functions; it does not clarify what a family is or how it is constituted. How does one belong, and how does one know that one belongs? Is family determined by blood, by a shared name, or simply by behavior, like love? Lessing offers all as possibilities in the drama. Leaving aside behavior for a moment, names and blood share certain significant attributes that are worth examining. As signs of belonging, both are presumed to circulate, to mark their carriers, to be legible at least to those who are part of the circuit. Both names and blood, as both the evidence and the inheritance of genealogical lineage, are narrative and classificatory. They also share a complex interdependence: the "true" family names sought in the drama are names that are conferred because of, and that are signs for, the shared blood of a family; and when names are missing, or confused, or misleading, the blood-affinities of which they would tell speak through the silence, and possess the strength to bring kin together. This is how the affinities felt by Saladin for the Templar and by the Templar for Recha can all too easily be read.

But there is, nonetheless, a difference between names and blood: it is the difference between words and things. Identifying the significance of this difference is one of the central problems with which the play struggles. It is the difference between notation and matter, between that which is humanly designated, and changeable, and that which is presumed "real," opposed to or prior to the conceptual. It therefore behooves us to examine how both operate; we shall begin with names.

The names that are of concern in the play include given and family names, as well as attributive names like "father" and "brother," all of which are tested by the drama for their power either to explain or to compel a network of human relationships. At first reading, the search for and the mapping of names might appear to be a viable project: the final family embrace is made possible, after all, because Nathan finally uncovers the Templar's "true name." This has led more than one critic to identify an "uncompromised faith in language" throughout the play.[22] Closer scrutiny, however, reveals that names—of any sort—are far from reliable guide-posts for any useful knowledge, much less for structuring community through a network of particular relationships.[23] Instead, the "telling names" of the characters, as Hendrik Birus aptly phrased it, function narratively, constituting texts of genealogical continuity that are interpretable only once a context (that is, the system of relations they represent) is more or less firmly in place.[24]

The Templar's layering of multiple first and last names evades any attempt to fix his identity thereby. His two given names (Curd and Leu) do not mean the same thing; however, each aligns with a name of his father. His original name, Leu, means lion; his adopted name, Curd, means wolf. The names of his father are Assad (lion) and Wolf.[25] Thus his original name is a romanization of the Arabic lion (as he is, in effect, a romanized derivation of his Arabic father), and his adopted name mirrors, both in its meaning and in its status as a second name, the adopted name of his father. As a further complexity, the adopted name is also similar to Conrad, the name of the uncle who adopted him—in effect, this second name marks him as the son of a second father. In each guise, the Templar's name labels him as an extension of his father—or fathers. In a world reliant upon patrilineal identification, such marking generates confusion rather than protecting from it. The Templar himself, who believes that his name makes clear his paternity, reveals how easily misinterpreted both can be. In identifying himself to the probing Nathan, the Templar declares, "I'm named after [my father]. Curd is Conrad."[26] According to the Templar, one need only know in advance that Curd and Conrad are exchangeable, one is the other. But of course, Conrad is not his real father, but rather his uncle; and Curd, according to Nathan, is not the same as Conrad but rather the same as Wolf. The challenge of translation here is obvious: while Curd is a translation of Wolf, the two are not the same, any more than the son is the same as his father. But this aside, Nathan will later reveal that Curd is not the Templar's "real" name anyway.

Recha also has two first names: Recha, the name Nathan gave her, and Blanda, her "original" name and one which, if we are guided by the Templar's response to its revelation, we are to identify explicitly as her Christian name. Recha is, after all, identified as "an abandoned Christian child."[27] However, if Recha's "real name" is supposed to confirm her true identity, both in terms of her original family and in terms of her true religion, "Blanda" is a deliberately obfuscating choice. For one thing, "Blanda" is not clearly identifiable as a Christian name, but was, in fact, also a popular Jewish name.[28] Not only do the two names fail to differentiate the two religious identities of the woman they signify, but, as Birus has noted, Recha and Blanda are names with the same meaning in Latin and Hebrew.[29] In effect, they name the same quality in different languages, they have the same signifying value in different currencies. In name at least, Blanda is not the original of Recha, but both stand equidistant from their common signified, the adjective "gentle." Although the end of the play offers original, or "real" names as if they carry the knowledge of origins and provide the requisite condition for starting the world and its social networks anew, the actual unraveling of Lessing's name game suggests that, at least in Recha's case, the apparently original name is no more authentic than, and in fact, not significantly different from, the adopted name. Thus if the Templar's set of names implies that one's lineage, and therefore true identity, is told by a uniquely significant original name, the case of Recha / Blanda is an equally illustrative contradiction thereof.

These name-riddles are an element of the drama's hermeneutic play that may captivate a reader, but the value—or the lack thereof—of the translated significance of the names is not something the characters take up.[30] At the end of the drama, Nathan still expresses faith in the existence of a true name as a method of social demarcation, asserting that confusions might have been averted had the Templar from the start offered up his "true name"—that is, the name of his father. Such a true name, simply by being spoken, would have made clear the network of relations among the various individuals, a form of knowledge which, if known, produces social harmony and staves off the social chaos resulting from ignorance.[31]

And yet, even Nathan recognizes that there is not such a thing as a singular true name, the likes of which would identify the Templar (or Recha) unproblematically within the social world. Nathan readily enough admits that the Templar himself might not have known his "real" name and was therefore unaware that he was un-identified. Additionally, the revelation of the true name, "von Filnek," is, for Nathan, the real name of the Templar's father and is the information he sought throughout the play. But for Saladin, "von Filnek" is an unknown second name for Assad; thus even if it *had* been spoken, the name would have failed to identify the Templar as Assad's son. For Saladin, the true family name would have been yet another name, one that is never identified in the play and that belongs instead to a reservoir of answers remaining inaccessible to the audience.[32]

Thus, a "true name" is both needed and impossible as a universal identifier—impossible because people are renamable, because names (like the people to whom they refer) are not static. In the drama, both Recha and the Templar, who supposed themselves to be named by their fathers once and for all, are nonetheless subjected to renamings by others. Further, while characters are not in control of their names, neither do names fix or limit their characters; names are multiple, they mislead, they can get lost. But even as they are used to establish identities, so those identities can be ordered into families, religions, or language cultures. This applies not only to proper names, but to functional relational names (father, child, brother), and to religious or attributive names (Jew, Christian, "the wise," "the good") as well.[33]

When Nathan refers to Recha as "Blanda," the Templar believes that he has freed her of a particular identity. Declaring, "God! You're disowning her! You're giving her back her Christian name!,"[34] the Templar believes that the mere articulation of the original name performs a renunciation and a return to an original state of being. Nathan immediately corrects him, reminding him that Recha is and remains his daughter (and therefore the Templar himself, as her brother, is finally welcomed by Nathan in an extension of adoptive filiation as his child). In this exchange, the Templar understands Recha / Blanda's character to reside in the choice of proper names; but for Nathan, it is not "Recha" or "Blanda," but "daughter" that identifies and defines the relationships in question. "*Tochter*" in this case indicates a particular relationship of love between one person who is a child and another person who is a parent; it is not primarily a social signifier of nationality or religion, like a family name, but is instead foremost a marker of a particular interpersonal dynamic. I say "foremost" because the two options do not exclude each other: Nathan's use of "*Tochter*" itself radiates a series of relationships that impact upon nationality and religion, as witnessed by the challenging questions posed by the proposal that the Templar might now consider himself Nathan's son. At stake is not an either/or of the social versus the interpersonal, but the very important question of which meaning is prior to, and takes a definitive priority over, the other.

Fatherhood is even more complicated, as an abundance of criticism will testify.[35] Nathan is, in some form or another, acknowledged by all to be Recha's father: the Friar's analysis of Nathan's paternity is the most detailed, acknowledging that fatherhood must entail a process of transmission of self to child and the certainty of seeing oneself reflected in that child.

Nathan had to choose to raise Recha either as a daughter or as a Christian. It was only by disregarding the law—by aligning himself with a sense of right and wrong that exists beyond or before worldly law—and by raising Recha in his own tradition that Nathan was able to love her fully as a daughter. The Friar knows that Nathan could not have loved her were she a Christian. Or, more correctly, he would not have loved her had he not regarded her as his own child, who by implication is the recipient of his own beliefs and values. The Friar acknowledges, "Oh really, if you had been smarter you would have let the Christian girl be raised as a Christian girl by someone else. But then you wouldn't have loved your friend's little child. And at that age children need love."[36] Nathan did well, following his own prescription of *"gut handeln."* He faced a conflict in identifying the good action: in the words of the Friar, Nathan had to choose between acting cleverly or acting with love. According to the law upheld by both the Patriarch and Saladin, Nathan should have set aside his own interests (his desire to raise the child, whom he regarded as the replacement for his seven murdered sons, as his own) and raised the child "second hand." However, the virtuous lack of interest this would have represented is, in fact, a clever cheat: it is pursued in the greater context of self-interest, and it would have been Nathan's option only had he been most concerned with his own professional and political status. Instead, his failure to be clever, seen also as a selfish disregard for the law in the "theft" of a child, is, in fact, the "good" that combines an outward-flowing love and interest for the child with the self-interest that accrues with love: the virtue that is the sharing of love is not compromised by the fact that Nathan himself gains as well. In this model of fatherhood, the simultaneity of loving and being loved unites self-interest with genuine virtue.

While, according to the Friar, Nathan could have served the law and done, by one account, the "right thing," by raising her a Christian on the one hand while being a (Jewish) father to her on the other, this rational plan, in realistic human terms, would exclude the more important element of the parent-child relationship, which is the kind of love that requires identification. What kind of identification? By implication, the father must see himself in his child; the child must learn herself through her father. There is, at the root of the relationship, a shared self, whatever that shared self is composed of. But here, a tension is identified between the shared self of the hereditary family line and that of the hereditary religious-political line. And in this instance of adoption, the hereditary law—derived from "truths" of family—is placed by the Patriarch within the domain of political Christendom.

By this reading, the love that Nathan gives to Recha, the love that defines that model of fatherhood that is emancipated from the tyranny of blood-ties, is merely a substitute. Recha, as the adopted child, is Nathan's child because she functions successfully as a surrogate for something "real." According to the Friar, Nathan can only love Recha if she is his child; she does not become his child because he loves her. Nathan himself says of his adoption of Recha that it was literally his love for seven dead sons that first bound him to the newly received infant and that, if he were to lose her, he would lose his seven sons yet again.

Such a defense of Nathan's paternity expands upon the familiar argument that the knowledge of paternity is the requirement for parental (paternal) investment in a child, but the defense redefines what it is to "know" one's child. Lessing shifts the primary criterion from biological to cultural sameness, from "knowing" that a child share's one's blood to recognizing that a child share's one's values.

If Nathan is Recha's father, however, he is not her only father. Assad and Wolf, who we are to believe are the Muslim and presumably Christian incarnations of one and the same man, are both also her "real" father, having engendered her before sending her to Nathan. And Saladin, too, at the end, is her "real" father—not because she accepts his offer to regard him as such, but because he has legal jurisdiction as her uncle and is therefore, by law, a replacement father. This is really too many fathers, if paternity is to determine her place in the world. And in fact there is no final determination of Recha's "paternity"—certainly no single answer that unites in one person the legal, the biological, and the emotional (love-based) ties that she shares with various characters. With which father should she identify, and with whom do her moral obligations rest: with the law, with the blood, or with the heart?

The excessive claims to paternity in a drama that revolves around familial identity underscore a point made repeatedly by various characters in (and critics of) the play: that fatherhood is not singularly a matter of physiological connection by blood, nor strictly a cultural phenomenon derived from particular behavior and interaction.[37] A confusion over what is meant by "father," accompanied by multiple reasons for valuing knowledge of fatherhood, occurs early in the play when, for particular reasons unbeknownst to the audience, Nathan gently resists the Templar's suit for the hand of his daughter Recha. The young man is astonished: did not Nathan, in his outpourings of gratitude to the Templar for saving Recha's life, clearly convey hope that the two would unite? And does not the Christian do the Jew a great honor by such an offer of marriage? But instead of welcoming the suitor into his family, Nathan avoids answering the appeal and instead presses for detailed information of the young man's paternity. Ostensibly concerned less with identifying bloodbonds than preventing blood-crimes, he seeks to assure himself of the lack of a blood-relationship between the Templar and Recha before declaring them a match. The family name of "von Stauffen" given by the Templar may or may not indicate a genealogical link to Recha;[38] Nathan therefore, without explaining his concerns, presses the Templar for a more precise account of his paternity, trusting that a sufficient knowledge of the young man's name will disclose the nature and degree of their relationship.

Neither the questions nor the answers are so straightforward for the Templar, however, who prefers not to acknowledge his own uncertainty regarding the identity of the man who engendered him. Not surprisingly, he presumes that Nathan is concerned with establishing his legitimate social rank and answers questions of his paternity with information about the man to whom he earlier referred as "My uncle himself—or my father, I should say," the man who raised him.[39] This confusion of uncle and father leads Nathan to insist that the Conrad von Stauffen named by the young man as his father could not have been his old friend, who himself was a Templar and unmarried—and thus presumably childless. The Templar, angry and defensive at Nathan's insistent prying, remarks that such considerations by no means preclude his uncle having a son. In the face of Nathan's confusion, he asserts: "What difference does it make? So what if I'm a bastard? We're not such a contemptible breed."[40] He then refuses to say any more, marking the limits of the information to be shared with the audience for some time. The story of the Templar's parentage is told only at the end of the play; until then (and, I will argue, even beyond), the audience is uncertain both of the Templar's paternity and of his legitimacy.

The Templar, too, is evidently uncertain, or at least unsatisfied with whatever understanding he has of his "father." Based on his behavior, the open question of his paternity is unbearable: it is a void that he struggles to fill in any way possible, motivating the search for a new father (with all its implied paradox) that catalyzes much of the dramatic action. At the outset of the meeting with Nathan, which prompts the Templar's outburst cited above—the meeting that highlights different possible meanings of the word "father"—it is, in fact, the Templar's desire for a father more than for a wife that emerges from the exchange. The Templar, responding to Nathan's question of how he liked Recha, stammers a confusing response: " . . . promise me right now that I'll be able to see her again and again, forever." The lack of clarity baffles Nathan, who responds, "How am I supposed to understand that?" As the situation will reveal, there are plural ways to understand the Templar's request simply to have the right of access to Recha, among which are as a husband or as a brother. In response to Nathan's request for clarification, the Templar simply exclaims, "My father!" From this point, the dialogue enters a cycle of repetition that further emphasizes the real focus of the Templar's desire:

Templar: My father!
Nathan: Young man!
Templar: Not "son"? I beg you, Nathan!
Nathan: Dear young man!
Templar: Not "son"? I beg you, Nathan! I implore you, by the first bonds of nature! Don't prefer the chains that came later![41]

What pains the Templar so unbearably is Nathan's refusal to embrace him as son: the first line begins with his impetuous claim, "my father" and ends with the question, "not 'son'?," a question that, in its spondaic emphasis, punctuates the high emotional pitch of the question. When Nathan howsoever gently resists the Templar's plea, the halting, spondaic "not son" [*nicht Sohn?*] is repeated, jarring the rhythm of the verse (keeping in mind the blank-verse form of the original) at the beginning of a line. While we tend to presume that the Templar "really" means he wants to marry Nathan's daughter, it is his explicit desire for a father / son relationship that triggers a crisis here.

The Templar in the end will get exactly what he asked for, which was to be called "son" by Nathan, and as the brother of Nathan's child he will, indeed, be allowed to see Recha "for ever" as he requests. But when he is initially rejected by Nathan (who will begin his search to identify the Templar as the brother of his daughter and therefore his son), the Templar—not to be without a father—denounces Nathan and initiates an unholy alliance with the father-Patriarch. When his conscience puts a halt to this action, he pledges himself "completely yours" to Saladin, who will be his legal father at the end of the drama. (Complaining to Saladin, the Templar extends the drama's ironic name game by calling Nathan, the father he wants but cannot have, "this Jewish wolf"—that is, the Jewish configuration of his father Wolf.) All of this underscores a fundamental challenge posed by the Templar to biological fatherhood and to the customary direction of genealogy, since it is he who seeks to name his father rather than wait to be identified as a son.

But to return to the exchange at hand: at stake are two definitions of "father" which, at least within the context of this unsuccessful conversation, are in no way interchangeable. Nathan seeks knowledge of the Templar's biological progenitor; the Templar identifies as his father the man who raised, loved, and educated him. The positions Nathan and the Templar take in this particular exchange are directly opposed to those by which they tend to be critically identified: Nathan is, of course, read as the embodiment of and the defense for love as the defining criterion for parenthood, whereas the Templar, for the most part, is usually viewed as an advocate for the truth of blood. This reversal of roles is, in many ways, consistent with Lessing's famous distrust of consistency, and it should discourage any impulse to read the characters allegorically. There is not one among them who could be shown to signify a singular, unwavering position within the play's highlighted issues; instead, each is complex and ambivalent, responding to the contingencies of particular situations as best he or she can.

The issue of paternity, as it is initially raised here, previews a primary interpretive crisis of the drama: Nathan understands "father" as a signature of physiological identity, whereas the Templar insists upon its reference to social identity, such that it therefore properly denotes his adoptive parent. The word "father," upon which multiple identities rest, has too many meanings. This instability underscores its function as a term that represents an idea rather than a fact or a thing. But on another level, the exchange between Nathan and the Templar, in raising and not addressing the possibility of legitimacy, opens up a question about the value and possibility of such knowledge at all.

BASTARD OR *BANKERT*?

Consider again the Templar's retort: "So what if I'm a bastard?"[42] The German doubles the term for bastard, doubling the Templar's indignation and the explosive force of his diction. More closely translated, the text reads, "What if it were so? Something like bastard [*Bastard*] or *Bankert*?"[43] The word "*Bankert*" is both unusual and particularly strong, guaranteeing that, although the theme of the Templar's legitimacy might not dominate the drama, the audience will not soon forget it. While bastardy is, in effect, smuggled into the play as a minor theme, Lessing underscores its presence through a highly unorthodox word choice that proved successful in chafing the sensitive eyes and ears of his audience.[44]

The term *Bankert* is designated as slang in Campe's dictionary of 1807–11 and identified (incorrectly) as Lessing's neologism; in addition to its own entry, *Bankert* is joined with the larger heading for "bank":

> [. . . .] "To lie under the bank," literally; and figuratively, to be despised or unknown. "To stick something under the bank," as to hide something shameful. "To pull something out from under the bank," to bring it from concealment into the light. . . ." To fall from the bank with someone," to conceive an illegitimate child with her. *Lessing derives "Bankert" from this meaning.*[45]

Campe claims that Lessing derives his term from the idiomatic turn of phrase for illegitimate conception, "to fall from the bank" ["*von der Bank fallen*"]. Important here are the moral markers connected to the term: a *Bankert* by definition is a child conceived "under the table," a place of traffic for those things or beings which are despised, hidden, unknown or unknowable. The either/or condition of life under the table is alternatively "*unbekannt*" or "*verachtet*"; the "*oder*" linking the two terms suggests they are either exchangeable equivalents or exclusive alternatives. Either way, the pairing implies that anything removed from the known and the visible is suspect, and exists "as something shameful."

The term *Bankert* and its derivation from *Bank* further tie the bastard conceptually to monetary circulation and gambling, to exchange and uncertainty. Campe continues his definition of "bank": "In an extended meaning, the table of a money changer, and the money found upon it, as well as the money that is laid upon a table as a wager during particular games of chance." The bank is the table on which currency exchange takes place, whether through the moneychanger or through gaming, both of which were stigmatized if not outright sinful; the bank is also the money that may be found on that table, whether offered up for or left over from exchange or anted up on a bet.[46] The bastard child is made under that table, connected to it but out of sight. That the connection is not incidental, but rather a structural component of the "bank," is suggested by the synonym provided by Campe, *Bankbein* (literally, "bank-leg"). The bastard is the illegitimate issue that nonetheless supports the table on which exchange is made.

These definitions suggest a revealing link between illegitimacy and bad currency (which may be bad because of how it is minted or because of how it is exchanged). We do well to remember Kant's identification of the bastard child with "smuggled goods." And, lest we forget just how despicable smuggled goods are, the comparison sufficed for Kant to condone the bastard child's murder. If we acknowledge a link between the bastard and (bad) currency or trade, we have to question whether there is a productive connection posited between the Templar as a bastard and Nathan as a merchant and *Wechsler* or "exchanger" (as possessor of currency so desperately needed by Saladin), both social signifiers of his identity as a Jew.[47]

Does the Templar fit as a *Bankbein* under the table of Nathan the Exchanger? Can he be figured as the excess that falls from the table, that disappears under the table, but that nevertheless proves vital in keeping the table standing? In fact, neither the Templar nor, for that matter, Recha is a product of Nathan's activity; or, perhaps, they both are, insofar as their uncertain lineage is only brought to light through Nathan's tireless tracing of a series of exchanges. Both the Templar and Recha are the unaccounted for, the excess issue of not a monetary but a sexual and religious exchange. And Nathan the merchant, who supplies either "cash money" or contingent fictions where appropriate, is the person who is compelled to account for the exchange and identify what is hidden. The Templar, in the scheme of the drama, can only be counted as smuggled goods when he assumes a name that is not "his"—that is, a name that fails to indicate his paternity. As a smuggled von Stauffen, he is disguised and dangerous. If he knew himself to be Conrad's bastard, he would be harmless to all; as Assad's bastard he would be (he is) welcomed by Saladin and related to Recha. It is not, in the end, the legality of his origin that is of concern. A knowledge of his bloodline is crucial not for political but for physiological reasons. Such smuggling in Nathan's world is a problem only when it threatens the incest taboo—a taboo that Buffon, as Lessing well knew, had famously identified as a natural law protecting the human race against corruption and degeneration. Here the law of Lessing's day and human needs are at odds: the law dictates that a bastard belongs to his mother and should take only the mother's name and family, but the drama, in the case of the Templar, illustrates potentially serious consequences. Along with other nurturing father figures, one must know who one's biological father is if incest is to remain taboo. The fact that the Templar has been accepted as a legitimate "von Stauffen" (a bastard could not have been a Templar) makes him, according to Kant, smuggled goods. On the other hand, the label under which he has passed through society—that is, his mother's name, "von Stauffen"—is the name imposed upon him by the law. So the law plays a role in masking his "true name," or at least an open acknowledgement of his paternity. Thus laws devised to prevent the crime of illicit generation and transmission of names might well be responsible for making possible the illicit and taboo (de)generation of people. Such a consequence is only prevented in the drama by the efforts of Nathan the Exchanger, the Jew threatened by the law of the Patriarch and by the initial trickery of Saladin, to capture the identities between the legitimate and the spurious, the traced and the untraceable.

Campe's repeated emphasis upon the despicable and the hidden when describing the bastard raises a connection between the hidden and the hated that is very much to the point of Lessing's drama. What, then, do we make of the fact that this valuation is expressly contradicted in the text as soon as the specter of illegitimacy is raised? Immediately after the Templar flings out the term *Bankert*, he insists that the very term "despise" does not apply to the charge or mark of illegitimacy ("*Der Schlag ist auch nicht zu verachten*"). Again we find ourselves in the vocabulary of currency: illegitimacy is a *Schlag*, an imprint or a minting which, despite its inauthentic or unauthorized origin, should *not* be despised. The *Schlag* or the trace, the *Spur* of the bastard or the *spurius*, is not contemptible and should neither be hidden nor remain unknown. Nevertheless, it is ultimately a trace that is an antitrace; the *spurius* or *Bankert* remains throughout the drama an unexamined though essential mystery. This being said, however, it is not hidden (having been mentioned) nor is it despised.

The Templar's hidden and unknown birth in fact gives rise to various speculations concerning his illegitimacy, but—contrary to his own fears—in no instance does this minting jeopardize the esteem in which the other characters holds him. The issue of his paternity is critically problematic, but not for the reasons that make legitimacy a concern for either political or moral law. On the contrary, if the Templar were, in fact, the illegitimate child of Conrad von Stauffen, Nathan's fears of possible incest would be alleviated and he could allow the marriage to Recha. Alternately, Saladin and Sittah speculate almost hopefully that he might be the bastard son of Assad, thereby explaining the perceived resemblance and confirming a longed-for connection to their lost sibling. Sittah asks why Saladin has not inquired of the Templar's parentage, since, as Saladin remarks, it is entirely probable that Assad would have had a (presumably illegitimate) child by one of the many Christian woman who found him attractive:

> Oh, nothing would be more possible! Since Assad was so welcome with pretty Christian ladies, and so intent on pretty Christian ladies, that there was once a rumor that . . . Well, well, I'd rather not discuss that.[48]

They do not imagine that Assad might have had a legitimate child with a Christian woman. For that reason Saladin emphasizes that he should have asked the Templar not for the identity of his father (implying that even if Assad were the father, the Templar would not have known the answer); rather, he should have asked, "and especially about his mother? Whether his mother might never have been here in this land? Right?"[49] As an eighteenth-century reader would know, legitimate children are known socially through the father, but bastards are known through the mother. Assad's behavior, in fact, produced rumors of a sort that Saladin will not repeat. What they might be, we can only speculate; the story that *might* be the narrative of the Templar's origin is at once elided and accentuated by a hyphen. Whatever Saladin knows of Assad's possible issue is something not to be spoken aloud. And so the audience speculates: Was there an illicit marriage? A liaison without a marriage? A religious conversion? We do not know what happened to Assad, or how much Saladin knows about his brother's departure from the royal house. Saladin's decisive silence magnifies the Templar's own, a silence surrounding Assad's life and the Templar's birth that the Templar himself insists upon maintaining even in the final scene of the drama. When Nathan begins to narrate what he knows of the story of his father and mother, the Templar interjects, "Enough! Please!"[50] and nothing more is said.

The audience receives no explanation for how the Templar was raised in Germany and Recha orphaned in Persia; nor is a satisfactory explanation offered for why the Templar bears the family name of his mother (and uncle) rather than that of his purported father, something that served as a legally enforced signal of illegitimacy.[51]

There is a further provocative suggestion complicating matters: when Saladin speaks of the day Assad left the house never to return, he reminds Sittah of her "older sister Lilla," who did not want to let Assad out of her arms that morning, and who died heartbroken when he never returned. Since incest is a sin by Muslim as well as by Christian and Jewish law, are we to understand that Lilla is Sittah and Saladin's "sister" because she was married to Assad? Did this marriage then compromise a subsequent union, rendering both Recha and the Templar illegitimate? Recha's birth is just as unclear: it is attested to by the Friar, to whom Wolf handed a baby, with no account of the missing mother. Which wife was she? Lilla or the Stauffen? or one of the other admiring Christian women with whom Assad was suspected to consort?

These possibilities, all inferred through the play, remain unresolved. The silence maintained by Nathan, by the Templar, and by Saladin—all of whom may share a truth, or each preserve and hide a different one—contains, beyond the question of bastardy, uncharted conversions: name changes, country changes, marriage, adoption, religious shifts, even a confusing linguistic multiplicity (it is never clear which language the characters all share; the fact that Wolf preferred to speak Persian and that the breviary contains both a presumably Latin text and Arabic script suggest that multiple languages lie behind the play's German). These various translations create untraceable multiplicities of identity that render origins not only unknown but also unknowable. Whatever the circumstances of the Templar's and of Recha's origin and identity, they do not reach the level of communicability to become public or collective knowledge. We never get a clear picture of the origin either of the Templar or of Recha, despite the efforts of various characters to seek them out and despite the importance attached to them; on the contrary, such origins are repeatedly figured as untellable. Whether criminal, embarrassing, or taboo, we do not know. A host of possibilities, all unorthodox, are gently raised, and the absence of information must be read as a deliberate confusion of the overt attempts to establish genealogical clarity.

A LAW ABOVE LEGITIMACY?

If names, be they proper or attributive, fail to identify characters unambiguously within their proper familial domain, we must consider that, within the drama, the blood-bonds that the names fail to signify appear nonetheless to be legible or audible in and of themselves. Thus, despite Saladin's identification of the Templar as an enemy because he is "the Templar," the warring sovereign feels and acts upon an affinity that overrides the otherwise absolute social demarcation. The relentless Saladin spares the life of a captive and condemned Knight Templar simply because the young man resembles and thereby recalls to mind Saladin's younger brother. Saladin's sentiment is ultimately explained as recognition: his feelings of empathy are justified because the Templar is, in fact, his own flesh and blood, a deep affinity that speaks to him through the distractions of all other signs to the contrary. The language of the blood, in writing the parent onto the body and gestures and ineffable presence of the child, tells him that the Templar, despite national, religious, and probably linguistic difference, is not different at all. In fact, Saladin erases differences so thoroughly that the Templar is left without any particular identity at all, as we saw above with the final adoption.

Similarly, the Templar suffers a crisis of self-identity because of his attraction to Recha. Had he known she was a Jew, so he claims, he would have let her die in the fire as an enemy and infidel; some other inclination that he cannot identify or defend, however, compelled him to save her life. Afterward, the fact that he is drawn to her, a Jew, provokes an identity crisis. From what source of the self could come this feeling, utterly contradicting the antipathy his Templar-self knows is right?[52] The affinity toward an unexpected other that overpowers both Saladin and the Templar ought not to be heralded as evidence of the power of friendship or common humanity or any other enlightened ideal that might overcome prejudice, since these particular relationships are ultimately justified as the natural consequence of blood-kinship.

That is what we would have to conclude if we accept the natural truth of the final family network established at the end of the play. But does the blood speak truly in these instances? If we, as readers, were certain that the kinship ties celebrated at the end of the play were established without ambiguity, then those critics would be correct who have argued that the drama represents no enlightened ideal of reason and friendship, but instead a triumph of blood bonds over the shaping powers of culture.[53] I maintain, however, that this is a false either/or, rendering far too simple the complexities of Lessing's play. If a series of astonishing coincidences do occur to bring together a scattered family, the "proofs" are the result of a complex hermeneutic that relies in great part upon an interconnection between dream-like (uncertain, alternate, unreal) memories and the characters' desire to invent original connections that bind people together, abetted by visual analogs and by textual histories, all of which can only remain questionable.

Nonetheless, this hermeneutic is premised upon the material reality of the body, its status within a line of physiological (blood-bound) transmission, and its availability as a text to be read—its availability as evidence to reestablish on firm ground the family structures that have otherwise faltered (i.e., Saladin's family splintered by Assad's departure, the uncertain origins of both Recha and the Templar). The Templar is the first of the characters to argue for the truth of the bodily sign as a marker for interior identity. As part of a vain attempt to recruit the Templar as a spy for the Patriarch against Saladin, the Friar tries to dissuade the young man from any sense of loyalty or gratitude to the Sultan for saving his life, arguing that (according to the wisdom of the Patriarch) one owes nothing for a service—even for the sparing of his life—that was not performed specifically on one's own behalf; in this case, the Friar reveals, Saladin pardoned the Templar's life not for the benefit of the youth but out of the sentimental conviction that, in both his manner and his being, "something in your face, in your being reminded him of his brother." The Templar—ignoring the implication of mere approximation, responds:

> Ah, Saladin! What? Nature should have put just *one* of my features in your brother's form, without this corresponding to anything in my soul? What this corresponded to, could I suppress it to please a Patriarch? Nature, you don't lie like this! Nor does God contradict himself in his work![54]

What began as the Templar's sense of honor in refusing to betray the man who spared his life becomes in this passage an argument linking both his body and soul to Saladin. The kinship that Saladin recalls when looking at his face establishes, according to the Templar, a natural claim that reaches beyond the young man's features to his innermost self. The Templar may or may not suspect that the resemblance Saladin sees is based on a real blood-bond (his final line of the play, referring to the dreams of his childhood, leaves this unclear); important here is the presumption that any link to brotherhood that Saladin reads on his features, be it material or metaphorical, must be echoed by his soul. Literally (written in the language of body and blood), something in his soul must express or correspond to [*entsprechen*] the trait expressed in his features, suggesting that the physiological comprises both legible form and corresponding spirit.

And yet there is a telling confusion in the Templar's declaration: "Nature should have put just *one* of my features in your brother's form." We might have expected the transfer of features to move from the brother to the Templar, referring to a trait from Assad's form that nature planted into his own. Only thus would the statement accord with the biological genealogical line that it seems the purpose of the play to reveal. However, his statement actually reverses the line of transmission, implying that the Templar's features have been incorporated onto Assad.

The Templar's outburst indicates a dynamic for linking people through time that is truer of memory than of biology: as we shall see, Saladin does remember, or reassemble Assad via the Templar's image as much as the other way around. This said, it does not matter to the Templar what kind of connection (or lack thereof) his words might imply; he refuses to spy for the Patriarch because he *wants* to feel himself bound to Saladin as evidenced in his embrace and amplification of the claim—from kinship or from kindness—that was read upon his body.

A tension between genealogy, with its transmission of identifying traits from father to son, and memory, with a transmission of traits from son to father, resurfaces in the scene between Saladin and Sittah and underscores the degree to which the genealogical connection, presumed to be *a priori* a natural fact, functions instead as a psychological artifact produced by longing and the tricks of memory. Saladin's initial "recognition" of the Templar is nothing more than a passing fancy, as evidenced by the fact that he promptly forgets both the incident and the young man and has to be reminded of both by Nathan. An interest in the degree of resemblance is renewed by Saladin's serendipitous discovery of an old miniature of Assad on the very morning that the Templar has been summoned to the palace. Showing the picture to Sittah and reciting the circumstances of Assad's disappearance, Saladin's pain at the loss of his brother rises to the surface. Fatalistically shrugging aside his sadness, he remarks that he will be curious nonetheless to compare the picture with the Templar to see "how badly my imagination deceived me." Not *if*, but *how badly*. The power of that fantasy is stronger than Saladin's skepticism; he then impatiently anticipates hearing the Templar's voice, in the hope that it, too, will awaken a sleeping memory of his brother: "Assad's voice [*Ton*] still sleeps somewhere in my soul!"[55]

Impressed by the Templar and by what he sees as a resemblance to the miniature, Saladin feeds the fancy of his comparison, and soon he begins to speak as if the Templar were, in fact and in person, a renewed version of his long-lost brother. Saladin does not recognize a bond with the Templar as a related individual so much as indulge a series of associations: the Templar stands in for lost memories, the lost memories are a (poor) substitute for the lost brother. Saladin collapses these associations and behaves initially as if the Templar were an identical Assad, a replacement Assad, the return of that which was lost; but even he knows that he cannot sustain that illusion. Saladin looks at the Templar and admits ruefully that he longs to address him as Assad, to find out where he has been in the intervening years. He would ask such things, sighs Saladin, "if I only saw you and not myself too." The fantasy of the Templar as the returned, still youthful Assad cannot survive its initial, sentimental moment, because Saladin inhabits the present: he himself is now older and cannot play the brother to the youth standing before him. If Saladin wants to replace his lost kin with some combination of memory and the Templar, the substitution will require a newly configured relationship, i.e., father and son. Although the Templar is not the same as Assad (as Saladin is not the same as the younger Saladin), Saladin contents himself with the degree of similarity that enables him to reconstruct his memory. He is content with the fiction, the memory, the dream as an end to which the Templar's presence is simply a means: "There's so much truth in this sweet daydream that an Assad should bloom again in the autumn of my life."[56]

Sittah, too, recognizes the delusion produced by her brother's longing. When, at the Templar's exit, Saladin demands that his sister participate in the comparison of the two men, Sittah criticizes the structure of his comparison, noting that he is not really recalling Assad; he does not find traces of Assad in the Templar, but rather he uses the Templar to engender a new, Templar-like Assad.

The reverse transmission apparent in both the Templar's and Saladin's references to Assad illustrates the function of genealogy as an idea that longing—rather than biological fact—produces. Over the course of the play, biology will be filled in after the fact. Important as this recognition is, it leads only to another question: Why, we must ask, is the longing felt by the characters answered solely by family, rather than by friendship (as the most particular of relationships) or by the bonds of an inclusive, universal humanity (as the most general)?

Lessing's answer seems to be that the friendship for which his character Nathan is famous, and which in aggregate ought, in principle, to bind all humanity through its network of particular relations, is not a viable foundation for a stable community. It is rationally pleasing (because rationally based) but emotionally unsatisfying. We see the Templar's rejection of Nathan's friendship when he is not allowed to transform the relationship into one of father and son. We see Saladin's violation of his pledge of friendship to Nathan when he tempts Recha to reject her adoptive father and accept him instead. The smaller allegiances of kinship—even obviously artifactual, contractual kinship—between parent and child are desirable enough to eliminate promises of friendship between "*Menschen.*"

At the same time, those smaller allegiances of kinship are powerful enough to undergird a complex network of good-will and indebtedness. Because Saladin is reminded of his brother, he extends brotherly protection to the Templar and spares his life. Because he is compared to a lost brother, the Templar feels bound to Saladin over and above his commitment to the institutional authority of his church. Because the Templar, having just been set free by Saladin, saves Recha's life, Nathan credits Saladin with saving both the Templar and his daughter, and he explains to Saladin, "how your grace toward him has flowed from him to me."[57] There is a generous supplement to the bonds kin (even substitute kin) share in the guises of duty, service, and kindness. Nathan and the Templar agree "we must, must be friends," emphasizing their choice to bind themselves and to feel bound.[58]

The circulation of variously understood debts of kindness seems to be what connects the concentric circles of family, community, state, and humanity: they are debts that extend from the family outward, beginning with family-bound interest. Nathan took a child when he was childless; Saladin spared a life when reminded of his brother's. These were acts that combined self-interest (the need for family) with altruism, acts of love extended to a stranger, triggered by a psychological state of longing and recollection.

In similar fashion, Saladin demonstrates a general inclination to place people with whom he has contact into one of two categories: family or enemy. Al-Hafi, when talking to Nathan about the Sultan, remarks that every instance of his famed generosity includes an incorporation of the recipient into his *Haus*. Al-Hafi criticizes this, unwilling to accept that Saladin can kill relentlessly on a grand scale (waging war) but then, in the words of one critic, "pose as a humanitarian with individuals."[59] This implies, of course, that there is something genuine about Saladin's aggression and something false about his kindness; this implies that Saladin's inconsistency must necessarily compromise the better of the two opposing elements, rather than the worse. Aside from this odd interpretive bias, the either/or stance that judges Saladin's generosity to be false is based on a misunderstanding of the dynamic involved in his separation of friend and foe. Saladin's differentiated behavior is based less on a division between groups and individuals than it is upon how people are grouped. In fact, particular individuals who receive his attention and his generosity do not remain either individuals or members of a universal human population, but they are brought instead into the small and specific circle of Saladin's *Haus*. When generosity is extended, the recipients must, as a part of the bargain, become part of a smaller network of allegiance, the (extended) family; those who exist outside of this (expandable) circle may be ignored or killed without compunction. Saladin's behavior exemplifies a tendency not merely to treat family better than non-family, but to consider those whom one treats well as family, revealing a tendency to reduce the world to family and non-family.

Rather than simplifying this tendency into a twentieth-century formulation of public and domestic spheres, it is more productive to understand Lessing's presentation of "family"—in the context of eighteenth-century theories of small-group allegiance—as an unavoidably compelling idea continually recast to fit present needs rather than as either a biological or even a sociologically determinable reality. Shaftesbury articulated well the notion that particular inclusion, which brings with it exclusion, is a human need. Whereas "the World in general" is a "remote Philosophical Object," by contrast a smaller group, a "more contracted Publick," provides its members the "Visible Band" necessary for common feeling.[60] Relying on the appeal of an abstract idea to an individual's reason, he continues, leads only to disaffection and aggressive factionalism. Instead, smaller alliances with others who are known, a group with visible boundaries, is required for the acknowledgment of common humanity, for intersubjective respect, to flourish.

Common humanity is thus not something all humans share, but something celebrated within the family. Binding large groups of people together under the organizing rubric of an idea—even lofty ideas like universal humanity or particular friendship—fails to engage them, and as a result, "the social Aim is disturb'd, for want of certain Scope. The close Sympathy and conspiring Virtue is apt to lose itself, for want of Direction, in so wide a Field."[61]

But what about the great theme of friendship with which *Nathan* is so often identified? The Scottish physician and philosopher John Gregory, too, believed that community (understood as investment in a large and ultimately national group) could only exist as an extension of intimate allegiances—although Gregory admits both kinship and friendship among these foundational bonds:

> Love of a Country and of a Public cannot subsist among Men, who neither know nor love the individuals which compose that Public. If a Man has a family and friends, these give him an interest in the Community, and attach him to it; because their honour and happiness, which he regards as much as his own, are essentially connected with its welfare.[62]

For Gregory, both family and friends constitute those whose "honor and happiness" are regarded as being as important as one's own. The "as much as" is significant: otherwise worded, a man's regard for his own honor and happiness is a given and functions as the standard by which his regard to others is measured. Family and friends are such because he regards them as highly as he regards himself; he transfers his self-regard to them, and they are similar to self. In Nathan's world, this kind of relationship is restricted to the family realm; friendship—at least for Nathan—operates entirely differently. Friendship, as modeled by Nathan himself, is a kind of love based on the otherness of the other. The bond of friendship is a wondrous and great thing, but it is not reliable in a crisis and inevitably defers to the still closer bonds of kinship—be they real or imagined, be they biological or contractual.

Saladin's mode of friendship, on the contrary, is to see himself in the other. When the Templar accuses Nathan of religious intolerance (both in replacing Recha's "true" religion with Judaism and in rejecting the Templar as a suitor), Saladin's commitment of friendship to Nathan is momentarily strained; he remarks to the Templar that, should the young man be correct in all he asserts, then "I can hardly find myself in such a Nathan."[63] Saladin's extension of friendship depends upon the possibility of seeing himself in the other—just as his extension of love and generosity (as to the Templar, who is regarded only in his Assad-like qualities; as with recipients of help who are incorporated into the Sultan's *Haus*) requires an erasure of differences in order to see even more of the self in the other. The links forged in the play between love and sameness, and between difference and hatred (primarily in the context of religion), echo Lessing's engagement of Burke and the notion of "Sympathy."[64] Lessing singles out the observation that sympathy is too often falsely identified as the inclination to place not the self in another's place, but another in one's own; this positioning is not to be judged as positive but as a signal of weakness of character, as a failure of discernment. Similarly, hatred is identified as the clear recognition of difference between the self and the other.[65] When critics accept the ending of *Nathan the Wise* as a rationalized explanation of the sympathetic inclination of characters to each other—reducing sympathy to recognition of one's own blood in the other—they fail to account for Lessing's engagement of Burke's critique of the selfsame dynamic.[66] Instead, we should see the seeming explanation as ironically tinged. Perhaps the audience, like the characters, are provided a foundational belief system, namely the family fiction, because, in the Templar's words, they are all still fools clinging to the familial faith until the breaking of a brighter truth.

The process of substitution that makes kin of strangers amounts to a substitution for a substitution, because kin—as the Friar observes—are those in whom one sees oneself. In the case of Nathan's fatherhood of Recha (and Saladin's of the Templar), the relationships are substitutions for or patterned on a familial, shared self. If one can substitute for the blood-tie, does the blood-tie substitute for something also, or is it authentic and original? Is it also a script, a sign, a substitute, a material marker, a way of making sense, a way of narrowing the field of interest to something manageable? Or is it the origin of human interaction, both on a historical species level and at the level of each individual's emotional reality, i.e., the generating pattern for human consciousness, both phylo- and ontogenetically? Are we to understand that the people one loves will always be a parent, a child, or a sibling, or a substitute for one thereof?

Are we to believe that all relationships are reducible to variously modulated instances of self-reflection, or, at least, that all relationships must be similar to or function as familial bonds? The instances of friendship, which are considered by some critics to be Nathan's strength counterpoised against the blood-allegiances, are problematic for a number of reasons. First, they are bonds that fail under pressure, as we see with Saladin and the Templar, both of whom are ready to betray Nathan the Friend when more pressing personal needs arise. Second, as we have seen, insofar as they are resilient, they are surrogates for family ties, not antithetical to them.

So back to our original question—in what ways is genealogy matter, and in what ways does it matter in *Nathan the Wise*? The answer seems to be that it is not matter and does not matter much. All close relations in the drama are family-like, and all family-like relations involve seeing one's self. This being the case, it is the *idea* of bodily matter and its continuity through generations and family lines that is crucial to people in understanding their relationships with those whom they call "family." This idea is accepted as real when necessary, and dismissed when expedient.

Recha is typical in the coexistence of her beliefs both that kinship is dismissible, and that a blood-bond *must* speak, and truly, at least to kin. Begging Saladin at his feet not to allow anyone to separate her from her father Nathan, she cries that all she wants is:

> No more, no less, than to let me keep my father, and to let him keep me! I still don't know who else claims, or can claim, to be my father. Nor do I want to know. But is it only blood that makes the father? Only blood?[67]

Saladin concurs with a dismissal of blood: "Truly blood, blood alone does not make the father. It hardly makes the father of an animal! At the most it confers the right to earn that name!" Even a biological father's status as father is unstable, subject as he is to the work of earning.

On the other hand, Saladin is also quick to confirm the essential and prescriptive truth of the blood-bond: when the Templar recoils from the revelation that Recha is his sister, Saladin accuses him of being an impostor, since "Everything about you is a lie: face and voice and walk! Nothing is yours!"[68] In other words, Saladin tells the Templar that he is not singular but shared, and that precisely this truth—the state of being shared, being always self and other—is the strength of kinship. Saladin thereby confirms that the blood-bond is not only a truth by which they must abide, but it is a truth that displays its signs for all to see. Recha, dismayed by the Templar's initial rejection, declares herself and Nathan to be impostors [*Betrieger*], thereby echoing the language of the parable: like the chastened brothers, she and Nathan are swindlers because they lay claim to knowledge and possession of something original, material, and powerful—in this case, not the ring, but the blood-bond. Recha insists that a sibling relationship existing between herself and the Templar must inevitably assert itself, and in predictable ways; thus, if the blood does not dictate the expected behavior, then the blood is not there. Saladin's interjection, however, dismisses the Templar's behavior as confused by idiosyncratic emotions, and affirms that the deeper, shared truth of blood-kinship is told, is evidenced on the bodies of the siblings, visible to anyone who can read the signs.

If we compare this final scene to the parable, it would seem that Saladin failed to learn a crucial lesson from Nathan's narrative; while he accepted the parable as an allegory of religious tolerance, he failed to understand just how closely the lines of blood-kinship proposed at the end of the play parallel the multiple rings. These blood ties ultimately function as an unverifiable possibility, but they stand for a possibility that must be accepted and acted upon. The challenge issued to the warring brothers and, I suggest, to the reconciled "family" of characters at the end of the play, is to perceive the heuristic fiction, either of the ring's history or of the kinship narrative, and to behave as if it were real, with one condition: the "as if" must somehow remain present. One must somehow preserve an awareness of the fiction, because to act upon the reality of a ring's history or a family's bloodline as fact is to become an ideologue and a bully. The brothers are reprimanded for having crossed that line; Saladin ends the play crossing it himself with his domineering claims to the loyalty of Recha and the Templar, and with his final warning: "Wait!"

THE BREVIARY AND THE ORIGINS OF THE CHILDREN

There is an additional piece of evidence to substantiate my claim to the spurious nature of the final family. Despite Saladin's insistence to the contrary, the signs that tell of the truth of the blood are not reliable as evidence; in fact, both he and Nathan must appeal to a disembodied script—namely, the breviary—to translate their desires and suspicions into knowledge of the origins of the children. The evidence that all accept at the end of the play is a *Büchlein*, a small book of prayers, discovered in the clothing of the dead von Filsneck and preserved in case it could be useful for another literate Christian. Since the Friar cannot read, he cannot know for certain what the book contains, but he was told that it included a list of relatives [*Angehörigen*]—in Arabic—of Wolf. Nathan looks into the book and finds there what he considers sufficient proof that Recha and the Templar shared, at least, a father, though precisely what he reads is not shared with the audience. Saladin, too, looks into the book—Saladin, whose urgent desire to establish a real connection between the Templar and Assad is clear, and for whom Nathan's statement that his friend Wolf von Filsneck "preferred to speak Persian" prompts Saladin to exclaim, "Persian? Persian? What more do I want? It's him! It was him! [. . . .] My brother! Quite certainly! My Assad! Quite certainly!"[69] This is, in fact, not "certain" at all—the only thing certain is Saladin's will. The visually oriented Sultan, who looks at bodies and sees family history, looks into the book and is struck by the sight of the handwriting, which he claims to recall as Assad's; this justifies his "recognition" of Assad's features in the Templar and serves to transform the breviary into a conveyor of knowledge, a book of begettings that authoritatively binds everyone together.[70]

Such is the play's *ex machina*: not a god, but a book—for most characters illegible, by most characters unread, its contents unseen by the audience and by most of the dramatic figures—is assigned the authority to reorder the human community in the world of the drama. Let us consider one of the many undetermined details of the breviary. It listed, we are told, the names of all those people related to Wolf von Filsneck. Are we to understand, then, that Saladin, if he is Wolf's brother, is among those listed? Perhaps not: the only proof Saladin actually claims to find in the book is the memory of his brother's handwriting. Or, perhaps so: Nathan, in handing Saladin the book, tells him to find assurance of his suspicions therein, as if he, too, read certainty there. Why is this all so mysterious, so elliptically presented?

If the breviary does indicate that the Templar and Recha are both Wolf's children, if it indicates that Wolf is Assad (two "ifs" that are not confirmed), then why not disclose this information immediately? Or, more specifically, what are the conditions under which Nathan might reasonably withhold the knowledge, insisting that the decision to reveal it is Saladin's alone? The single coherent explanation that is consistent with both the world of the drama and the world of Lessing is that Assad's children—if they are his—are illegitimate. This returns us to the world of the law and the theme of bastardy we already saw smuggled early into the play in the form of insinuation and unanswered questions.

If Recha and the Templar were unambiguously the legitimate offspring of Assad, we can presume there would be no secrecy; as bastards, however, Nathan is bound to reveal the hidden relationships only to the degree that he prevents incest. For, according to the law under which Lessing and his readers lived and wrote, the relationship between a bastard and his (or her) father could only be acknowledged and defined legally by the father. It makes sense in this context that Nathan would discreetly transfer any decision to Saladin: Nathan, in fact, could not rightfully establish a relationship between the children and the family of their illegitimate father, nor would it be proper for him to bring shame to Saladin's family by exposing sexual transgressions. Only Saladin, as the dead father's nearest male kin, is in the position to choose to acknowledge or not to acknowledge the bastards of his brother. And for Saladin, a man who has nurtured dreams of family throughout the play, the choice is simple and immediate: "Me, not recognize my brother's children? My niece and nephew—my children? Not recognize them? Me? Leave them to you?"[71] His repeated question may be taken literally: he is not compelled by law to recognize these people as kin. But his questions reveal his desire for connection in the intensification of the relationship he could potentially reject: they are progressively identified as first "my brother's children," followed by "my nephews" [a plural including both genders], and finally transformed as "my children." Having named Recha and the Templar as his children, he may choose between formal acknowledgement [*erkennen*] and dismissal [*dir wohl lassen*], between recognition and loss, and he chooses to recognize an illegitimate relationship that does not have to be recognized. This recognition—which includes by speech-act an adoption and a legitimizing *Aufhebung*—is preferable to life without kin.

Thus these children, neither of legal (or even certain) stamp, counterfeit in so many ways, are finally legitimized by a fiction of blood-kinship that is itself the product of longing and willful interpretations. If we read the drama in this way, appreciating that Lessing presents a drama about bastards who are never named as such, we must question why critics have failed to identify this theme of illegitimacy. While not an overt focus of the play, illegitimacy is one of its framing themes. Its presence is repeatedly alluded to—and illustrated—in the multiple narrative gaps that occur when the Templar's birth or Assad's conduct are discussed, marked by elision marks or abrupt silence. These gaps, which exclude the theme of bastardy from social discourse, mirror its existence outside of the law and legal discourse. The illicit must not be told in so many words; hence, we may understand that the part of the story that is constantly censured is, in fact, illicit. Less understandable than the textual gaps is the parallel narrative gap in the history of criticism: no one has identified the children as bastards, much less identified the theme of illegitimacy as playing a role in the drama. Are we to understand that critics have tended to share the delicacy of the characters in this matter? That they regularly succumbed to the invitation to inhabit rather than regard critically the fictional world, discreetly turning away from what should not be told and accepting the fictions of blood-certainty and universal brotherhood that are substituted?

There is a way to read Lessing's plot that suggests that all children are adopted, that they are always substitutes for loss, and that all families are artifacts of grief and willful bonding. The blood-bonds that may or may not circulate through the bodies of the characters are no more reliable in identifying and structuring community than the names which circulate socially. This is not so much a revelation of the play as one of its premises. Thus the drama of *Nathan the Wise* demonstrates ways in which humans in need of connections exploit a combination of blood's materiality and non-traceability to construct a real and legitimate ground for affinities. Neither blood nor handwriting, however, reveals anything truer than the desire of the reader to read connection in the other.

Postscript
Heredity's Time

It is with Lessing's insight into the necessary fiction of kinship that I end this book. The genealogical structures that comprise the drama reveals that lineage is always ultimately unknowable, and yet the play points to the political, religious, and psychological disorder that can result when an individual believes his or her biological lineage to be unclear. As an idea, the hereditary bloodline has answered fundamental questions of human society; it has traced connections among people and infused those connections with social, moral, and emotional prescriptions. Thus we are urged to take seriously the collective tendency to invent genealogical narratives (and the forms of knowledge necessary for their defense), and to refrain from subjecting it to analysis unless (until) it functions as an instrument of abuse or exclusion. Belief in the hereditary bonds that bind us—whatever they are, however they do so—must hover within the delicate philosophical balance of "as if": we believe as if they are indisputable, until we should not. This "as if" is not difficult to sustain, as long as it is shielded from analytic inquiry; as soon as the complex ties that heredity promises become the object of analysis, they become elusive. They are not the stuff of demonstrated argument and evidence. However, if we dismiss or dismantle genealogical "fictions" out of hand because they can not be substantiated as facts, we sacrifice their unique power to stimulate the moral imagination (with its extensions as empathy and altruism), and we are left with a "reality" that leaves people radically and dangerously disconnected from one another.

Human beings, it would seem, do not bear well the alienation which results from not belonging to a family in some way or another, and social institutions in the West continue to operate with traditional beliefs in the a priori value of the "natural" parent-child connection. If heredity were nothing more today than potentially alterable genetic codes and brain chemistry, then Staffan Müller-Wille would be right to declare that heredity is "as trivial as it is precarious."[1] However, a strong current of belief in a connection between hereditary kinship and fundamental human relationships continues: the numbers of adoptees who, as adults, seek their "real" parents attest to this, as does a recent argument in Britain over whether or not sperm or egg donor information should be marked on a child's birth certificate. Debates soar on the ethics of genetic information as it becomes available: do individuals have a "right" or an "obligation" to know their genetic heritage? Do potential marriage partners or one's children have similar rights or obligations?

Introducing this project, I used metaphors of Gordian knots and tangles to evoke heredity as a conceptual field that underscores and links biological, societal, metaphorical, and metaphysical ideas, facts, and practices. Because I am convinced that the network of connections is itself the locus of significance in pursuing heredity—because of the paths that connect gaps in the law with speculations of scientists, and with descriptions of the moral and the material world by philosophers, poets, and statesmen—it would be disingenuous to construct a single progressive path from one discourse or praxis to another. Out of respect for the Gordian challenge heredity poses, I shall not pretend to untie its tangle, nor shall I sever it with the sword of academic impatience, dismissing either the scientific or the transcendent, either the natural or the institutional, as residual or invalid or simply unimportant.

Instead, I shall presume here at the end of this book to follow one line along the tangle, knowing full well it is one among many options in a multidimensional network. While heredity as a concept is universal and counts among the fundamental cognitive building blocks used across time in the West (although its particular manifestations are historically bound), my study does respect the historical construct of eras—I write of the Enlightenment and of the "modern" and I am particularly interested in the way that the heredity complex as a whole lends respectability and resonance to the confluence of natural science and social order at the end of the eighteenth and the beginning of the nineteenth centuries.

At the end of the eighteenth century, concurrent with a widespread crisis of belief in (kinship-based) religious and political systems, there developed an increasing interest in substantiating the authority of the blood-tie within the emerging context of scientific knowledge. This might be read as a reauthorizing process, insofar as it offered up the biological materiality of the blood as an answer to the problem of grounding the origin and direction of civilization. According to this reading, we might grant this late eighteenth-century moment its modernity, in Bruno Latour's terms: "not because . . . it is finally liberating itself from the hell of social relationships, from the obscurantism of religion, from the tyranny of politics," all of which are customary elements in descriptions of the modern, but instead "because, just like all the others, it is redistributing the accusations that replace a cause—judiciary, collective, social—by a cause—scientific, nonsocial, matter-of-factual."[2]

We witnessed just such a shift over the course of this book from from the "judiciary, collective, social" manipulations of heredity to the "scientific, nonsocial, matter-of-factual" in a movement—by no means simple, by no means linear—from legal to scientific attempts at verifying a hereditary line. Early chapters provided instances of the law's anxiety to secure the fundamentally unsecurable paternal line. As medical and natural science research made increasing claims to knowledge of the processes of generation and transmission, legal theorists were quick to refer to scientific expertise in order to verify the natural basis for hereditary claims. The age-old faith in the truth of bloodlines to carry both family names and family virtues functioned rhetorically as the basis for an inheritance law that now could reach to the emerging laws of biological science for evidence. However, whereas the legal system, based upon tradition and custom and periodic change, was flexible and prepared to dismiss hereditary facts or fictions judiciously, science was invested in demonstrating immutable facts. If hereditary links were claimed to be real, then they were real, and all other meanings and consequences had to accommodate.

A particular challenge arises when the science of heredity acquires the authority to declare the concrete reality of "blood" relations. Here we witness a phenomenon that we might well label "modern," the impetus to harness individual reproductive activity for the physical, moral, and political improvement of the collective (be it a family, a nation, a race, or the species). Ideas of improvement and perfectibility themselves are "modern," insofar as they reflect an era's consciousness of itself as different from both the past and the future. I believe, however, that the interest in reproduction suggests further a sense of accelerated time, as if the future might be distinguished from the present within one carefully molded generation. Reinhard Koselleck identifies as hallmarks of *Neuzeit*, or modernity, both the "expected otherness of the future" and "the experience, at once disturbing and widely gaining acceptance, of acceleration by means of which one's own time is distinguished from the preceding time."[3] Just past the mid-century mark, in 1769, Friedrich II wrote of educating "a future generation entrusted to the oversight of the present generation: it is a new human race [*Menschengeschlecht*]."[4] The upcoming generation that he envisioned, cast as new kind of man altogether, was being created not in the image of, but according to the ideals of, the present "parent" generation. The transmission of values would transform not only history, but also the human kind that makes and experiences history. And Friedrich felt the process to be happening within the present, under his governing eyes.

Those writers throughout this study who grappled more directly with ideas of species, race, and reproduction during the long eighteenth century variously articulated that era's experience of being-in-time. We sense the perception of acceleration as races and species—newly conceptualized as long-term products of biological transmission and as carriers of hereditary cultural identities—become themselves subjects that may be affected by immediate changes in reproductive patterns that would direct the flow of physical, aesthetic, and moral inheritance from one generation to another. This articulation is a modern gesture, and the various and contradictory senses of the good thus generated are part of our own hybrid, modern inheritance, as long as we find ways to balance—for good—the hereditary bonds that bind us.

Notes

NOTES TO THE INTRODUCTION

1. Bruno Latour, *We Have Never Been Modern*, 3.
2. Friedrich Schiller, *Die Räuber. Ein Schauspiel*, 15. I cite from the original version of the play, published in 1781.
3. Ibid., 95.
4. Schiller, in his preface to the first edition of *Die Räuber*, wrote, 8: "I shall rightly grant my text, on account of its peculiar catastrophe, a place among other moral books."
5. This last is interpreted by the editor as "relatives make claims upon the heart" ["*Blutsfreunde treten ans Herz*"]. Wander, *Deutsches Sprichwörter-Lexikon*, 410–414.
6. Ibid., p. 413.
7. Eisenhart, *Grundsätze der deutschen Rechte*, 158.
8. Ibid., p. 156.
9. One can look back to Gottfried von Strassburg's medieval masterpiece, *Tristan*: the eponymous hero is drawn to the uncle he has not yet met because of the unknown ties of blood that unite them: "nu Tristan den künic sehen began, / er begunde im wol gevallen / vor den andern allen;/ sin herze in sunder uz erlas, / wan er von sinem bluote was: / diu natiure zoch in dar" (lines 3240–3245).
10. The Grimms' dictionary offers the following idiom under its heading *Blut*: "The spilled drop of blood cries for revenge" ["*Der gefallene Blutstropfe schreit um Rache*"]. Wander, p. 413 offers the following: "Blood cries to God" ["*Das blut schreiet zu gott*"] and "Innocent blood cries to heaven" ["*Unschuldig Blut schreiet zum Himmel*"] followed by the Biblical citation, "1 Moses, 4, 10." *Das Deutsche Wörterbuch*, 170–74.
11. For an analysis of the rhetoric of family in France during the same period, see Lynn Hunt, *The Family Romance of the French Revolution*.

NOTES TO CHAPTER 1

1. Michel Serres, *Hermes II*, 31.
2. Moser, *Familien=Staaats=Recht derer Teutschen Reichsstände*, 50ff.
3. Hugo Grotius argued that property should be passed through channels determined by the will of the bequeather; legal thinkers before and after maintained the obligation of familial passage, justified either legally or philosophically. This issue was linked to debates about the nature of private property, which themselves were undergoing renegotiation and definition

from the time of the "Reception" of Roman Law during the sixteenth and through the nineteenth century. See Brakensiek, et. al., *Generationengerechtigkeit? Normen und Praxis im Erb- und Ehegüterrecht 1500–1850*. For Hegel's comments, see, for example, §. 180 and the *Zusatz zu* §. 180 in the *Grundlinien der Philosophie des Rechts*, 151 and 333.
4. Moser, *Familien=Staaats=Recht*, 856.
5. See, for example, Kantorowicz, *The King's Two Bodies*; also Stollberg-Rilinger, *Der Staat als Maschine*.
6. Bodin's *Les six livres de la republique* is cited with comment by Dieter Schwab on p. 268ff. in his article "*Familie*," in Conze and Koselleck, eds., *Geschichtliche Grundbegriffe*.
7. The larger, familial *Haus* merely added elements thereto. See Schwab, ibid., for a discussion of the relationship of *Familie* to *Haus*.
8. Fichte, *Grundlage des Naturrechts*, 305.
9. This phenomenon has been addressed variously by literary critics, notably: Gail Hart, *Tragedy in Paradise* and Susan Gustafson, *Absent Mothers and Orphaned Fathers*. Fritz Breithaupt, in "Anonymous Forces of History," correctly notes a sudden surge in the representation of otherwise absent mother figures during the *Sturm und Drang* period, with a flurry of infanticide dramas.
10. From the fifth lecture, delivered in 1810 and titled "Wie sich in der natürlichen, allen Völkern der Erde gemeinschaftlichen Verfassung der Familie die lebendige Natur des Staates ausdrücke" in Adam Müller's *Die Elemente der Staatskunst*, 59–72.
11. Kant, *Political Writings*, 159.
12. Hobbes, *The Collected Works of Thomas Hobbes*, Vol 6, 147.
13. See Montesquieu, *Spirit of the Laws*, Book 1, Chapter 3 and Book 4, Chapter 1.
14. Montesquieu, *Spirit of the Laws*, Book 23, Chapter 6.
15. Eisenhart, 143, under the section heading "Das Kind gehöret zu der ärgern Hand," in his *Grundsätze der deutschen Rechte*.
16. Moser identifies, *Familien=Staats=Recht*, 785, the rare occurrence, and the subsequent legal complexity, of a child who wishes to be made heir of the mother and to take her name and station rather than those of the father.
17. ALR, 2.2.604–605.
18. Compare Ibid., 2.2.560, 2.2.639.
19. Justi, *Rechtliche Abhandlung*, 79. This formulation continued throughout the mid-nineteenth century, where it found expression by Savigny in the identification of families as the *Keime* or the seeds of the state. Cited by Schwab, "Familie," 289.
20. Justi, *Rechtliche Abhandlung*, 11.
21. Ibid., 29.
22. Ibid., 44.
23. Ibid., 11.
24. Eisenhart, *Grundsätze*, 151 and 154.
25. Frank, *System*, 286.
26. Included in Grotefend, *Das Allgemeine Preußische Landrecht*, 28.
27. ALR, 2.2.717.
28. See Moser, *Familien=Staats=Recht*, 724.
29. From the essay, "Versuch über die Eigenliebe als Moralprinzip," 200 and 203.
30. See Wächtershäuser, *Das Verbrechen Des Kindesmordes*, 28. He mentions further that extramarital sex was officially decriminalized in Prussia in 1799, 144.

31. See Moser's description of "das Odium" laid upon bastards, in his *Familien=Staats=Recht*, part 2, 886.
32. This is partially redressed by the *ALR*, 2.8.279, by which stipulation a person of illegitimate birth who attained a certificate of legitimization could no longer be excluded from an apprenticeship.
33. The limits placed upon the charity extended to illegitimate orphans and *Findlinge* are discussed in Meumann's, *Findelkinder, Waisenhäuser, Kindsmord*, especially 92 and 183ff. See also Grolle's *Bettelkinder, Findelkinder, Waisenkinder* and Pfeil's *Das Kind als Objekt der Plannung*.
34. Meumann, *Findelkinder, Waisenhäuser, Kindsmord*, 92 ff., also describes the plight of illegitimate children, who had little chance of public support. As further proof of their lesser human dignity, upon death, the corpses of unmarried mothers and illegitimate children were sent to anatomical labs along with criminals and unknown beggars.
35. Moser, *Familien=Staats=Recht*, part 2, p. 860ff.
36. Cited in Deppermann, *Der Hallesche Pietismus*, 115. The guilds were so rigid in preserving the moral purity of their ranks that a member was not allowed to marry a woman who had an illegitimate child. See Dülmen, *Frauen vor Gericht*, 95.
37. Ibid., see 105–15.
38. See ibid. for a lengthy account of Francke's 1698 privileges, the opposition they aroused, and in particular Brandenburg-Prussia's hostility toward the guilds; see also an account of this episode, with a list of Francke's programs and their relation to Prussian absolutist politics, in Fulbrook, *Piety and Politics*, 158–59.
39. See the "Cirkular=Verordnung vom 1. September 1798, an sämmtliche Regimentschefs und Commandeurs, betreffend das Heirathen der Offiziere und die Legitimation der unehelichen Kinder," p. 30 in Grotefend, *Das Allgemeine Preußische Landrecht*, reprinted under "Gesetze und Verordnungen." He expressly forbids the conferring of a father's name, nobility, and coat of arms, granting that for the purposes of "the better advancement in civic life among guilds, handworkers, and craftesmen, and for the prevention of accusations of illegitimate birth," a certificate of legitimation might be extended. But in such a case, the child would still carry the name of its mother rather than its father, thereby retaining the purity of the paternal lines.
40. See the "Allerh. Kabinets=Order vom 4. September 1798, betreffend die Verheirathung der Subaltern=Offiziere und die Legitimation der unehelichen Kinder," 31 ff. in Grotefend's *Das Allgemeine Preußische Landrecht*.
41. Justi, *Rechtliche Abhandlung*, 69.
42. Schwab, "Familie," 279ff., discusses the links between the official understanding of the father-role and the *Sittenpolizei*.
43. Justi, *Rechtliche Abhandlung*, 69.
44. This is taken from Friedrich's corrective decree in the Müller Arnold affair, recorded as an *Aktenstück* of 11 December 1779. My citation is from Christian Wilhelm von Dohm's *Denkwürdigkeiten meiner Zeit*. In the case of the infamous "Müller Arnoldsche Sache," Friedrich supported a miller's right to defend his claims to water access against a noble landowner who wished to drain a river to fill a fishpond. Friedrich seems to have abused his own authority over the law in order to proclaim the equality of all men before the law: he intervened on behalf of the miller, reversed a legal decision which had favored the nobleman (who was factually in the right), and publicly punished the jurists who had found for the nobleman, who received restitution under Friedrich Wilhelm II.
45. Milton, *Paradise Lost*, Book 5, 791–93.

46. Jonathan I. Israel, *Enlightenment Contested*, 545.
47. The classic investigation of this phenomenon, as a subject of English juridical debate during the Tudor reign, is Kantorowicz's *The King's Two Bodies*.
48. The *ALR* was completed under Friedrich Wilhelm II in 1791 and went into effect in 1794.
49. *ALR*, "Einleitung. Von Gesetzen überhaupt," §. 22.
50. Friedrich II, *Oeuvres Philosophiques* vol 8, 43. Borcke was the primary educator of Friedrich Wilhelm between 1751–1764.

NOTES TO CHAPTER 2

1. Significantly, the French Revolution's democratic reforms included the official end of the legal differentiation between legitimate and illegitimate children; as Marc Shell notes, *Children of the Earth*, 261 n. 141, "even children of adulterous unions were given the same right as others to inherit" under the Law of 12 Brumaire in 1793. Shell notes further that by 1803 "a new law entitled 'Paternity Affiliation in the Civil Code' returned France to its more traditional concerns with illegitimacy."
2. This is also true of legitimate children of "*Misheyrathen*": Moser writes in *Familien=Staats=Recht*, 848ff., that a child of an *unstandesmäßiges* marriage [presumed to be a noble man married to a common woman] cannot inherit the name, title or property of the father, although considered legitimate. These children are "not considered part of the line" and "not counted with the family"; however, they have to be supported—Moser suggests they receive private holdings from the father, that sons be supported at a university, etc.—which engenders a separate set of rules and regulations written into "*Stamm-*" or "*Familienverträge.*"
3. Eisenhart, *Grundsätze*, 146.
4. Parents could also sell their children. Exposed and rescued children were, until the reign of Justinian, automatically considered slaves. According to Schwab, the legal right of a parent to sell or kill a child was still disputed throughout the eighteenth century; see esp. "Familie," 279 n. 151.
5. For twentieth-century anthropological and socio-biological perspectives on infanticide in human communities, see the following: Martin Daly and Wilson, "A Sociobiological Analysis of Human Infanticide"; Dickemann, "Concepts and Classification in the Study of Human Infanticide," and Scrimshaw's "Infanticide in Human Populations." See also Hrdy, *Mother Nature*.
6. See Dülmen, *Frauen vor Gericht*, 21.
7. Cited in ibid. This rhetoric of a natural loyalty to one's own blood-family echoes remarks made by Seneca in a letter to Nero. He writes in *De Clementia*: "Even animals devoid of reason as they are and accused by us of cruel ferocity spare their own kind: wild beasts respect their own likeness." But Seneca's concern with the "fury of tyrants" who treat kin and strangers alike is translated here to the fear of the maternal monster who destroys only her own child. (Seneca passage cited in Shell, *Children of the Earth*, 133.)
8. See Pestalozzi, *Ueber Gesetzgebung und Kindermord*, vol. 7, 269.
9. See Dülmen, *Frauen vor Gericht*, 75.; also on pp. 28–29 he notes that until the sixteenth century, there were no secular officials appointed to monitor the crime; with the Carolina of 1532 came the first legal declaration of intent to seek out and prosecute infanticide.
10. The struggle between religious and secular control of marriage had a long history, but for a discussion of the decisive shift during the Reformation, see especially pp. 104ff. in Kroj, *Die Abhängigkeit der Frau*.

11. See Ellrichshausen, *Die Uneheliche Mutterschaft*, 29–31.
12. This was the "Edikt wider den Mord neugebohrner unehelicher Kinder, Verheimlichung der Schwangerschaft, und Niederkunft." Reprinted as *Anhang* 4 of Wächtershäuser's *Das Verbrechen des Kindesmordes*. For bibliography on illegitimacy statistics, see esp. p. 135, n. 5, in Beck's article "Of Two Minds About the Death Penalty."
13. See Dülmen, *Frauen vor Gericht*, 30.
14. For laws against and punishments for concealing pregnancy, see Schlegel's *Sammlung aller Sanitätsverordnungen für das Fürstenthum Weimar*.
15. Pestalozzi, *Ueber Gesetzgebung und Kindermord*, 269.
16. Kant, *Die Metaphysik der Sitten*, 234. While Kant's treatment was characteristic insofar as it arose from the death-penalty debates preoccupying legal and ethical thinkers, it was unique in its dispassionate treatment of the crime itself. Kant's response is also discussed by Wächtershäuser, *Das Verbrechen des Kindesmordes*, 29ff.
17. Wächtershäuser, *Das Verbrechen des Kindesmordes*, 34ff. See also Meumann, *Findelkinder, Waisenhäuser, Kindsmord*, 96ff., who discusses the prize essay, pointing out that *Kindsmord* was a more discussed problem than that of *Findelkinder*.
18. Barbara Becker-Cantarino describes the response of over 400 submissions to the contest in "Witch and Infanticide," 13: "The (exclusively male) authors debated and fictionalized sexual encounters leading to infanticide; they shaped and adapted social and individual conflicts about woman's procreative role in such a way as to foreground the moral argument and the woman's shame over her illegitimate child."
19. Pestalozzi, *Ueber Gesetzgebung und Kindermord*, 269–70.
20. Wächtershäuser, *Das Verbrechen des Kindesmordes*, 41ff.
21. Scholarly literature on eighteenth-century infanticide is abundant. See ibid., esp. p. 27ff. For a classic treatment of the "Sturm & Drang" infanticide literature, see Rameckers, *Der Kindermord in der Literatur der Sturm-und-Drang-Periode*. Recent works with additional bibliography include Beck, "Of Two Minds About the Death Penalty"; Dülmen, *Frauen vor Gericht*; Becker-Cantarino, "Witch and Infanticide"; see also Breithaupt, "The Case of Infanticide in the Sturm und Drang"; Goetzinger, "Männerphantasie und Frauenwirklichkeit"; and Kord, "Women as Children."
22. For a list of literary treatments during the late 18th century, see Rameckers, *Der Kindermord*, 4ff. Kord describes the portrayal of remorse on the part of the mothers in numerous literary examples, identifying their admission of guilt and horror as an implicit or explicit "long overdue warning to other—as yet innocent—young women"; see Kord, "Women as Children," 459. Dülmen, *Frauen vor Gericht*, 104, describes the Sturm & Drang treatment as characterized by a social agenda that had little to do with the actual situation of most real-life infanticides. He describes their concern as "vielmehr die Kritik am adligen Verhalten und am Mißbrauch des anständigen Bürgertums durch die tugendlosen Adligen."
23. According to Kord, "Women as Children," 459, there are no dramas written by women in Germany in the eighteenth century which treat the theme of infanticide.
24. Goetzinger; Kord. For discussions of the class-identification of most infanticides and the difference between reality and most dramatic representation, see Becker-Cantarino, "Witch and Infanticide." See also Rameckers, *Der Kindermord*; Dülmen, *Frauen vor Gericht*, esp. 76ff.; and Ulbricht, *Kindsmord und Aufklärung*.

25. See Wächtershäuser, *Das Verbrechen des Kindesmordes*, 148. Beck, "Of Two Minds" notes also, 136–37 n. 10, that the common death by beheading was merciful when compared to the other prevalent forms of execution.
26. Cited in Wächtershäuser, *Das Verbrechen des Kindesmordes*, 29.
27. Ibid. See also Herman Mostar, "Weltgeschichte höchst privat" S. 144.
28. The unwillingness to imagine women might be both mothers and violent aggressors appears in other contexts as well; for just one example, see Cornelius de Pauw's refutation of New World Amazons, cited by Zantop in *Colonial Fantasies*, 57.
29. See Kroj, *Die Abhängigkeit der Frau*, esp. p. 104ff., 136ff.
30. *ALR*, 2.1.19.
31. *ALR*, 2.1.20.
32. *ALR*, 2.1. Anhang § 64. Compare with 2.2. 19–39. A widower, on the other hand, is free to marry six weeks after his wife's death—that is, after an appropriate mourning period (§ 22–24). For a discussion of the status of women throughout the ALR, see Weber-Will's *Die Rechtliche Stellung der Frau*.
33. See Ploucquet's *Ueber die Physische Erfordernsse der Erbfähigkeit der Kinder*, 102.
34. *ALR*, 2.2.6.
35. Fischer, *Versuch über die Geschichte der Teutschen Erbfolge*, 21–22. Marc Shell points out (*Children of the Earth*, 97) that Montaigne (in his essay "Of the Affection of Fathers for Their Children") implies that "kinship claims are essentially literary fictions." Shell continues in note 5, 241, that Montaigne suggests the love that fathers bear their children is "based in fictional tales only, or *contes*."
36. Eisenhart, *Grundsätze*, 138.
37. The *ALR* accords with this, 2.2.1. A man disputing the "legal presumption" of paternity will only be heard if he can prove his absence or impotence during a stipulated period of possible impregnation. In such a case, the mother's testimony may not be used as evidence either for or against the child's legitimacy (see 2.2.6).
38. Eisenhart, *Grundsätze*, 138.
39. Ibid.
40. Social position is bequeathed by the state; it is not the parents' to give. Nor is it something a parent can withhold: see Moser, *Familien=Staats=Recht*, part 1, 58, in which he identifies the limits to a father's right to disinherit his son. Any *Reichsstand* which the father himself inherited must pass through him to his son regardless of his will in the matter.
41. Eisenhart, *Grundsätze*, 140. One might note that the adage favors the mother's declaration, not her certainty: the issue does not pretend to rest upon her knowledge but upon her speech act which has almost the force of law.
42. Mistakes might be made in the case of multiple sexual partners, or in the case of attendants at a birth switching a child so that even the mother does not know its "true" identity. Also, as amply illustrated throughout Renaissance literature, a mistake might be made because a woman slept with one man believing him to be another.
43. See Majer's *Teutsche Staatskonstitution*, 460.
44. For an introduction to the medical theories of generation before, during, and just after the eighteenth century, see Farley's *The Spontaneous Generation Controversy*; also his *Gamets & Spores*.
45. See Frank, *System*, viii.
46. Ibid., 3–4.
47. See Ibid., 313ff.

48. The sub-discipline of *Semiotik* was prevalent throughout the medical physiologies of the century; compare, for example, Loseke's *Lehre von den Zeichen der Krankheiten*, Metzger's *Grundsätze der Allgemeinen Semiotik*, and the later work by Sprengel, *Handbuch der Semiotik*.
49. Dülmen discusses the increasing reliance upon official medical testimony during the 18th century during infanticide cases, *Frauen vor Gericht*, 34. Especially critical was a medical determination (which was usually highly detailed and far from certain) of whether a child had been born alive and *lebensfähig*, i.e., not premature and likely to have died naturally soon after birth.
50. See Haller, *Vorlesungen über die Gerichtliche Arzneiwissenschaft*.
51. Ploucquet, *Ueber die Physische Erfordernsse der Erbfähigkeit*, 7.
52. Ibid., 9.
53. Ibid., 105ff.
54. Ibid., 106ff.
55. Ibid., 119.
56. Ibid., 121.
57. Ibid., 125-26.
58. Ibid.
59. Ibid., 132.
60. Voltaire, "Of the Different Races of Men," 7.
61. Ploucquet, *Ueber die Physische Erfordernsse der Erbfähigkeit*, 132.
62. Ibid.
63. Londa Schiebinger, *Nature's Body: Gender in the Making of Modern Science*, 95.
64. Ibid., 132-33.
65. For an interesting article on the term's use in botany, see especially the chapter on the "Doctrine of Reproduction" and the work of Joseph Gottlieb Koelreuter, who uses conventional kinship terms in describing plant hybridization and labels the products "bastards" in Frängsmyr's *The Quantifying Spirit*.

NOTES TO CHAPTER 3

1. See E. Mayr and P. D. Ashlock, *Principles of Systematic Zoology*.
2. Note here the allusions to and critique of Descartes and followers, perhaps even to Pascal's critique of Descartes. Diderot, *Encyclopédie*, 107.
3. Marcus IV, 4, *The Meditations*. Cited in Nussbaum, "Kant and Cosmopolitanism," 31.
4. The interest in an idea of "kinds" is central to Plato's work; he applies the concept not only to natural forms, but also to ethical, artificial, mathematical, political, and mundane kinds. For a brief discussion and references, see Johnson, "Aristotle and Natural Kinds."
5. The "*Système figuré des connoissance humanines*" is included at the end of the "*Prospectus de l'encyclopédie*," 1751.
6. See Kant's review essay on a speech given by the Italian anatomist Moscati, in which he discusses the significance of the human animal's upright stance in distinguishing him from other beasts. See pp.421-426 in *Kants Werke*, Akademie Textausgabe, vol. 2. The issue—an old one—was renewed by Linnaeus's inclusion of man (genus *Homo*) with apes and sloths as one among many quadrupeds in the order *Anthropomorpha*.
7. The quality of "kind" is specified by Marcus, and it is notably *not* a shared physical nature, but rather a quality of spirit. Nussbaum, p. 34 cites Marcus

reminding himself to relinquish feelings of anger against others because "the nature of the wrongdoer is of one kin with mine—not indeed of the same blood or seed but sharing the same kind, the same portion of the divine . . . " The ethical mandate linking all humans stems from a shared human portion of the divine (manifest in the capacity to reason) and pointedly *not* from shared blood or lineage.

8. Of course, this presupposes it is not atrocious for a man to eat a rabbit; one should bear in mind that there was a discussion at this time of the ethics of vegetarianism, including a contribution by Friedrich II in his *Anti-Machiavel*.
9. For a late eighteenth-century discussion of what was then considered an antiquated notion still in need of discussion, see the anonymous "Ueber den Ausdruck: adeliches Blut," in the *Schleswigsches Journal* of August, 1792.
10. Canguilhem, *Idéologie*, 129. Also cited in Atran, *The Cognitive Foundations of Natural History*, 261. For a discussion of the seventeenth-century understanding of species, see Roger, *Les Sciences de la Vie*, 81ff.
11. Buffon did identify the Linnaean system as arbitrary, declaring that it "is not a science, and is at most only a convention, an arbitrary language, a means of understanding; from it results no real knowledge [*connoissance réele*]." Cited by Sloan, "Buffon, German Biology," 117.
12. Diderot, *Encyclopédie*, vol. 5, 956.
13. Buffon can be cited as both an advocate for and a critic of the real, historical status of natural classificatory categories; however, the idea that seems to predominate in his writings is that species (singular) exists as a category *and* that species (plural) exist as real and historical phenomena. For an extended treatment of his challenge of the Linnaean system, see Sloan, "The Buffon-Linnaeus Controversy." Erich Voegelin, *Die Rassenidee in der Geistesgeschichte*, 28 points out that an historical, genealogical understanding of species predicated on fertile interbreeding did not, strictly speaking, originate with Buffon, but was anticipated by Ray.
14. Cited by Diderot in the *Encyclopédie*, vol. 5, 955. Always worried about the real versus conceptual status of his objects of study, Buffon writes elsewhere about the boundaries drawn generally between different natural entities, musing that "these lines of separation do not exist in nature; there are beings which are neither animals, vegetables, nor minerals, and which we in vain might attempt to arrange with either." Lyon and Sloan, *Readings from Buffon*, 203. Nevertheless, as indicated above, Buffon's faith in the natural fact of genealogical species division remained firm.
15. Buffon, "The Generation of Animals," 10 in *Readings from Buffon*, ed. Lyon and Sloan.
16. Species, writes Buffon in 1765, "are the sole beings of Nature, perpetual beings . . . we must no longer consider them as a collection or a series of similar individuals, but as a whole, independent of number, independent of time, a whole always living, always the same." Cited by Sloan, "Buffon," 119.
17. Buffon, *Barr's Buffon. Buffon's Natural history*, 187.
18. The French "chose" can be a thing, and it can equally refer to a more inclusive and indeterminate "matter," as in "the matter at hand."
19. Phillip Sloan ("Buffon") argues persuasively, 117 that Buffon, profiting from Wolff, "by 1749 had made the organic species the prime example of such a successional series, in which the *real* character is found in the continuity of reproduction." Sloan identifies "the metaphysical connexion of organic species with the immanence of time" to be Buffon's "critical innovation" for the species concept.
20. Sloan, "Buffon," 114.

Notes   167

21. We shall see that Kant acknowledges and separates the real and the ideal with more system and less irony. In the twentieth century, Husserl takes up the concept of species for phenomenology; he theorizes that "Species"—as the ideal—exists neither *externally* to thought nor *in* thought." See esp. *Logical Investigations*, 350.
22. Illiger, in 1800, deems it necessary to begin his comprehensive dictionary of natural history terminology with an essay on the terms "species" and "genera." He begins by defining *Art, Species* simply as: "the embodiment of all individuals who beget fertile offspring with each other," *Versuch einer Systematischen Vollständigen Terminologie*, xxvi. Further, xxxi he declares that "expert knowledge and experience with regard to fertile reproduction" is the sole arbiter [*Schiedsrichter*] of species.
23. Susan Shell, *Embodiment of Reason*, 192.
24. As will be discussed further below, the terminology for genus, species, and race is rendered inconsistently in German, complicating not only the task of translating, but also reflecting a conceptual imprecision typical of the period. For an example of how terminological confusion is thematized in the debates at the time, see p. 79–80 in Georg Forster's "Noch Etwas über den Menschenrassen," a direct response to Kant's theory of *Naturgeschichte* and its application to the human species and races.
25. Blumenbach, *Handbuch* 1791, 53–54. Blumenbach first addressed the issue in the third edition of 1788.
26. *Menschengeschlecht* can be grouped with other eighteenth-century favorites, like "*die allgemeine Menschheit*," or "*die Menschheitsfamilie*," all of which indicate the presence of *Menschlichkeit*, a moral, empathetic, humane quality.
27. Grimm, *Deutsches Wörterbuch*.
28. "Die natürliche folge vom vater in kindskind, das ein jglich glied derselben folge heisze ein geschlecht." Ibid.
29. Later anthropologists would include other, extinct species under the genus "*Homo*" but modern man, "*Homo sapiens*," remains the only extant species in the genus.
30. Blumenbach, *Handbuch* (1791), v-vi. This text remains consistent through the 1821 edition.
31. "Bastard" was for a time, in German, also *Zwitter* (which by the eighteenth century predominantly referred to hermaphrodites). *Zwitter* is Luther's occasional translation of the Latin *spurius* or *nothus*, and is defined by Grimm as the product of two beings of different kinds (*zwei wesen verschiedener art*); with regard to humans, it pertains most specifically to children born of foreign mothers (*von einer mutter fremden stammes*), thus underscoring a conflation of national or regional difference with natural kind. (Grimm, *Deutsches Wörterbuch*, vol. 32, 1408.) This highlights the combination of social and biological components that make up the notion of the foreign, the other art, the different variety or race.
32. Illiger, *Versuch einer Systematischen Vollständigen Terminologie*, 6, § 14: "Bastardart, Mittelart, *Species hybrida*, *Hybridum*, ein aus der Vermischung der beiden Geschlechter verschiedener Art entstandner organischer Körper."
33. It is significant here that Voltaire chooses "black" and "white" as the obvious examples of racial difference. Bernasconi and Lott, *The Idea of Race*, 6.
34. The term for the mixed-race child of a black and a white parent, "mulatto" (German: *Mulatte*) is, according to the *Duden Herkunft* etymological dictionary, derived from the sixteenth-century *mulo*, German *maultier*, English

mule. This conveys both a breeding that crosses naturally distinct kinds and that produces a child who is mule-like: that is, useful for work, visibly inferior in kind to its nobler parent, essentially ridiculous, and sterile. While sterility is, of course, not a biological result of mixed-race breeding, it was often a wishful association.

35. In fact, Blumenbach in several instances contradicts the fundamental reproductive premise of species-unity, suggesting that species can, on rare occasion, interbreed and generate fertile offspring. His qualifications, which are not picked up on by any of his contemporaries, effectively compromise the claim that "species" is real rather than conceptual.
36. We see a similar example in the continuation of the citation under examination: "... we learn already as children that *genus* also means gender [*Geschlecht*] in grammer, in the difference between words of masculine and feminine gender, etc." Here Blumenbach justifies the term *Geschlecht* via example of grammatical gender, raising the question of which predominates, the systematicity of grammar or the natural specificity of gender? One might also recall that this period of time also witnesses the use of a genealogical model for the development of languages themselves (grouped into historical "families"), as well as their textual traditions.
37. On species as organic entities with a lifespan and for a discussion of disputes about fossil records, see 147ff. in Laudan's *From Mineralogy to Geology*.
38. Blumenbach, *Handbuch* (1799), 22.
39. Metzger, "Noch ein Wort über Menschenracen." 508–512.
40. Note: in Kant's two-page chapter of the *Anthropology*—little more than an observation—on "The Character of Races," he includes the *Familienschlag*, along with varieties [*Variätaten*] and mutations [*Spielarten*] as differentiations found within races. The English translation that I use throughout this study translates *Familienschlag* here simply as "family". Kant, *Anthropology*, 236.
41. See Kant's chapter, "Der Charakter der Gattung," *Werke*, vol. 7, 321–333.
42. Kant's essay, "Von den verschiedenen Racen der Menschen," *Werke*, vol. 2, 430.
43. The project of trying to unify people by calling upon a presumably natural species-loyalty continues in precisely the same terms in later centuries: in 1949, UNESCO felt it productive to assert that "man-kind is one: all men belong to the same species." Cited in Baker's *Race*, 65. Consider also the MoMA's "Family of Man" photography exhibit following World War II, designed to reinforce an awareness of the common binding forces among all peoples. Curated by Edward Steichen, "The Family of Man" was mounted in 1955 in New York and then traveled the world for eight years.
44. Kant, *Anthropology*, 240–41.
45. Ibid., 251.
46. Interestingly, the Greek *polis*, a city-state, existed in contrast to the *ethnos*, or tribal state. On the history of the term "cosmopolitan" from classical times, see Toulmin, *Cosmopolis*, esp. 67.
47. See Nussbaum's "Kant and Cosmopolitanism," 31. See also pp. 27ff.
48. See Geiman's "Enlightened Cosmopolitanism," 521.

NOTES TO CHAPTER 4

1. For a discussion of attempts made to objectively render a "typical" subject from the seventeenth to the twentieth centuries, see Lorraine Daston and Peter Galison's, "The Image of Objectivity," 81–128.

2. See John H. Zammito, "Policing Polygeneticism in Germany," 35–54.
3. An excellent presentation of the debate over how and if to reconsider Kant's work in light of his writings on race is provided by Charles W. Mills, in his article, "Kant's *Untermenschen*." 169–193. On the need to reassess dominant understandings of Western philosophy in light of embedded racist attitudes limiting the identity of the moral "persons" included, see for example Lucius Outlaw, *On Race and Philosophy*. On Kant's racism in particular, and its impact upon "Kantian thought" as received by philosophy, see in particular Emmanuel Chukwudi Eze, "The Color of Reason," 103–40; Robert Bernasconi, "Kant as an Unfamiliar Source of Racism," 145–66.
4. See Robert Bernasconi, "Who Invented the Concept of Race?" 11–36. See also Zammito, *Kant, Herder, and the Birth of Anthropology*, and *The Genesis of Kant's Critique of Judgment*; Phillip R. Sloan has analyzed Kant's writings on natural science, including on race, from various angles of concern to the history and philosophy of science: see, for example, "Preforming the Categories," 229–253.
5. Bindman, *Ape to Apollo*, 17
6. Metzger, "Noch ein Wort über Menschenracen," 508–512.
7. Ibid., "Aeusserungen ueber Kant," 42–43.
8. Kant, "On the Use of the Teleological Principle," 186.
9. See Larrimore, "Sublime Waste," 113–114. He notes that "Kant's discussion of the unsuitability of race-mixing as a means to the achievement of true human diversity has ethical implications."
10. Kant, "Von den verschiedenen Racen," 438.
11. For a discussion of Kant's theory of *Keime* in the context of other scientific theories of the day and as it extended into his moral philosophy, see 239 ff. in Phillip R. Sloan, "Preforming the Categories."
12. Kant, "On the Use of the Teleological Principle," 186–187.
13. See in particular Ibid., Kant's last essay on race. See also Larrimore, "Sublime Waste," 110 ff.
14. Kant, *Reflexionen zur Anthropologie* Akademische Ausgabe Vol. 15, 500. (Hereafter referred to as AA.)
15. Emmanuel Chukwudi Eze, "The Color of Reason: The Idea of 'Race' in Kant's Anthropology," 231.
16. Larrimore, "Sublime Waste," 100.
17. Kant, "Entwürfe zu dem Colleg über Anthropologie aus den 70er und 80er Jahren," in AA, Vol. 15, 878.
18. Larrimore, "Sublime Waste," 118.
19. Patrick Brantlinger, *Dark Vanishings. Discourse on the Extinction of Primitive Races, 1800–1930*.
20. Kant, AA, Vol. 15, 590.
21. Ibid., 598.
22. Susan M. Shell, "Kant's Conception of a Human Race," 69.
23. Larrimore suggests that, according to Kant, all individuals, all races, and ultimately all species are dispensable in the greater unpredictable patterns of nature's "sublime waste." Is it possible that this is a philosophical position devised to come to terms with the evisceration of New World peoples by Old World conquerors? See, for example, the language used by Cornelius de Pauw in his description of the massacres of Americans in his *Recherches philosophiques* of 1768, cited in Zantop, *Colonial Fantasies*, 49; see also his remarks, cited p. 64.
24. The Prussian Code declares that all human beings, even unborn children, have rights because of their status as Menschen. It also clearly limits a

170   Notes

woman's role in civic and domestic life, and authorizes a degree of paternal authority over children that we now regard as extreme. See chapter one of the present work.
25. On Forster's experience in the Pacific Islands and his ideas of race contrasted with those of his contemporaries, see Vanessa Agnew, "Pacific Island Encounters and the German Invention of Race."
26. Ibid., 180.
27. Herder, *Ideen*, 179. This rejection of race is directed against Kant (and Kant's lectures on Physical Geography) and is an important moment in their dispute during the later 1780s.
28. Bindman, *Ape to Apollo*, 13. For charges of organicist xenophobia among nineteenth-century German writers, see Leon Poliakov, *The History of Anti-Semitism*; Liah Greenfeld, *Nationalism: Five Roads to Modernity*, 368–69; Rogers Brubaker, *Citicenship and Nationhood in France and Germany*.
29. Nicholas Hudson, "From 'Nation' to 'Race,'" 248.
30. See for example, F. M. Barnard, *Self-Direction and Political Legitimacy: Rousseau and Herder*; Muthu, *Enlightenment Against Empire*; and La Vopa, "Herder's Publikum."
31. Helmut Walser Smith, *The Continuities of German History*, 41.
32. Two examples of rich readings of Fichte, in particular, are Anthony J. La Vopa's study *Fichte. The Self and the Calling of Philosophy, 1762–1799*; and Helmut Walser Smith's briefer but equally interesting treatment in his *The Continuities of German History*.
33. Herder, 251, *Essay on the Origin of Language*, cited by from Muthu, *Enlightenment Against Empire*, 236.
34. Ibid., 192–93.
35. Herder, *Ideen*, 239.
36. Ibid., 245.
37. Ibid., 243. The addition of the plant metaphor to the family/state analogy is a common trope of the period. Its ubiquity is evident in the language itself: one need think only of the family tree ("*Stammbaum*"), the "*Stamm*" itself, references to a child as a "*Sprößling*," etc. And the comparison of a child to a growing plant was a favorite with the 18th-century pedagogues.
38. Muthu, *Enlightenment Against Empire*, 249.
39. Herder, *Ideen*, 180.
40. Ibid., 243–244.
41. Ibid., 244. He argues that, with regard to final causes, nature created diversity among peoples so the entire world could not fall subject to any single despot.
42. Vick, "Greek Origins and Organic Metaphors," 488.
43. Anthony J. La Vopa, "Herder's Publikum," 12.
44. Herder's essay, "Haben wir noch das Publikum" (1795), cited ibid.
45. Planert, "Wann beginnt der 'moderne' deutsche Nationalismus?" 43.
46. Greenfeld, *Nationalism*, 18. See also Kramer, "Historical Narratives and the Meaning of Nationalism," 527.
47. Greenfeld, *Nationalism*, 368.
48. Ibid., 369.
49. Helmut Walser Smith, *The Continuities of German History*, 62.
50. Clark, *Iron Kingdom*, 386.
51. Deutsch, *Der Nationalismus und Seine Alternativen*, 9.
52. Herder, *Ideen*, 239. We might be justified in hearing an anticipation of Hegel.
53. Ludwig, *Grundriss der Naturgeschichte der Menschenspecies*, 77.
54. Ibid., 99

55. Ibid., 213.
56. Ibid., 206.
57. Ibid., 79.
58. Ibid., 77 and 192.
59. Ibid., 228.
60. Ibid., 89.
61. Ibid., 226–227.
62. What interest remained in morphology was focused increasingly on anatomy and embryology, thus restricting the perception of differences to specialists. See Atran's discussion of the relation between folk and scientific taxonomy and the role of vision for both, *Cognitive Foundations of Natural History*.
63. This is still an issue today: genetic scientists argue, and are continually quoted as stating, that the genetic differences between races per se are fewer than the differences between any two individuals of the same race; nonetheless, the truth of racial difference survives as a tenet of folk belief. People seem to need to believe that the patterns of difference they see are somehow meaningful. See Zantop's *Colonial Fantasies* for interesting discussion of the travel literature of the seventeenth and eighteenth centuries, and in her accounts of Christian Meiners and Alexander Humboldt.
64. Zantop, *Colonial Fantasies*, 82, citing Sömmering.
65. From his "Von den Varietäten und Abarten der Neger" of 1790, cited p. 177 in Dougherty, "Christoph Meiners." On the range of representations of Africans in German writing during the eighteenth century, see Sadji's *Der Negermythos am Ende des 18. Jahrhunderts*.
66. See Zantop, *Colonial Fantasies*, particularly chapters 4 and 5. For a detailed account of the debate between Meiners and Blumenbach, see Dougherty, "Christoph Meiners und Johann Friedrich Blumenbach im Streit um den Begriff der Menschenrasse."
67. Blumenbach, *Handbuch* (1791), 54.
68. Blumenbach, *Beyträge zur Naturgeschichte*, 81.
69. Both Bernasconi and Zammito have discussed Blumenbach's adoption of the term and the influence of Kant's work upon his decision. See for example: Robert Bernasconi, "Kant and Blumenbach's Polyps"; Robert Bernasconi, "Who Invented the Concept of Race?"; John Zammito, "Policing Polygeneticism in Germany." See also Phillip R. Sloan, "Preforming the Categories."
70. With a few notable exceptions—Bernasconi, Sloan, Lenoir, and Zammito cited above and below—most references to Blumenbach in the context of racial thinking reduce his contribution to one or two statements in support of the achievements of "Negroes" as evidence of his objections to racist thinking. See Stephen Jay Gould, "On Mental and Visual Geometry," 503; Philip D. Curtin, *The Image of Africa*, 47; Gustav Jahoda, *Crossroads between Culture and Mind*, 87; Londa Schiebinger, "The Anatomy of Difference," 390; Robin Hallett, "The European Approach to the Interior of Africa," 200, note 24.
71. Johann Friedrich Blumenbach, *Abbildungen Naturhistorischer Gegenstände*.
72. Ibid., "Preface"; the book is unpaginated.
73. Marx, "Life of Blumenbach," 12.
74. On relevant debates concerning generation and race, see Sloan, "Preforming the Categories." Also Phillip R. Sloan, "Buffon, German Biology, and the Historical Interpretation of Biological Species," 109–53. C. Correia, *The Ovary of Eve*. Timothy Lenoir, "Kant, Blumenbach, and Vital Materialism in German Biology," 77–108. On the development and context of

Blumenbach's position, see Bernasconi, "Kant and Blumenbach's Polyps"; Zammito, "Policing Polygeneticism"; Frank William Peter Dougherty, *Gesammelte Aufsätze zu Themen der Klassischen Periode der Naturgeschichte*.
75. Sara Eigen [Figal], "Self, Race, and Species: Blumenbach's Atlas Experiment."
76. Blumenbach, *Abbildungen*, unpaginated. [emphasis in original]
77. Foster, *The Return of the Real*, 178.
78. Vanessa Agnew, "Pacific Island Encounters and the German Invention of Race," 91.
79. Homi Bhabha, *The Location of Culture*, 37.
80. Forster, *Werke*, Vol. 8, 193.
81. Zantop, Susanne, "The Beautiful, the Ugly, and the German," 23.
82. Ibid., 33.
83. Cited in Baum, *The Rise and Fall of the Caucasian Race*, 85.
84. Ibid., 86.
85. François Bernier, "A New Division of the Earth," in Bernasconi and Lott, *The Idea of Race*, 4.
86. Ibid.
87. Chardin, *Travels in Persia*, 190.
88. Blumenbach, *Handbook*, 269.
89. Sara Eigen Figal, "The Caucasian Slave Race," article in progress.
90. Felicity Nussbaum, *The Limits of the Human*, 256.

NOTES TO CHAPTER 5

1. Ludwig, *Grundriss der Naturgeschichte*, 5 and 13.
2. Helmut Zedelmaier, *Der Anfang der Geschichte*, 251–255.
3. Carolyn Burdett, "Introduction: Eugenics Old and New," 7.
4. For a provocative analysis of the historical (and current) relationship between "eugenics" and "genetics," see Diane B. Paul, *The Politics of Heredity*, especially chapters six and eight.
5. We should keep in mind that "objective terms" for the late eighteenth century were radically different than the statistical compilations produced by nineteenth-century hereditary science. See López-Beltrán, "Storytelling, Statistics, and Hereditary Thought."
6. Steele, "From My Own Apartment," see pp. 512–517.
7. Ibid., 514.
8. This is written in the wake of the English Revolution of 1688 and the 1701 Act of Settlement, which had sought to limit monarchical powers in favor of parliament, particularly the House of Commons. Steele and Addison, both of Whiggish sympathy, began publishing the *Tatler* pseudonymously in 1709; when their identities were discovered, it was shut down by the Tories in 1711.
9. Hence while this might offer a challenge to the aristocratic hold on power, it is not exactly replacing it with power to the people.
10. "Inoculate," initially meaning to engraft or implant, is significantly adopted by medicine, suggesting that inoculating against disease should be understood as a similar—familiar, visible—process of grafting for health and beauty. Paradoxically, however, it is used not to signal a process of refining a complex specimen, but one of protecting the specimen from an external assault.
11. Steele, "From My Own Apartment," 516.
12. Ibid., 516–17

13. Wheeler, *The Complexion of Race*, 7.
14. This recalls Buffon's dilemma with conceptualizing the species as a whole. See prior chapter.
15. Within the emergent field of experimental physiology, debates over the legitimacy of animal experimentation and whether they could yield information pertinent to the human organism challenged what seemed elsewhere to be an all-too-easy comparison of animals and humans. See especially chapter four of Hubert Steinke, *Irritating Experiments*.
16. My emphasis. See Gregory, *A Comparative View*, 27.
17. Charles Augustin Vandermonde, p. 91. Vandermonde was editor of *the Journal général de la médicine* and identifies himself on the title page of his book as "Docteur-Régent de la Faculté de Médecine de Paris." He is mentioned by Hilts, p. 259.
18. Vandermonde, *Essay on the Manner of Pefecting the Human Species*, 92.
19. Maupertuis, *Venus Physique*, 133.
20. Immanuel Kant, "Von der verschiedenen Rassen der Menschen," 1777. In English, see Immanuel Kant, "Of the Different Human Races," trans. John Mark Mikkelsen, in *The Idea of Race*, ed. Robert Bernasconi and Tommy L. Lott, 8–22.
21. This is a modified translation from *Outlines of an Historical View of the Progress of the Human Mind: being a posthumous work of the late M. de Condorcet*, 291–292. (Translated from the French).
22. Darwin, *The Temple of Nature, or The Origin of Society*, Additional Notes, XI.
23. See Atran, *Cognitive Foundations of Natural History*.
24. For a discussion of heredity and generation within scientific debates and experiments throughout the eighteenth century, see Mary Terrall, "Speculation and Experiment in Enlightenment Life Sciences."
25. See particularly Farley's *The Spontaneous Generation Controversy* and Roger's *Les Sciences de la Vie*. See also Hilts' "Enlightenment Views on the Genetic Perfectibility of Man," Laqueur's *Making Sex*, López-Beltrán's "Storytelling, statistics, and hereditary thought," and Geyer-Kordesch's *Medizin*.
26. It was published in 1794 as *Abhandlung über die erblichen Krankheiten: Eine gekrönte Preißschrift*.
27. Rougemont, *Abhandlung über die erblichen Krankheiten*, 41. Note: he himself refers to Gregory here.
28. Ibid.
29. See Johanna Geyer-Kordesch, *Pietismus, Medizin und Aufklärung*. See also Geyer-Kordesh, *Psychologie*, for the influence of these theories upon the collaborative aesthetic efforts of G. E. Lessing, Moses Mendelssohn, and Friedrich Nicolai.
30. Schaarschmidt, *Physiologie*, 5.
31. Rougemont, *Abhandlung über die erblichen Krankheiten*, 41. His reference to "die moralischen Ursachen"—that is, the moral original causes—does give a kind of a priori existence to the moral realm, which might well be an accommodation of religious sentiment. But while the moral has some originary force, it is only activated in the real human world through the conditions of the individual human body.
32. López-Beltrán, "The Medical Origins of Heredity," 123.
33. Roy Porter maintains in his "Medical Science and Human Science in the Enlightenment" that, while Frank's image of the *"médecin-philosoph"* appealed to French thinkers, the practice of medical police remained for the most part confined to German-speaking territories.

34. See Broman, *The Transformation of German Academic Medicine*, esp. pp. 51ff for discussion of the medical police in the context of the changing status of medicine at the end of the eighteenth century. See also Lindenfeld, *The Practical Imagination*.
35. Isabel Hull, *Sexuality, State, and Civil Society*, 156.
36. Bernt, *Systematisches Handbuch der Staats=Arzneykunde*, 11.
37. Pieper, "Der Körper des Volkes," 106.
38. Osterhausen, *Ueber medicinische Aufklärung*, 9.
39. Unzer, *Der Arzt*, "Preface to the first edition," unpaginated preface.
40. Bucholtz, *Beyträge zur gerichtlichen Arzneygelahrheit*.
41. Baldinger, *Neues Magazine*, issue 7, 1785, 77.
42. Karl Härter and Michael Stolleis, *Repertorium*, 2.
43. Berg, *Handbuch des Teutschen Policeyrechts*, vol. 4, 737.
44. Berg, *Handbuch*, vol. 2, 212; vol. 4, 692.
45. In describing the move by eighteenth-century physicians to proclaim "a new vision of medicine that stressed its utility to society and state," Thomas Broman writes: "These activities received a tremendous boost in 1779 with the publication of the first volume of Johann Peter Frank's epochal *System einer vollständigen medicinischen Polizey* ... At the universities, medicinische Polizey became the basis for new courses and textbooks with a more applied orientation. During the last two decades of the century, a rising flood of treatises, articles, and periodicals on *medizinische Polizey* appeared, each following the trail Frank had marked." "University Reform in Medical Thought," 38. For a more extended history of the work's reception, see Harald Breyer, *Johann Peter Frank*; also see Anke Pieper, *Medizin in aufgeklärten Absolutismus*. Pieper points out, 158, that *"medicinal Polizey"* was taught by the Vienna medical faculty until 1875, and a steady production of new books (that she calls *"epigonale Nachahmungen"*) appeared in various European lands.
46. Baldinger, *Neues Magazin*, issue 6, 65.
47. This last, of course, raises interesting questions about the readership. Other works focused upon issues of pre- and post-natal care addressed a female readership while also ostensibly arguing for policy change.
48. Frank, *System*, v.
49. Ibid., x. For an overview of European and American writing on regulated breeding, see Victor Hilts, "Enlightenment Views on the Genetic Perfectibility of Man." Acknowledging the increasing interest in the topic, Frank points out that, "nevertheless there remain numerous important ideas about which an unbroken silence has been maintained; it shall become clear in the following that such topics deserve our fullest attention," vii.
50. For a discussion of these theories in the German context, see especially part two of Robert J. Richards, *The Romantic Conception of Life*.
51. Frank, *System*, 353.
52. Ibid., 353–354.
53. Ibid.
54. Unzer, Johann August. *Medicinisches Handbuch. Nach den Gründsätzen seiner medicinischen Wochenschrift, Der Arzt, Zweyter Theil. vom neuen ausgearbeitet*. (Vienna: Joh. Thom. Edeln von Trattnern, 1791), 67.
55. Gregory, *A Comparative View of the State and Faculties of Man with those of the Animal World*, 85–86
56. Ibid., 67.
57. Works that picked up on this theme, generally citing Frank, include: G. H. Berg's *Handbuch des Teutschen Policeyrechts*, esp. 737ff; E. G. Baldinger's

Neues Magazin für Aerzte; Johann Daniel Metzger's *Kurzgefaßtes System der gerichtlichen Arzneiwissenschaft*, esp 370 ff.; W. H. S. Bucholtz's *Beyträge zur gerichtlichen Arzneygelahrheit und zur medicinischen Polizey*, and J. Bernt's *Systematisches Handbuch der Staats=Arzneykunde zum Gebrauche für Aerzte, rechtsgelehrte, Polizeybeamte und zum Leitfaden bey öffentlichen Vorlesungen*. See also Rousseau's *Emile*, esp. 152; Campe's *Vätherlicher Rath*, esp. 154; and Oest, *Höchstnöthige Belehrung*, 18.
58. Ludwig, *Grundriss der Naturgeschichte*, 258.
59. Frank, *System*, x.
60. Ibid., 321.
61. Ibid., 26.
62. Ibid., xiii.
63. Illiger, *Versuch*, 7, § 15.3.
64. On the attempts to make eighteenth-century medicine more "scientific" (including various attempts at mapping disease onto a taxonomic framework), see Porter, "Medical Science and Human Science in the Enlightenment."

NOTES TO CHAPTER 6

1. Samuel Gottlieb Vogel, from the preface, xi, to Adolph Friedrich Löffler's *Beobachtungen aus der Arzneykunst*.
2. Ludwig Joseph Schmidtmann, *Ausfuehrliche praktische Anleitung zur Gruendung einer vollkommen Medizinal-Verfassung und Polizey*, 238.
3. Ibid., 355.
4. Frank, *System*, 4.
5. Johann Albert Heinrich Raimerus, *Untersuchung der vermeinten Nothwendigkeit eines autorisirten Kollegii medizi und einer medizinischen Zwang-Ordnung*, 14–15.
6. Frank, *System*, xviii.
7. Frank, *Akademische Rede*, 31.
8. Ibid., xxi.
9. Frank, *System*, xix. For Frank's engagement with Rousseau, see Breyer, *Johann Peter Frank*, esp. 54–55.
10. Robert Bartlett, *The Idea of Enlightenment*, 5.
11. Frank, *System*, xix.
12. Isabel Hull, *Sexuality, State, and Civil Society*, 238.
13. Frank, *System*, 353 and 367. In the Prussian *Allgemeines Landrecht* of 1794, the grounds for reasonable prohibition of marriage on the part of a legal guardian include "epileptic episodes, consumption, venereal or other infectious diseases" (Theil II, I.64); and conditions allowing the dissolution of an engagement contract include the following: "If after an engagement there is discovery of a disgusting [*ekelhaften*], infectious, particularly venereal or any incurable disease on the part of one party, the other party can withdraw the promise of marriage" (Theil II, I.103).
14. Michel Foucault, "The Politics of Health in the Eighteenth century," 172.
15. Frank, *System*, 312–313.
16. Blumenbach, *Abbildungen*, unpaginated preface.
17. Herder, "Die Liebe und nicht die Konvention soll die Erbanlagen im Kind zusammenführen," 215.
18. Vandermonde, vii.
19. Ibid., 170.
20. Ibid., 448.

21. Frank, *System*, 448.
22. Laurence Sterne, *Tristram Shandy*, 6.
23. See also Anne Vila, *Enlightenment and Pathology*, 84.
24. Herder, in his *Ideen*, writes 193 that "diseases and characteristic form" as well as "inclinations and dispositions" are passed though the generations.
25. Frank, *System*, 355.
26. Ibid., 207.
27. Another example which makes several similar points is Lenz's essay, "Über die Soldatenehe" written in 1775, copies of which he intended both for the Weimar court and the French Ministry of War. See Lenz, *Werke*, vol. 2, 787–827
28. Frank, *System*, 356. The Swiss system is a favorite comparison, also praised by Lenz in his essay on "Soldatenehe." See note above.
29. This contradicted most other writings on the subject, which tended to advocate for the prohibition of marriage among the very poor, simply because of the high risk that the children would end up as burdens upon the state. See, for example, Berg, *Handbuch*, 692–709.
30. Frank, *System*, 354–55. The notion of relocating children is not new with Frank. Plato launches the Timaeus with just such a suggestion; and programs to relocate orphan children have proliferated throughout modern times.
31. Ibid., 357.
32. Ibid., 450–451.
33. Ibid., 459–62. He cites and discusses an ordinance from the Parliament of Dijon.
34. Ibid., 463.
35. Ibid., 321–322.
36. Ibid., 352.
37. Ibid. He notes that the Chinese have small feet, which he claims began with a custom of binding and then became an inherited trait. He also refers to the disputed belief that, as a result of such modification, Jewish boys are often born circumcised.
38. This is not an unusual position. Vandermonde, too, begins an interesting discussion of what beauty is by discussing the different standards of different cultures with the example of northern cultures valuing white skin and the black cultures valuing dark skin, so that their devils are painted white and ours are painted black. He makes interesting observations on the cultural relativity of beauty, using the same example of the Chinese preference for small feet, adding the French preference for small waists, and he suggests that tolerance is the best approach to these opinions since all are imaginary beauties (*Essay*, esp. 11–12).
39. Herder, *Ideen*, 194–96.
40. Ibid., 452.
41. Vandermonde, *Essay*, 110.
42. Ibid, 113.
43. Ibid., 108.
44. Ibid.
45. Vandermonde writes, Ibid.: "It is in part because of this that port cities, which are almost always flourishing, and which abound in foreigners, possess more geniuses in proportion to other cities."
46. Ibid.
47. Ibid., 111.
48. Ibid. Here again is evidence of the preoccupation with the role of beautiful female slaves who share a particular national and racial identity.
49. Ibid.

50. Ibid., 453.
51. Ibid., 452.
52. Frank, *System*, 454. Both are commonplace observations in travel accounts and anthropological writings.
53. Frank, *System*, 456.
54. Ibid.
55. Ibid. Frank cites Peter Simon Pallas, *Rüssische Reisen.*
56. Ibid., 458–59.
57. Charles Darwin explained his identification of "sexual selection" (and distinguishes it from "natural selection") in *The Descent of Man*, 1871. My anachronistic use does not presume that Frank's theories connect directly to Darwin's zoological theory of competition and selection; however, I do think it might productively be included among the intellectual and conceptual antecedents that filter into subsequent discourse.
58. Anne Vila, *Enlightenment and Pathology*, 80.
59. Ibid, 88.

NOTES TO CHAPTER 7

Note: Unless otherwise indicated, all citations from the play are taken from the English translation by Ronald Schechter. G. E. Lessing. *Nathan the Wise. With Related Documents*, trans., ed., and intro. Ronald Schechter. Boston, New York: Bedford/St. Martin's, 2004. When necessary, I refer to and note the German edition: *Sämtliche Schriften*, ed. Karl Lachmann and Franz Muncker. Stuttgart, Leipzig, and Berlin: Göschen, 1968. This is noted in the text as LM, followed by a volume and page number.

1. Many critics focus on what they identify as the problem of Nathan's exclusion from the final blood-family at the end, a point we shall discuss later in detail. Compare Hans Mayer, "Der Weise Nathan und der Rauber Spiegelberg," 364; Benjamin Bennett, *Modern Drama and German Classicism*, 84–87. Peter Erspamer compares Nathan to Moses, insofar as "he leads his people (not only Recha, but also Curd, Saladin, and Sittah) to the border of the utopia/promised land, but he cannot enter it himself," *The Elusiveness of Tolerance: The 'Jewish Question' from Lessing to the Napoleonic Wars*, 36.
2. The literature on this subject is far too vast to cite here; I will provide a few representative views. For an overview on the play's reception history, see Hans-Friedrich Wessels, *Lessings 'Nathan der Weise.' Seine Wirkungsgeschichte bis zum Ende der Goethezeit*. Contemporaries of Lessing responded either by praising the play's enlightened tolerance or by railing against the perceived critique of the absolute truth of Christianity; compare Erspamer, *The Elusiveness of Tolerance*, 41ff; Wessels, *Lessings 'Nathan der Weise,'* 39–41. Late twentieth-century supporters of a utopian reading include Günter Saße, *Die Aufgeklärte Familie: Untersuchungen zur Genese, Funktion und Realitätsbezogenheit des Familialen Wertsystems im Drama der Aufklärung*, 248 and 291–306. Henry Schmidt describes Nathan's ending as a "heroic attempt [. . .] to fuse warring religions in a universal embrace." He places this in the context of the end of the *Sturm und Drang* plays focused on familial conflict. Henry Schmidt, *How Dramas End*, 38. Schröder affirms the "menschliche[. . .] Brüderlichkeit" which suffuses the drama, *Gotthold Ephraim Lessing*, 263–64. Erspamer on "utopian intent," *The Elusiveness of Tolerance*, 36–54. See also Demetz, who identifies Lessing's particular genius in his deft extension of a (mere) family story to invoke "the utopia of a family of humanity without conflict," *Lessing's Nathan der Weise*, 126.

3. Gustafson, *Absent Mothers*, 258.
4. Saße questions whether the final tableau can be a portrait of the *Menschheitsfamilie* when the Patriarch, Daja, Friar and Al-Hafi are all absent, and they specifically each, for different reasons, stand for separations based alternately on nationality, religion, and class or caste, *Die Aufgeklärte Familie*, 254ff.
5. Gustafson, *Absent Mothers*. For other objections to a utopian reading, see Waniek, "Wunder und Rätsel: die Gute Tat in Nathan der Weise."
6. Schmidt, *How Dramas End*, 27.
7. Klaus Briegleb, *Unmittelbar zur Epoche des NS-Faschismus*, 201.
8. Cited by Schmidt, *How Dramas End*, 9.
9. This echoes in the later version, when Saladin and Sittah discuss an attempt (probably historically accurate) to create a set of marriage alliances with the house of Richard of England, thereby ending the wars in the region. LM 3, 42.
10. I disagree with Sørensen, *Herrschaft und Zärtlichkeit*, 97, who reads this otherwise. Because Saladin claims that the marriage bond between the two houses (and thus the two religions) would produce "*Menschen*," Sørensen regards this as placing faith in attempt to achieve political harmony through an extension of the family. In my view, it is important to differentiate between the functioning of legal and blood ties that constitute such a "family."
11. Demetz, *Lessing's Nathan der Weise: Dichtung und Wirklichkeit*, 157. See Kowalik, "Nathan as a Work of Mourning."
12. Lessing's choice is original: for refutation of the claim that Voltaire used the term for his "Guèbres," see Dominik König, *Natürlichkeit und Wirklichkeit*, 155. König discusses Lessing's choice with an analysis of various terms employed throughout the *Hamburgische Dramaturgie*, noting that Lessing differentiates between "*Gattung*" and "*Geschlecht*" in his labeling system. König claims that the "*dramatisches Gedicht*" is a "*Geschlecht*," an "*Überbegriff*." He further cites Jürgen Schröder, 251 who echoed an old belief that Lessing, with his label, draws attention away from the action and the characters to focus it upon language primarily because he wrote the drama with readers rather than viewers in mind. Helmut Göbel declares: "The *Nathan* drama constitutes its own genre." *Bild und Sprache bei Lessing*, 195.
13. Certainly, Lessing was in the habit of resisting the marriage plot: one need think only of *Miß Sara Sampson*, *Emilia Galotti*, or *Der Jude* for examples of promised or possible unions pointedly unfulfilled. *Minna von Barnhelm* is the sole exception, but here the complexities of the personal relationship between Minna and Tellheim and the difficulties surrounding the marriage make the bond the more complex of the various possible solutions and not the final panacea expected of the comic genre. Saße also remarks on Lessing's decision to avoid the expected marriage-plot, 223. On the marriage plot and eighteenth-century drama, see Kord, "All's Well That Ends Well?"
14. Lessing, *Nathan*, 114 and 115.
15. Most obviously, the law is counterpoised against the good in the positions of the Patriarch and Nathan with regard to his raising of Recha: the Patriarch wields the law as a material record of proscriptions and prohibitions. His target is precisely what we come to understand as Nathan's goodness, a manifestation of the spirit in which the law was initially constructed.
16. There are critics who accept the final tableau (itself a much-used convention of eighteenth-century family drama signaling emotional and social reconciliation) as the emblem of the spiritual and political harmony espoused by the work. On the final tableau in *Nathan* as a conventional end to a family drama, see Saße, *Die Aufgeklärte Familie*, 217ff.

17. Bennett, *Modern Drama and German Classicism*, 87 regards Nathan as "both a Jew and a non-Jew, both a father and a non-father, which in practice means neither-nor. His life is one of unceasing self-restraint and unfulfillment."
18. Bennett presupposes that Recha/Blanda will have to assume "a new family, a new name, and a new religion." Ibid., 80.
19. Erspamer, *The Elusiveness of Tolerance*, 35 writes of Nathan as training Recha to take a role "within a larger group context" which "is nothing less than a multicultural circle, representing a utopian condition." It is worth noting that not all readers find this "multicultural circle" a positive utopia: in fact, the play has been a consistent failure in Israel, where it is regarded as condescending and assimilationist.
20. Compare Bennett on the unanswered questions of the Templar's and Recha's fate at the end. I disagree with him when he writes: "If Saladin had kept quiet about the breviary, Recha and her brother could have gone back to Europe and led a relatively uncomplicated existence," *Modern Drama and German Classicism*, 82. Nothing in the play signals that that were ever a possibility. On the contrary, we have already witnessed the Templar renounce his past for his new birth at the hand of Saladin.
21. See Schwab, "Familie."
22. Schröder, *Gotthold Ephraim Lessing: Sprache und Drama*, 251.
23. Contrast Gustafson, *Absent Mothers*, who argues 253 that the stress upon naming in the drama is connected to Kristeva's suggestion "that the process of naming is one of the primal separations necessary for the establishment of a patriarchal-Symbolic order." She continues, 254: "Multiple rings, names, and familial relationships make it impossible to determine the identity of the one true Father." I agree with her observations but differ in how they are best interpreted. She is right to observe that. "the characters of *Nathan der Weise* render the concept 'family' so fluid, that it has essentially no determinable meaning." However, this can be an effective starting point for questioning its function, not a conclusion.
24. See Hendrik Birus, *Poetische Namengebung: Zur Bedeutung der Namen in Lessings 'Nathan der Weise'*, who also discusses at length the division of name investigations in the play. He notes, 91 that in the first half of the drama, the preocupation with names concerns the exposition of character and the concretization of the worldly themes of the drama. It is different in the second half, when Nathan's right to be called Recha's father becomes an issue.
25. Birus, *Poetische Namengebung*, 175.
26. Lessing, *Nathan*, 77.
27. Ibid., 87.
28. Birus, 170.
29. Ibid.
30. One of the more interesting examples is Lessing's name-game with Nathan, modeled after but not named for Boccaccio's Melchisedek. See Birus, *Poetische Namengebung*, 157.
31. The examples here are incest and the murder of one's kin: that is, incest between Recha and the Templar, and the near-death of the Templar at the hand of Saladin.
32. Interestingly, he is identified by his social function, a "Templar," and not by any of his given names throughout the drama. The decision to identify him as "Templar" is a choice made all the more clear when one looks at the earlier draft of the play, in which throughout he is called Curd. There might be several ways to read this decision: it might signal that the name we know, Curd,

is not the real one; it implies that he is more truly identified by his belonging to the Knights Templar than by his belonging to a family via a given name; and/or that he can't be known beyond his social function.
33. See, for example, Sittah's criticism of the Christian obsession with whether or not people are labeled as Christian, while simultaneously disregarding the responsibility to embody the qualities that the name should represent, LM3, p. 43.
34. Lessing, *Nathan*, 113.
35. Sørensen, *Herrschaft und Zärtlichkeit*, 95 writes that paternity is to be found in the traces of education and the formation of character, not in the body. Sørensen overlooks the fact that, even if we accept the blood-ties posited at the end, Saladin's "paternity" is a legal artifact and therefore just as much an instance of "cultural fatherhood" as Nathan's claim.
36. Lessing, *Nathan*, 93.
37. Gustafson, *Absent Mothers*, 258 sets these up as an either/or.
38. Nathan remarks that there must be several distinct lines marked by that name. LM3, 66.
39. Lessing, *Nathan*, 59.
40. Ibid., 78. The original reads: "Was wärs denn nun? So was von Bastard oder Bankert! Der Schlag ist auch nicht zu verachten."
41. Ibid., 77.
42. Ibid., 78.
43. LM3, 102.
44. This is not the only stylistically discordant element, but one of the sharpest. See Wessels, *Lessings ‚Nathan der Weise.' Seine Wirkungsgeschichte bis zum Ende der Goethezeit*, on the early reviews. On "Bankert," see Demetz, *Lessing's Nathan der Weise*, 131 discussing the function of "profane words and idioms."
45. Emphasis added. See volume 1, 375 of Campe's *Wörterbuch der Deutschen Sprache*. Under the separate heading for the slang term *Bankert*, Campe lists as synonyms "*Bänkling*," with a citation from Ramler, and "*Bankbein*," 376.
46. Only at the end of his definition does Campe associate a "*Bank*" with the public institution of securing money against interest, 376.
47. Even as sophisticated a dramatist as Schiller excised a section for production because he felt the details of Nathan's trade concerns compromised his stature as the protagonist of a serious drama. See Demetz, *Lessing's Nathan der Weise*, 145. This is of course evaluated differently in our century, in which Erspamer can maintains that "in writing from a nascent middle-class perspective, Lessing forms a close association between morals and business." *The Elusiveness of Tolerance*, 37.
48. Lessing, *Nathan*, 88.
49. Ibid.
50. Ibid, 113.
51. As we know from the previous chapter, the child of a married couple was given the father's name, and only the illegitimate child was condemned to bear the mother's. Nathan generously suggests that perhaps his uncle adopted him, thus explaining why the Templar never knew his "real" name, the name of his father.
52. In the early version of the play, the explanation comes sooner, with the Templar's memories of his mother.
53. See Saße, *Die Aufgeklärte Familie*, 258 and 260; Birus, *Poetische Namengebung*, 93; Schröder, *Gotthold Ephraim Lessing*, 263.
54. Lessing, *Nathan*, 41.

55. Ibid., 84.
56. Ibid., 85.
57. Ibid., 75.
58. Ibid., 57.
59. Bennett, *Modern Drama and German Classicism*, 79ff. .
60. Shaftesbury, *An Old-Spelling, Critical Edition of Shaftesbury's Letter Concerning Enthusiasm and Sensus Communis*, 174.
61. Ibid., 175.
62. Gregory, *A Comparative View of the State and Faculties of Man with Those of the Animal World*, 137–38.
63. Lessing, *Nathan*, 87. Translation slightly altered.
64. Lessing began (though did not complete) an essay treating this problem, entitled *Bemerkungen über Burke's philosophische Untersuchungen*, focusing among other things upon Burke's formulation of sympathy. Lessing, *Sämtliche Schriften*, vol. 14, 223ff.
65. Ibid., 225.
66. Birus, *Poetische Namengebung*, 93 note 8.
67. Lessing, *Nathan*, 109.
68. Ibid., 113.
69. Ibid., 114.
70. Bennett suggests that when Nathan allows Saladin to make the final decision, he signals that the revelation of Assad's paternity may not be necessary; it might not be "in everyone's best interest to reveal the whole truth." Bennett, *Modern Drama and German Classicism*, 82.
71. Lessing, *Nathan*, 114.

NOTES TO THE POSTSCRIPT

1. Staffan Müller-Wille, "Figures of Inheritance, 1650–1850," 178.
2. Latour, *We Have Never Been Modern*, 84.
3. Reinhart Koselleck, *The Practice of Conceptual History*, 168.
4. Friedrich II, "Brief eines Genfers über Erziehung an Herrn Burlamaqui, Professor in Genf," in *Friedrichs des Großen Pädagogishe Schriften*, 220.

Bibliography

Agnew, Vanessa. "Pacific Island Encounters and the German Invention of Race." In *Islands in History and Representation*, ed. Rod Edmond and Vanessa Smith. London: Routledge, 2003.
Anonymous. "Auszug eines Briefes aus London." *Deutsches Museum* 2 (1776): 759.
Anonymous. "Blumenbach, J.F.: Abbildungen Naturhistorischer Gegenstände. H.1. No. 1–10. Göttingen: Dieterich 1796.: Rezension." *Magazin für das Neueste aus der Physik und Naturgeschichte* 1 (1797), unpaginated.
Anonymous. "Ueber den Ausdruck: Adeliches Blut." *Schleswigsches Journal* August (1792): 407–16.
Ashlock, P.D., and E. Mayr. *Principles of Systematic Zoology*. New York: McGraw-Hill, 1991.
Atran, Scott. *The Cognitive Foundations of Natural History*. Cambridge: Cambridge Univ. Press, 1993.
Baldinger, E.G. *Neues Magazin für Aerzte*, Zweyter Band. Leipzig: Friedrich Gotthold Jacobäer und Sohn, 1780.
Banneker, Benjamin. *Benjamin Banneker's Pennsylvania, Delaware, Maryland and Virginia Almanack and Ephemeris For the Year of Our Lord 1792*. Baltimore: Printed and Sold, Wholesale and Retail, by William Goddard and James Angell, 1791.
Baker, J. R. *Race*. Oxford: Clarendon Press, 1974.
F. M. Barnard, *Self-Direction and Political Legitimacy: Rousseau and Herder*. Oxford: Clarendon Press, 1988.
Bartlett, Robert C. *The Idea of Enlightenment: A Post-Mortem Study*. Toronto, Buffalo, London: Univ. of Toronto Press, 2001.
Baum, Bruce. *The Rise and Fall of the Caucasian Race: A Political History of Racial Identity*. New York: NYU Press, 2006.
Beck, Hamilton. "Of Two Minds About the Death Penalty: Hippel's Account of a Case of Infanticide." *Studies in 18th-Century Culture* 18 (1988): 123–40.
Becker-Cantarino, Barbara. "Witch and Infanticide: Imaging the Female in *Faust I*." *Goethe Yearbook* 7 (1994): 1–22.
Bennett, Benjamin. *Modern Drama and German Classicism: Renaissance from Lessing to Brecht*. Ithaca and London: Cornell Univ. Press, 1979.
Berg, Günther Heinrich von. *Handbuch des Teutschen Policeyrechts*. Hannover: Verlag der Gebrüder Hahn, 1804.
Bernasconi, Robert. "Kant and Blumenbach's Polyps: A Neglected Chapter in the History of the Concept of Race." In *The German Invention of Race*, ed. Sara Eigen [Figal] and Mark Larrimore. Albany: State Univ. of New York Press, 2006.

184 Bibliography

———, "Kant as an Unfamiliar Source of Racism." In *Philosophers on Race: Critical Essays*, ed. Julie K. Ward and Tommy L. Lott, 145–166. Malden, MA: Blackwell, 2002.

———, "Who Invented the Concept of Race? Kant's Role in the Enlightenment Construction of Race." In *Race*, ed. Robert Bernasconi, 11–36. Malden, MA: Blackwell, 2001.

Bernasconi, Robert and Tommy L. Lott, ed. *The Idea of Race*. Indianapolis: Hackett, 2000.

Bernier, François. "A New Division of the Earth," *The Idea of Race*, ed. Bernasconi and Lott. Indianapolis: Hackett, 2000.

Bernt, J. *Systematisches Handbuch der Staats=Arzneykunde zum Gebrauche für Aerzte, rechtsgelehrte, Polizeybeamte und zum Leitfaden bey öffentlichen Vorlesungen, Erster Theil*. Wien: Kupffer und Wimmer, 1816.

Bhabha, Homi. *The Location of Culture*. New York: Routledge, 1994.

Bindman, David. *Ape to Apollo: Aesthetics and the Idea of Race in the 18th Century*. Ithaca: Cornell Univ. Press, 2002.

Birus, Hendrik. *Poetische Namengebung: Zur Bedeutung der Namen in Lessings ‚Nathan der Weise'*. Göttingen: Vandenhoeck & Ruprecht, 1978.

Blakely, Allison. *Blacks in the Dutch World*. Bloomington and Indianapolis: Indiana Univ. Press, 1993.

Blumenbach, Johann Friedrich. *Abbildungen Naturhistorischer Gegenstände. Nr. 1–100*. Göttingen: Heinrich Dieterich, 1810.

———. *Beyträge zur Naturgeschichte, Erster Theil*. Göttingen: Johann Christian Dieterich, 1790.

———. *Handbuch der Naturgeschichte*. Göttingen: Johann Christian Dieterich, 1791, 1799.

———. *Über den Bildungstrieb*. Göttingen: Johann Christian Dieterich, 1791.

Brakensiek, Stefan, Michael Stolleis and Heide Wunder. *Generationengerechtigkeit?: Normen und Praxis im Erb- und Ehegüterrecht 1500–1850*. Berlin: Duncker & Humblot, 2006.

Brantlinger, Patrick. *Dark Vanishings. Discourse on the Extinction of Primitive Races, 1800–1930*. Ithaca and London: Cornell University Press, 2003.

Breithaupt, Fritz. "The Case of Infanticide in the Sturm und Drang," *New German Critique: An Interdisciplinary Journal of German Studies* 79 Winter (2000): 157–76.

Breyer, Harald. *Johann Peter Frank*. Leipzig: S. Hirzel Verlag, 1983.

Briegleb, Klaus. *Unmittelbar zur Epoche des NS-Faschismus: Arbeiten Zur Politischen Philologie 1978–1988*. Frankfurt am Main: Suhrkamp, 1990.

Brilliant, Richard. *Portraiture*. Cambridge: Harvard Univ. Press, 1991.

Broman, Thomas H. *The Transformation of German Academic Medicine: 1750–1820*. Cambridge: Cambridge Univ. Press, 1996.

———. "University Reform in Medical Thought at the End of the Eighteenth Century." *Osiris* 5 (1989): 38.

Brubaker, Rogers. *Citizenship and Nationhood in France and Germany*. Cambridge: Harvard Univ. Press, 1992.

Bucholtz. W.H.S. *Beyträge zur gerichtlichen Arzneygelahrheit und zur medicinischen Polizey*. Weimar: Carl Ludolf Hoffmanns seel. Witwe und Erben, 1782.

Buffon, Georges Louis Leclerc, comte de. *Barr's Buffon. Buffon's Natural history. Containing a theory of the earth, a general history of man, of the brute creation, and of vegetables, minerals, &c. &c. &c. From the French. With notes by the translator. In ten volumes*. Vol. 5. London, 1797.

Burdett, Carolyn. "Introduction: Eugenics Old and New." *New Formations: A Journal of Culture/Theory/Politics* 60 Spring (2007): 7–12.

Campe, Joachim Heinrich. *Väterlicher Rath für Meine Tochter (1796)*. Paderborn: M. Hüttemann, 1988.
———. *Wörterbuch der Deutschen Sprache*. 5 vols. Brunswick: Schulbuchhandlung, 1807–11.
Canguilhem, Georges. *Idéologie et Rationalité dans l'Histoire des Sciences de la Vie*. 2nd ed. Paris: Vrin, 1981.
Casey, Edward S. *The Fate of Place: A Philosophical History*. Berkeley, Los Angeles: Univ. of California Press, 1998.
Clark, Christopher. *Iron Kingdom: The Rise and Downfall of Prussia, 1600–1947*. Cambridge: Harvard Univ. Press, Belknap Press, 2006.
Condorcet, Jean A. de. *Esquisse d'un Tableau Historique des Progrès de l'Esprit Humain*. Paris: Flammarion, 1988.
———. *Outlines of an Historical View of the Progress of the Human Mind*. Philadelphia: Lang & Ustick, 1796.
Correia, C. *The Ovary of Eve: Egg, Sperm, and Preformation*. Chicago: Univ. of Chicago Press, 1997.
Curtain, Philip D. *The Image of Africa: British Ideas and Action, 1780–1850*. Madison: Univ. of Wisconsin Press, 1964.
Dahlmann, F.C. *Die Politik, auf den Grund und das Mass der Gegebenen Zustände Zurückgeführt*. 2 ed. Leipzig: 1847.
Daly, Martin and Margo Wilson. "A Sociobiological Analysis of Human Infanticide." In *Infanticide: Comparative and Evolutionary Perspectives*, ed. Glenn Hausfater and Sarah Blaffer Hrdy, 487–502. New York: Aldine, 1984.
Darwin, Erasmus. *The Temple of Nature: Or, the Origin of Society, a Poem with Philosophical Notes*. London: Jones and Company, 1825.
Daston, Lorraine and Peter Galison. "The Image of Objectivity." *Representations* 40, Special Issue: Seeing Science (1992): 81–128.
de Boor, Helmut, ed. *Das Nibelungenlied*. Mannheim: Brockhaus, 1988.
Demetz, Peter. *Lessing's Nathan der Weise: Dichtung und Wirklichkeit*. Frankfurt am Main: Ullstein, 1966.
Deppermann, Klaus. *Der Hallesche Pietismus und der Preußische Staat unter Friedrich III (I)*. Göttingen: Vandenhoeck & Ruprecht, 1961.
Deutsch, Karl W. *Der Nationalismus und seine Alternativen*, Munich: Piper, 1972.
Dickemann, Mildred. "Concepts and Classification in the Study of Human Infanticide: Sectional Introduction and Some Cautionary Notes." In *Infanticide: Comparative and Evolutionary Perspectives*, ed. Glenn Hausfater and Sarah Blaffer Hrdy, 427–438. New York: Aldine, 1984.
Diderot, Denis. *Diderot on Art, Volume II: The Salon of 1767*, ed. and trans. John Goodman. Intro. Thomas Crow. New Haven and London: Yale Univ. Press, 1995.
Diderot, Denis and Jean le Rond D'Alembert, ed. *Encyclopédie*. Paris: 1751–1780.
Dohm, Christian Wilhelm von. *Denkwürdigkeiten Meiner Zeit oder Beiträge zur Geschichte vom Lezten Viertel des Achtzehnten und vom Anfang des Neunzehnten Jahrhunderts 1778 bis 1806*. 3 vols. Lemgo and Hannover: Verlage der Meyerschen Hof=Buchhandlung und Commission der Helwingschen Hof=Buchhandlung, 1814-19.
Dougherty, Frank William Peter. "Christoph Meiners und Johann Friedrich Blumenbach im Streit um den Begriff der Menschenrasse." In *Gesammelte Aufsätze zu Themen der Klassischen Periode der Naturgeschichte*, 176–190. Göttingen: Klatt, 1996.
Dougherty, Frank William Peter. *Gesammelte Aufsätze zu Themen der Klassischen Periode der Naturgeschichte*. Göttingen: Klatt, 1996.

Dülmen, Richard van. *Frauen vor Gericht: Kindsmord in der Frühen Neuzeit.* Frankfurt am Main: Fischer, 1991.
Eigen [Figal], Sara. "Self, Race, and Species: Blumenbach's Atlas Experiment," *German Quarterly* 78 (2005): 277–298.
Eisenhart, Johann Friederich. *Grundsätze der Deutschen Rechte in Sprüchwörtern mit Anmerkungen Erläutert.* Helmstädt: Christian Friederich Weygand, 1759.
Ellrichshausen, Egon Conrad. *Die Uneheliche Mutterschaft im Altösterreichischen Polizeirecht des 16. bis 18. Jahrhunderts.* Berlin: Duncker & Humblot, 1988.
Erspamer, Peter R. *The Elusiveness of Tolerance: The 'Jewish Question' from Lessing to the Napoleonic Wars.* Chapel Hill and London: Univ. of North Carolina, 1997.
Eze, Emmanuel Chukwudi, "The Color of Reason: The Idea of 'Race' in Kant's Anthropology." In *Anthropology and the German Enlightenment: Perspectives on Humanity*, ed. Katherine M. Faull. *Bucknell Review* 38:2 (1995): 200–241.
Farley, John. *Gamets & Spores. Ideas About Sexual Reproduction 1750–1914.* Baltimore and London: Johns Hopkins Univ. Press, 1982.
———. *The Spontaneous Generation Controversy from Descartes to Oparin.* Baltimore and London: Johns Hopkins Univ. Press, 1974.
Fauconnier, Gilles and Mark Turner. *The Way We Think: Conceptual Blending and the Mind's Hidden Complexities.* New York: Basic Books, 2002.
Fichte, Johann Gottlieb von. *Grundlage des Naturrechts nach Prinzipien der Wissenschaftslehre.* Jena, Leipzig: Gabler, 1796.
Fischer, Friedrich Christoph Jonathan. *Versuch über die Geschichte der Teutschen Erbfolge.* 2 vols. Mannheim: C.F. Schwan, 1778.
Forster, Georg. "Beschluß der im Vorigen Monat Angefangenen Abhandlung des Herrn G. R. Forsters über die Menschen-Rassen." *Teutscher Merkur* 1786: 150–66.
———. "Noch Etwas über den Menschenrassen." *Teutsche Merkur* 1786.
———. *Werke*, Vol. 8. Berlin: Akademie Verlag, 1958.
Foster, Hal. *The Return of the Real: The Avant-Garde at the End of the Century.* Cambridge and London: MIT Press, 1996.
Foucault, Michele. "The Politics of Health in the Eighteenth century." In *Power/Knowledge. Selected Interviews and Other Writings, 1972–1977.* Ed. Colin Gordon. New York: Pantheon Press, 1980.
Frängsmyr, Tore, J.L. Heilbron, and Robin E. Rider. *The Quantifying Spirit in the 18th Century.* Berkeley: Univ. of California Press, 1990.
Frank, Johann Peter. *Akademische Rede vom Volkselend als der Mutter der Krankheiten (Pavia 1790). Oratio Academica De Populorum Miseria, Morborum Genitrice (Ticini 1790).* 1790.
———. *System einer Vollständigen Medicinischen Policey. Erster Band. Von Fortpflanzung der Menschen und Ehe=Anstalten, von Erhaltung und Pflege Schwangerer Mütter, Ihrer Leibesfrucht und der Kind=Betterinnen in Jedem Gemeinwesen.* Zwote, verbesserte Auflage. Mannheim: Schwan, 1784.
Friedrich II. *Friedrichs des Großen Pädagogishe Schriften*, trans. Jürgen Bona Meyer. Scriptor Reprints. Ed. Jörn Garber. Königstein/Ts.: Scriptor, 1978 (1885).
Friedrich II. *Anti-Machiavel, oder Prüfung der Regeln Nic. Machiavells von der Regierungskunst eines Fürsten Mit Historischen und Politischen Anmerkungen Aus Dem Französischen Übersetzet.* Göttingen: Königliche Universitets= Buchhandlung, 1741.
Fulbrook, Mary. *Piety and Politics: Religion and the Rise of Absolutism in England, Württemberg and Prussia.* Cambridge: Cambridge Univ. Press, 1983.
Geiman, Kevin Paul. "Enlightened Cosmopolitanism: The Political Perspective of the Kantian 'Sublime'." In *What Is Enlightenment? Eighteenth-Century*

Answers and Twentieth-Century Questions, ed. James Schmidt, 517–532. Berkeley, Los Angeles, London: Univ. of California Press, 1996.

Geyer-Kordesch, Johanna. "Die Medizin im Spannungsfeld zwischen Aufklärung und Pietismus: Das Unbequeme Werk Georg Ernst Stahls und dessen Kulturelle Bedeutung." *Wolfenbütteler Studien zur Aufklärung* 15 (1989): 255–74.

———. "Die Psychologie des Moralischen Handelns: Psychologie, Medizin und Dramentheorie bei Lessing, Mendelssohn und Friedrich Nicolai." Ph.D. Univ. of Massachusetts, 1977.

———. *Pietismus, Medizin und Aufklärung in Preußen im 18. Jahrhundert: Das Leben und Werk Georg Ernst Stahls*. Hallesche Beiträge zur Europäischen Aufklärung, no. 13. Tübingen: Max Niemeyer, 2000.

Göbel, Helmut. *Bild und Sprache bei Lessing*. München: 1971.

Goethe, Johann Wolfgang von. *Werke. Hamburger Ausgabe*. 14 vols. Munich: Deutsche Taschenbuch Verlag, 1988.

Goetzinger, Germaine. "Männerphantasie und Frauenwirklichkeit. Kindermörderinnen in der Literatur des Sturm und Drang." In *Frauen-Literatur-Politik*, ed. Annegret Pelz et al., 263–286. Hamburg: Argument-Verlag, 1988.

Gould, Stephen Jay, "On Mental and Visual Geometry." Isis 89.3 (1998): 503.

Greenfeld, Liah. *Nationalism: Five Roads to Modernity*. Cambridge: Harvard Univ. Press, 1992.

Gregory, John. *A Comparative View of the State and Faculties of Man with Those of the Animal World*. London: Routledge, 1994.

Grimm, Wilhelm and Jacob, ed. *Deutsches Wörterbuch*. 33 vols. Munich: Deutscher Taschenbuch Verlag, 1991 (1854–1971).

Grolle, Ingeborg. *Bettelkinder, Findelkinder, Waisenkinder 1600–1800*. Hamburg: Behörde für Schule, Jugend und Berufsbildung, 1991.

Grotefend, G. A., ed. *Das Allgemeine Preußische Landrecht und die Gesetze und Verordnungen für den Preußischen Staat aus der Zeit vor 1806*. Düsseldorf: L. Schwann'schen Verlagshandlung, 1879.

Gustafson, Susan. *Absent Mothers and Orphaned Fathers: Narcissism and Abjection in Lessing's Aesthetic and Dramatic Production*. Detroit: Wayne State Univ. Press, 1995.

Haller, Albrecht von. *Vorlesungen über die Gerichtliche Arzneiwissenschaft. Aus einer Nachgelassenen Lateinischen Handschrift Übersetzt*. 3 vols. Bern: bey der neuen typographischen Gesellschaft, 1782.

Hallett, Robin. "The European Approach to the Interior of Africa in the Eighteenth Century." The Journal of African History 4.2 (1963): 200, note 24.

Hart, Gail K. *Tragedy in Paradise. Family and Gender Politics in German Bourgeois Tragedy 1750–1850*. Columbia: Camden House, 1996.

Härter, Karl and Michael Stolleis, eds. *Repertorium der Policeyordnungen der Frühen Neuzeit. Band 1: Deutsches Reich und geistliche Kurfuerstentuemer (Kurmainz, Kurkoeln, Kurtrier)*. Frankfurt am Main: Klostermann, 1996.

Hegel, Georg Wilhelm Friedrich. *Grundlinien der Philosophie des Rechts und Naturrecht und Staatswissenschaft im Grundrisse*. Leipzig: Felix Meiner, 1911 (1821).

Henrichs, Hermann. *Kurze Geschichte des Princen Heraclius, und des gegenwärtigen Zustandes von Georgien*. Flensburg: Korten, 1793.

Herder, Johann Gottfried. "Die Liebe und nicht die Konvention soll die Erbanlagen im Kind zusammenführen." In *Herder Lesebuch*, ed. Siegfried Hartmut Sunnus. Frankfurt/M, Leipzig: Insel Taschenbuch, 1994.

———. *Ideen zur Philosophie der Geschichte der Menschheit*. Bodenheim: Syndikat, 1995.

Hilts, Victor. "Enlightenment Views on the Genetic Perfectibility of Man." In *Transformation and Tradition in the Sciences: Essays in Honor of I. Bernard*

Cohen, ed. Everett Mendelsohn, 255–271. Cambridge, etc.: Cambridge Univ. Press, 1984.
Hobbes, Thomas. "A Dialogue between a Philosopher and a Student of the Common Laws of England." In *The Collected Works of Thomas Hobbes*, ed. William Molesworth. Vol. 6. London: Routledge/Thoemmes Press, 1994.
Hrdy, Sarah Blaffer. *Mother Nature: A History of Mothers, Infants, and Natural Selection*. New York: Pantheon, 1999.
Hudson, Nicholas. "From 'Nation' to 'Race': The Origin of Racial Classification in Eighteenth-Century Thought." *18th-Century Studies* 29.3 (1996): 247–64.
Hull, Isabel V. *Sexuality, State, and Civil Society in Germany, 1700–1815*. Ithaca: Cornell Univ. Press, 1996.
Humboldt, Wilhelm von. *Humanist Without Portfolio: An Anthology of the Writings of Wilhelm von Humboldt*, trans. Marianne Cowan. Detroit: Wayne State University Press, 1963.
Hunt, Lynn. *The Family Romance of the French Revolution*. Berkeley, Los Angeles: Univ. of California Press, 1992.
Husserl, Edmund. *Logical Investigations*, trans. J. N. Findlay. Vol. 1. London: Routledge & Kegen Paul, 1982.
Illiger, Johann Karl. *Versuch einer Systematischen Vollständigen Terminologie für das Thierreich und Pflanzenreich*. Helmstädt: C. G. Fleckeifen, 1800.
Israel, Jonathan I. *Enlightenment Contested. Philosophy, Modernity, and the Emancipation of Man, 1670–1752*. New York: Oxford Univ. Press, 2006.
Jahoda, Gustav. *Crossroads between Culture and Mind: Continuities and Change in Theories of Human Nature*. Cambridge: Harvard Univ. Press, 1993.
Johnson, Mark. *Aristotle and Natural Kinds*. 2000. http://www.chass.utoronto.ca/~mojohnso/aristotle.htm. 2001.
Justi, Johann Heinrich Gottlob von. *Rechtliche Abhandlung von denen Ehen, die an und vor Sich Selbst Ungültig und Nichtig Sind (De Matrimonio Putativo Et Illegitimo) Wobey Zugleich von dem Wesen der Ehe und dem Großen Einflusse der Ehegesetze in die Glückseligkeit des Staats Gehandelt Wird*. Leipzig: Bernhard Christoph Breitkopf, 1757.
Kant, Immanuel. *Kants Werke*. Akademie-Textausgabe. Berlin: Walter de Gruyter, 1968.
———. "On the Use of the Teleological Principle in Philosophy." In *Kant*, trans., ed., and intro. Gabriele Rabel. Oxford: Oxford Univ. Press, 1963.
———. *Political Writings*, ed. Hans Reiss, trans. H. B. Nisbet. Cambridge: Cambridge Univ. Press, 1991.
———. "Vom Straf- und Begnadigungsrecht." *Die Metaphysik der Sitten. Erster Theil. Metaphysische Anfangsgründe der Rechtslehre*. Königsberg: Friedrich Nicolovius, 1803.
Kantorowicz, Ernst H. *The King's Two Bodies: A Study in Medieval Political Theology*. Princeton: Princeton Univ. Press, 1957.
Kirschke, Siegfried. "Zur Herausbildung der Neuzeitlichen Biologischen Anthropologie im 18. Jahrhundert." In *Grundlinien der Geschichte der Biologischen Anthropologie*, ed. Siegfried Kirschke, 106–117. Halle (Salle): 1990.
König, Dominik von. *Natürlichkeit und Wirklichkeit: Studien zu Lessings 'Nathan der Weise'*. Bonn: Bouvier Verlag Herbert Grundmann, 1976.
Kord, Susanne. "All's Well That Ends Well? Marriage, Madness and Other Happy Endings in Eighteenth-Century Women's Comedies." *Lessing Yearbook* 28 (1996): 181–97.
———. "Women as Children, Women as Childkillers: Poetic Images of Infanticide in Eighteenth-Century Germany." *18th-Century Studies* 26.3 (1993): 449–66.

Koselleck, Reinhart. *The Practice of Conceptual History. Timing Hisotry, Spacing Concepts*. Trans. Todd Samuel Presner and Others. Stanford: Stanford University Press, 2002.

Kowalik, Jill Ann. "Nathan as a Work of Mourning." *Lessing Yearbook* 21 (1989): 1–17.

Kramer, Lloyd, "Historical Narratives and the Meaning of Nationalism." *Journal of the History of Ideas* 58.3 (1997): 525–545.

Kroj, Karen. *Die Abhängigkeit der Frau in Eherechtsnormen des Mittelalters und der Neuzeit als Ausdruck eines Gesellschaftlichen Leitbilds von Ehe und Familie*. Frankfurt: Peter Lang, 1988.

Lakoff, George and Mark Johnson. *Metaphors We Live By*. Chicago: Chicago Univ. Press, 1980.

———. *Philosophy in the Flesh: The Embodied Mind and its Challenge to Western Thought*. New York: Basic Books, 1999.

Laqueur, Thomas. *Making Sex: Body and Gender from the Greeks to Freud*. Cambridge: Harvard Univ. Press, 1990.

Larrimore, Mark. "Sublime Waste: Kant on the Destiny of the 'Races'." *Canadian Journal of Philosophy* 25 (Supplementary) (1999): 99–125.

Latour, Bruno. *We Have Never Been Modern*. Cambridge: Harvard Univ. Press, 2007.

Laudan, Rachel. *From Mineralogy to Geology: The Foundations of a Science, 1650–1830*. Chicago and London: Univ. of Chicago Press, 1987.

Lavater, Johann Caspar. *Physiognomische Fragmente, zur Beförderung der Menschenkenntniss und Menschenliebe*. Leipzig: Weidmanns Erben und Reich, 1775.

———. *Physiognomische Fragmente, zur Beförderung der Menschenkenntnis und Menschenliebe*, 4 vols. Zürich: Orell Füssli, [1775–78] 1968.

La Vopa, Anthony J. "Herder's Publikum: Language, Print, and Sociability in Eighteenth-Century Germany." *Eighteenth-Century Studies* 29.1 (1996) 5–24.

———. *Fichte. The Self and the Calling of Philosophy, 1762–1799*. Cambridge: Cambridge University Press, 2001.

Lenoir, Timothy. "Kant, Blumenbach, and Vital Materialism in German Biology." *Isis* 71 (1980): 77–108.

Lenz, Jakob Michael Reinhold. *Werke und Briefe in Drei Bänden*, ed. Sigrid Damm. Frankfurt am Main: Insel, 1992.

Lessing, Gotthold Ephraim. *Gotthold Ephraim Lessings Sämmtliche Schriften*, ed. Karl Lachmann and Franz Muncker. 12 vols. Berlin: Voß'schen Buchhandlung, 1840.

———. *Nathan the Wise*. With Related Documents, trans., ed., and intro. Ronald Schechter. Boston, New York: Bedford/St. Martin's, 2004.

———. *Sämtliche Schriften*, ed. Karl Lachmann and Franz Muncker. Stuttgart, Leipzig, and Berlin: Göschen, 1968.

Lindenfeld, David F. *The Practical Imagination: The German Sciences of State in the Nineteenth Century*. Chicago and London: Univ. of Chicago Press, 1997.

Löffler, Adolph Friedrich. *Vermischte Aufsätze und Beobachtungen aus der Arzneykunst, Wundarzneykunst, Geburtshülfe und Gerichtlichen Arzneykunde. Heraugegeben mit einer Vorrede, Zusätzen und Bemerkungen von Dr. Samuel Gottlieb Vogel*. Stendal: Franzen und Grosse, 1801.

López-Beltrán, Carlos. "'Les Maladies Héréditaires': 18th Century Disputes in France." *Revue d'histoire des sciences* 48 (1995): 307–50.

———. "Storytelling, Statistics, and Hereditary Thought: the Narrative Support of Early Statistics." *Studies in History and Philosophy of the Biological and Biomedical Sciences* 37 (2006): 41–58.

190 Bibliography

———. "The Medical Origins of Heredity." in *Heredity Produced: At the Crossroads of Biology, Politics, and Culture 1500–1870*, eds. Staffan Müller-Wille and Hans-Jörg Rheinberger, 105–132. Cambridge, London: MIT Press, 2007.
Loseke, Johann Judwig Leberecht. *Joh. Judw. Leberecht Losekens, der Arztneygelahrheit Doctors, Semiotik, oder, Lehre von den Zeichen der Krankheiten. Zweyte Auflage.* Dresden and Warsaw: In der Gröllischen Buchhandlung, 1768.
Lovejoy, Arthur O. *The Great Chain of Being.* Cambridge and London: Harvard Univ. Press, 1964 (1936).
Ludwig, Christian Friedrich. *Grundriss der Naturgeschichte der Menschenspecies.* Leipzig: 1796.
Lyon, John and Phillip R. Sloan, ed. *From Natural History to the History of Nature: Readings from Buffon and His Critics.* Notre Dame, London: Univ. of Notre Dame, 1981.
Majer, Johann Christian. *Teutsche Staatskonstitution.* Hamburg: Carl Ernst Bohn, 1800.
Marin, Louis. "Towards a Theory of Reading in the Visual Arts: Poussin's *The Arcadian Shepherd*." In *The Reader in the Text*, ed. S. R. Suleiman and I. Crossman. Princeton: Princeton Univ. Press, 1980.
Marx, K.F.H. "Life of Blumenbach," In *The Anthropological Treatises of Blumenbach and Hunter*, ed. and trans. Thomas Bendyshe. Boston: Longwood Press, 1865, 1978.
Mason, Peter. *Infelicities: Representations of the Exotic.* Baltimore: Johns Hopkins Univ. Press, 1998.
Maupertuis, Pierre Louis Moreau de. *Venus Physique: Lettre sur le Progres des Sciences.* Paris: Aubier Montaigne, 1980.
Mayer, Hans. "Der Weise Nathan und der Rauber Spiegelberg." In *Lessings 'Nathan der Weise,'* ed. Klaus Bohnen, 350–373. Darmstadt: Wissenschaftliche Buchgesellschaft, 1984.
McCausland, Richard, Joseph Planta, Jos. Brant Thayendanega and John Butler. "Particulars Relative to the Nature and Customs of the Indians of North-America. By Mr. Richard Mc Causland, Surgeon to the King's or Eighth Regiment of Foot. Communicated by Joseph Planta, Esq. Sec. R. S." *Philosophical Transactions of the Royal Society of London* 76 (1786): 232.
Metzger, Johann Daniel. *Aeusserungen ueber Kant, seinen Charakter und seine Meinungen.* Koenigsberg: 1804.
———. *Grundsätze der Allgemeinen Semiotik und Therapie: Ein Lehrbuch.* Königsberg: Gottlieb Leberecht Hartung, 1785.
———. *Kurzgefaßtes System der gerichtlichen Arzneiwissenschaft.* Königsberg und Leipzig: Verlag der Hartungschen Buchhandlung, 1793.
———, "Noch ein Wort über Menschenracen," In *Neues Magazin für Aerzte* Zehnten Bandes Sechstes Stück, ed. Ernst Gottfried Baldinger. 1788.
Meumann, Markus. *Findelkinder, Waisenhäuser, Kindsmord. Unversorgte Kinder in der Frühneuzeitlichen Gesellschaft.* Munich: R. Oldenbourg, 1995.
Mills, Charles W. "Kant's *Untermenschen*." In *Race and Racism in Modern Philosophy*, ed. Andrew Valls, 169–193. Ithaca and London: Cornell Univ. Press, 2005.
Montesquieu, Charles Louis de Secondat, baron de La Brède et de. "De l'Esprit des Lois." *Oeuvres Complètes, Vol. 2.* Paris: Gallimard, 1951.
Moser, Johann Jacob. *Familien=Staats=Recht derer Teutschen Reichsstände; Nach denen Reichs=Gesezen und dem Reichs=Herkommen, Wie auch aus denen Teutschen Staats=Rechts=Lehrern, und Eigener Erfahrung; Mit Beygefügter Nachricht von Allen Dahin Einschlagenden Öffentlichen und Wichtigen Neuesten Staats=Geschäfften, So Dann denen Besten, oder Doch*

Neuesten, und in Ihrer Art Einigen, Schrifften. Erster Theil. Frankfurt and Leipzig: Johann Gottlieb Garbe, 1775.
———. *Familien=Staats=Recht Derer Teutschen Reichsstände. Zweyter Theil.* Frankfurt and Leipzig: Johann Gottlieb Garbe, 1775.
Mosse, George. *Nationalism and Sexuality: Respectability and Abnormal Sexuality in Modern Europe.* New York: Howard Fertig, 1985.
Muthu, Sankar. *Enlightenment Against Empire.* Princeton: Princeton Univ. Press, 2003.
Müller, Adam Heinrich. *Die Elemente der Staatskunst.* Based on original 1808–09 ed. Berlin: Haude & Spenersche Verlagsbuchhandlung, 1936.
Staffan Müller-Wille, "Figures of Inheritance, 1650–1850" In *Heredity Produced. At the Crossroads of Biology, Politics, and Culture 1500–1870,* eds. Staffan Müller-Wille and Hans-Jörg Rheinberger. Cambridge, London: The MIT Press, 2007.
Nussbaum, Felicity. *The Limits of the Human: Fictions of Anomaly, Race, and Gender in the Long eighteenth Century.* Cambridge: Cambridge University Press, 2003.
Nussbaum, Martha. "Kant and Cosmopolitanism." In *Perpetual Peace: Essays on Kant's Cosmopolitan Ideal,* ed. James Bohman and Matthias Lutz-Bachmann, 25–57. Cambridge and London: MIT Press, 1997.
Oest, Johann Friedrich. *Höchstnöthige Belehrung und Warnung für Jünglinge und Knaben die Schon zu Einigem Nachdenken Gewöhnt Sind (1787).* Ed. Johannes Merkel und Dieter Richter. München: Wiesmann Verlag, 1977.
Osterhausen, J. K. *Ueber medicinische Aufklärung.* Zurich: Heinrich Geßner, 1798.
Outlaw, Lucius. *On Race and Philosophy.* New York: Routledge, 1996.
Paul, Diane B. *The Politics of Heredity: Essays On Eugenics, Biomedicine, and the Nature-Nurture Debate.* Albany: State Univ. of New York Press, 1998.
Pestalozzi, Johann Heinrich. "Ueber Gesetzgebung und Kindermord." *Pestalozzi's Sammtliche Schriften.* Vol. 7 & 8. Stuttgart and Tübingen: J.F. Cotta'schen Buchhandlung, 1821.
Pfeil, Sigurd Graf von. *Das Kind als Objekt der Planung: Eine Kulturhistorische Untersuchung über Abtreibung, Kindestötung und Aussetzung.* Göttingen: Otto Schwartz & Co., 1979.
Pieper, Anke. *Medizin in aufgeklärten Absolutismus: Das Programm einer 'vollständigen medicinischen Polizey' und die Reformtätigkeit Johann Peter Franks in Pavia 1785–1795.* MA Thesis. Kiel: Christian Albrechts Universität, 1994.
Pieper, Markus. "Der Körper des Volkes und der Gesunde Volkskörper: Johann Peter Franks 'System einer Vollstaendigen Medicinischen Polizey.'" *Zeitschrift für Geschichtswissenschaft* 2 (1998): 101–19.
Planert, Ute. "Wann beginnt der 'moderne' deutsche Nationalismus?" In *Die Politik der Nation,* ed. Jörg Echternkamp und Sven Oliver Nüller, 25–60. Munich: Oldenbourg Verlag, 2002.
Plato. *Phaedrus.* The Persius Digital Library 2001. http://www.perseus.tufts.edu/cgi-bin/ptext?lookup=Plat.+Phaedrus+276a
Ploucquet, Wilhelm Gottfried. *Ueber die Physische Erfordernsse der Erbfähigkeit der Kinder.* Tübingen: Jakob Friedrich Heerbrandt, 1779.
Poliakov, Leon, *The History of Anti-Semitism.* 3 Vol. Philadelphia: Univ. of Pennsylvania Press, 2003.
Porter, Roy. "Medical Science and Human Science in the Enlightenment." In *Inventing Human Science: Eighteenth-Century Domains,* eds. Christopher Fox, Roy Porter, and Robert Wokler, 53–87. Berkeley, Los Angeles: Univ. of California Press, 1995.

Raimerus, Johann Albert Heinrich. *Untersuchung der vermeinten Nothwendigkeit eines autorisirten Kollegii medizi und einer medizinischen Zwang-Ordnung.* Hamburg: Carl Ernst Bohn, 1781.
Rameckers, J.M. *Der Kindermord in der Literatur der Sturm-und-Drang-Periode, ein Beitrag zur Kultur und Literaturgeschichte des 18. Jahrhunderts.* Rotterdam: Nijgh & van Ditmar's Uitgevers-Maatschappij, 1927.
Rau, Wilhelm Thomas. "Gedanken von dem Nutzen und der Notwendigkeit einer medizinischen Polizeyordnung in einem Staat" Ulm: 1764, 1771.
Richards, Robert J. *The Romantic Conception of Life: Science and Philosophy in the Age of Goethe.* Chicago and London: Univ. of Chicago Press, 2002.
Rieckmann, Christian. "Von dem Einfluß der Arzneiwissenschaft auf das Wohl des Staates und dem besten Mittel zur Rettung des Lebens." Jena: 1771.
Roger, Jacques. *Les Sciences de la Vie.* Paris: Albin Michel, 1993 (1963).
Rougemont, Joseph Claudius. *Abhandlung über die Erblichen Krankheiten. Eine Gekrönte Preißschrift. Aus der Französischen Handschrift Übersetzt von Wegeler, Friedrich Gerh., Doktor und Professor zu Bonn.* Frankfurt am Main: Johann Georg Fleischer, 1794.
Rousseau, Jean-Jacques. *Émile ou de l'Education.* Oeuvres Complètes. Vol. 3. Paris: Éditions du Seuil, 1971.
Sadji, Uta. *Der Negermythos am Ende des 18. Jahrhunderts in Deutschland.* Frankfurt am Main, Bern, Las Vegas: Peter Lang, 1979.
Saße, Günter. *Die Aufgeklärte Familie: Untersuchungen zur Genese, Funktion und Realitätsbezogenheit des Familialen Wertsystems im Drama der Aufklärung.* Tübingen: Max Niemeyer Verlag, 1988.
Scammell, Geoffrey. "The Other Side of the Coin: The Discovery of the Americas and the Spread of Intolerance, Absolutism and Racism in Early Modern Europe." *America in European Consciousness.* John Carter Brown Library, 1991.
Schaarschmidt, Samuel. *Physiologie, das ist, Betrachtung der Veränderungen des menschlichen Körpers in dem gesunden Zustande mit Zusätzen vermehrt von Ernst Anton Nicolai.* Berlin: Joh. Jac. Schützen, 1751.
Schiebinger, Londa. "The Anatomy of Difference: Race and Sex in Eighteenth-Century Science." Eighteenth-Century Studies 23.4, Special Issue: The Politics of Difference (1990): 390.
———. *Nature's Body: Gender in the Making of Modern Science.* Boston: Beacon Press, 1993.
Schlegel, Julius Heinrich. *Sammlung Aller Sanitätsverordnungen für das Fürstenthum Weimar.* Jena: Joh. Christ. Gottfr. Göpferdt, 1803.
Schmidt, Henry J. *How Dramas End: Essays on the German Sturm und Drang, Büchner, Hauptmann, and Fleisser.* Ann Arbor: University of Michigan Press, 1992.
Schmidtmann, Ludwig Joseph. *Ausfuehrliche praktische Anleitung zur Gruendung einer vollkommen Medizinal-Verfassung und Polizey.* Hannover: Bey den Gebruedern Hahn, 1804.
Schröder, Jürgen. *Gotthold Ephraim Lessing: Sprache und Drama.* München: Wolhelm Fink, 1972.
Schwab, Dieter. "Familie." *Geschichtliche Grundbegriffe.* Eds. Werner Conze and Reinhart Koselleck, Otto Brunner. Vol. 2. Stuttgart: Ernst Klett, 1975. 253–301.
Scrimschaw, Susan C. M. "Infanticide in Human Populations: Societal and Individual Concerns." *Infanticide: Comparative and Evolutionary Perspectives*, ed. Glenn Hausfater and Sarah Blaffer Hrdy, 439–462. New York: Aldine, 1984.
Shaftesbury, Anthony Ashley Cooper, Third Earl of. *An Old-Spelling, Critical Edition of Shaftesbury's Letter Concerning Enthusiasm and Sensus Communis:*

An Essay on the Freedom of Wit and Humor. Edited by Richard B. Wolf. New York & London: Garland Publishing, 1988.
Shell, Marc. *Children of the Earth: Literature, Politics, and Nationhood.* New York, Oxford: Oxford Univ. Press, 1993.
Shell, Susan M. "Kant's Conception of a Human Race." In *The German Invention of Race*, eds. Sara Eigen [Figal] and Mark Larrimore, 55–72. Albany: State Univ. of New York Press, 2006.
———. *The Embodiment of Reason: Kant on Spirit, Generation, and Community.* Chicago and London: Univ. of Chicago Press, 1996.
Slessarev, Helga. "Nathan der Weise und Adam Smith." In *Nation und Gelehrtenrepublik: Lessing im Europäischen Zusammenhang*, ed. Winfried und Albert M. Reh Barner, 248–256. Sonderband Zum Lessing Yearbook. Detroit: Wayne State Univ. Press, 1984.
Sloan, Phillip R. "Buffon, German Biology, and the Historical Interpretation of Biological Species." *British Journal for the History of Science* 12.41 (1979): 109–53.
———. "Preforming the Categories: Eighteenth-Century Generation Theory and the Biological Roots of Kant's a Priori." *Journal of the History of Philosophy* 40.2 (2002): 229–53.
———. "The Buffon-Linnaeus Controversy." *Isis*.67 (1976): 356–75.
———. "The Gaze of Natural History" *Inventing Human Science: Eighteenth-Century Domains*, ed. Roy Porter, Christopher Fox, and Robert Wokler. Berkeley, Los Angeles, London: Univ. of California Press, 1995.
Smith, Helmut Walser. *The Continuities of German History. Nation, Religion, and Race Across the Long Nineteenth Century.* Cambridge, 2008.
Sørensen, Bengt Algot. *Herrschaft und Zärtlichkeit: Der Patriarchalismus und das Drama im 18. Jahrhundert.* München: C. H. Beck, 1984.
Sprengel, Kurt Polycarp Joachim. *Handbuch der Semiotik.* Halle: Johann Jacob Gebauer, 1801.
Steele, Richard. "From my own Apartment, September 30." In *The Tatler: Edited with an Introduction and Notes by Donald F. Bond*, ed. Donald F. Bond, 512–517. Vol. 1. Oxford: Clarendon Press, 1987.
Steele, Richard and Joseph Addison. "No. 75, Saturday, October 1, 1709." In *The Tatler: Edited with an Introduction and Notes by Donald F. Bond*, Ed. Donald F. Bond, 512–517. Vol. 1. Oxford: Clarendon Press, 1987.
Steinke, Hubert. *Irritating Experiments: Haller's Concept and the European Controversy on Irritability and Sensibility, 1750–90.* Amsterdam: Rodopi, 2005.
Sterne, Laurence. *The Life and Opinions of Tristram Shandy, Gentleman.* Oxford, New York: Oxford University Press, 1983.
Stollberg-Rilinger, Barbara. *Der Staat als Maschine: Zur Politischen Metaphorik des Absoluten Fürstenstaats.* Berlin, 1986.
Strassburg, Gottfried von. *Tristan und Isold.* Berlin: Weidmann, 1978.
Sulzer, Johann George. *Allgemeine Theorie der Schönen Künste in Einzeln, nach Alphabetischer Ordnung der Kunstwörter auf Einander Folgenden Artikeln Abgehandelt.*, Vol. 3, 4 vols. Leipzig: in der Weidmannschen Buchhandlung, 1793.
Terrall, Mary. "Speculation and Experiment in Enlightenment Life Sciences," in *Heredity Produced: At the Crossroads of Biology, Politics, and Culture 1500–1870*, eds. Staffan Müller-Wille and Hans-Jörg Rheinberger, 253–275. Cambridge, London: MIT Press, 2007.
Tönnies, Ferdinand. *Gesellschaft und Gemeinschaft: Grundbegriffe der Reinen Soziologie.* 3 ed. Berlin: Curtius, 1920.
Toulmin, Stephen. *Cosmopolis: The Hidden Agenda of Modernity.* New York: The Free Press, 1990.

Turner, Mark. *Death is the Mother of Beauty: Mind, Metaphor, Criticism*. Chicago: Chicago Univ. Press, 1987.
Ulbricht, Otto. *Kindsmord und Aufklärung in Deutschland*. München: R. Oldenbourg, 1990.
Unzer, Johann August. *Der Arzt: Eine medicinische Wochenschrift. Neueste von dem Verfasser Verbesserte und viel bemehrte Ausgabe. Zweyter Druck*. Hamburg, Lüneburg and Leipzig: Gotthilf Christian Berth, 1769.
Vandermonde, Charles Augustin. *Essai sur la Manière de Perfectionner l'Espece Humaine*. 2 vols. Paris: Vincent, 1756.
Vick, Brian. "Greek Origins and Organic Metaphors: Ideals of Cultural Autonomy in Neohumanist Germany from Winckelmann to Curtius." *Journal of the History of Ideas* 63.3 (2002): 483–500.
Vick, Brian. "The Origins of the German Volk: Cultural Purity and National Identity in Nineteenth-Century Germany." *German Studies Review* 26.2 (2003): 241–256.
Vila, Anne C. *Enlightenment and Pathology: Sensibility in the Literature and Medicine of Eighteenth-Century France*. Baltimore and London: Johns Hopkins Univ. Press, 1998.
Voegelin, Erich. *Die Rassenidee in der Geistesgeschichte von Ray bis Carus*. Berlin: Junker und Dünnhaupt, 1933.
Voltaire. "Of the Different Races of Men." *The Idea of Race*. Ed. Robert Bernasconi and Tommy L. Lott. Indianapolis and Cambridge: Hackett, 2000.
Wächtershäuser, Wilhelm. *Das Verbrechen des Kindesmordes im Zeitalter der Aufklärung. Quellen und Forschungen Zur Strafrechtsgeschichte*. Berlin: Erich Schmidt, 1973.
Wahrig, Gerhard, ed. *Wörterbuch der Deutschen Sprache*. München: Deutsche Taschenbuch Verlag, 1981.
Wander, Karl Friedrich Wilhelm, ed. *Deutsches Sprichwörter-Lexikon: Ein Hausschatz für das Deutsche Volk*. Augsburg: Weltbild, 1987 (1867).
Waniek, Erdmann. "Wunder und Rätsel: die Gute Tat in Nathan der Weise." *Lessing Yearbook* 14 (1982): 133–60.
Weber-Will, Susanne. *Die Rechtliche Stellung der Frau im Privatrecht des Preußischen Allgemeinen Landrechts von 1794*. Frankfurt am Main, Bern, New York: Peter Lang, 1983.
Wessels, Hans-Friedrich. *Lessings ‚Nathan der Weise.' Seine Wirkungsgeschichte bis zum Ende der Goethezeit*. Königstein/Ts.: Athenäum, 1979.
Wheeler, Roxann. *The Complexion of Race. Categories of Difference in Eighteenth-Century British Culture*. Philadelphia: Univ. of Pennsylvania Press, 2000.
Wise, M. Norton. "How Do Sums Count? On the Cultural Origins of Statistical Causality." *The Probabilistic Revolution. Volume 1: Ideas in History*, ed. Lorenz Krüger, Lorraine J. Daston, and Michael Heidelberger, 395–425. Cambridge and London: MIT Press, 1987.
Zammito, John. *Kant, Herder, and the Birth of Anthropology*. Chicago: Univ. of Chicago Press, 2002.
———. "Policing Polygeneticism in Germany, 1775: (Kames) Kant and Blumenbach." In *The German Invention of Race*, ed. Sara Eigen [Figal] and Mark Larrimore, 35–54. Albany: SUNY Press, 2006.
———, *The Genesis of Kant's Critique of Judgment*. Chicago: Univ. of Chicago Press, 1992.
Zantop, Susanne. *Colonial Fantasies: Conquest, Family, and Nation in Precolonial Germany, 1770–1870*. Durham and London: Duke Univ. Press, 1997.
———. "The Beautiful, the Ugly, and the German. Race, Gender, and Nationality in Eighteenth-Century Anthropological Discourse." In *Gender and Germanness.*

Cultural Productions of Nation, ed. Patricia Herminghouse and Magda Müller, 21–35. Berghahn Books, 1998.

Zedelmaier, Helmut. *Der Anfang der Geschichte. Studien zur Ursprungsdebatte im 18. Jahrhundert.* Hamburg: Felix Meiner Verlag, 2003.

Zimmermann, Johann Georg von. *Von der Erfahrung in der Arzneykunst.* Vol. 1 and 2. Zürich: bei Heidegger und Compagnie, 1763.

Zur Mülhen, Patrik von. *Rassenideologien: Geschichte und Hintergründe.* Berlin, Bonn, Bad Godesberg: Dietz, 1977.

Index

A

absolutism, 14, 21–25, 67, 161n 38, 174n 45
adage, 19, 25, 31, 164n 41. *See also* idiom
adoption, 19, 131, 136–138, 140, 155
Agnew, Vanessa, 80, 170n 25
Allgemeines Landrecht (ALR, Prussian Legal Code),18, 19, 23, 32–33, 161n 32, 162n 48, 164n 32, 164n 37, 175n 13
anatomy, 42–43, 171n 62
animal: animal nature, 27, 162n 7; mixing of animals and humans, 37–39; human as animal, 44; human-animal border, 56, 85, 108, 165n 6, 166n 14; Africans as animals, 76; animal breeding, 91–93, 100, 122; animal experimentation, 173n 15
anthropology, 42, 96; and Kant, 55–57, 64–66, 168n 40
Arndt, Ernst Moritz, 69, 71, 72
Atran, Scott, 166n 10, 171n 63

B

Baldinger, Ernst Gottfried, 97
bastard (bastardy), 8, 14, 17, 20–26, 28, 31; product of mixed races, 37, 52, 71; and animals, 38, 39; as infertile, 51, 52; as monstrous, 52; as superior, 113, 114, 120, 127; and Kant, 142; and Lessing's *Nathan the Wise*, 139, 141–144, 154–155. *See also* hybrid; miscegenation; legitimacy; natural children
Berg, Günther Heinrich von, 98, 176n 29

Bernasconi, Robert, 63, 64, 77, 169nn 3–4, 171n 69, 171n 70, 172n 74
Bernier, François, 82
Bernt, Joseph, 96, 175n 57
Bhabha, Homi, 80
Bindman, David, 63, 68
Birus, Hendrik, 134–135, 179n 24, 179n 30
blood: blood-bond and kinship, 1, 4–7, 10, 11, 19–20, 25, 29–30, 85, 114, 128, 130, 132, 133, 134–142, 145–147, 151–153, 155; bloodline, 6, 9–10, 13–14, 17, 25, 33–40, 87–92, 114, 121, 142, 156–158 ; and transmission of traits, 12; and character, 6; foreign blood, 35, 118–124; and nation, 69, 71; and disease, 102–104, 116–117; "hot-blooded," 125
Blumenbach, Johann Friedrich, 49–55, 60, 63, 73–79, 83, 110, 168nn 35–36, 171nn 69–70
Bodin, Jean, 14, 160n 6
botany, 52, 165n 65
Brantlinger, Patrick, 66
Breithaupt, Fritz, 160n 9, 163n 21
Broman, Thomas, 174n 34, 174n45
brotherhood: rhetoric of, 2–5, 7, 15, 20, 42, 60–61; manifestation of moral good, 11; and race, 61, 68; signs of, 147, 155
Bucholtz, W.H.S., 97, 174n 40, 175n 57
Buffon, Georges-Louis Leclerc, Comte de, 9, 47–48, 142, 166n 11, 166nn13–14, 166n 16, 166n 19, 171n 74, 173n 14
Burdett, Carolyn, 86

C

cameralism, 96
Campe, Joachim Heinrich, 15, 141–143, 175n 57, 180nn 45–46
Canguilhem, Georges, 41, 46
Caucasian, 67, 78–84, 125
character: inherited moral character, 1, 6, 11, 55, 65, 90, 95, 112; genetic character, 68; national character, 70–71, 105, 118–119; 121; family character, 91, 92; 168n 40
Chardin, Jean, 82–83
Circassian, 82–83, 121
citizens: and family, 14–17, 20, 102, 120; and orphans, 21; and illegitimacy, 25; and species, 43, 57; improvement of, 87, 92, 95, 98, 101–111, 114–116; and race 123, 125
clan, 6, 50
Clark, Christopher, 72
common seed, 48. *See also Familienschlag*
Condorcet, Jean de, 92–93
cosmopolitanism, 43, 57, 88, 120

D

Darwin, Erasmus, 93–94
Darwinism, 66
degeneration, 51, 66, 77, 80–88, 92–93, 100–101, 104, 113, 116–126, 142; as aberration, 5
Demetz, Peter, 177n 2, 180n 44, 180n 47
Deutsch, Karl, 72
Diderot, Denis, 42–47, 56
Dohm, Christian Wilhelm von, 161n 44
Dougherty, Frank William Peter, 171n 66, 172n 74
Dülmen, Richard van, 27, 161n 36, 162n 9, 163nn 21–22, 163n 24, 165n 49

E

Efendi, Jusuf Aguiah (alt. Yusuf Agah Efendi), 79–80
Eisenhart, Johann Friedrich, 6, 8, 17, 19, 25–26, 33–34
Encyclopédie, 43, 47. *See also* Diderot
epigenesis, 57, 100
Erspamer, Peter, 177nn 1–2, 179n 19, 180n 47
eugenics, 66, 86, 90, 114, 126
Eze, Emmanuel, 63, 65, 169n 3

F

Familienschlag (family stamp): 55, 62, 168n 40. *See also* common seed
Farley, John, 164n 44
fatherland, 2–3, 72, 76, 102, 110, 122
Fauconnier, Gilles, 4
Ferguson, Adam, 8
Fichte, Gottlieb, 15, 69
Fischer, Friedrich Christoph Jonathan, 12, 22, 33
Forster, Georg, 63, 68, 81, 167n 24, 170n 25
Foster, Hal, 79
Foucault, 109
Francke, August Hermann, 21, 161n 38
Frängsmyr, Tore, 165n 65
Frank, Johann Peter, 10, 19, 35–36, 98–127, 174n 45, 174n 49, 177n 57
Friedrich II ("the Great") of Prussia, 20, 22–24, 28, 30, 67, 158, 161n 44, 166n 8
Friedrich Wilhelm II of Prussia, 21, 161n 44, 162n 48

G

Galton, Francis, 86
genealogy, 5, 7, 10–11, 15–18, 23–24, 40, 42, 47–48, 59, 90, 99–101, 107, 114, 140, 147–148, 152
generation: as reproductive process, 1, 3, 7, 35, 40, 47, 89, 94, 99, 100, 103, 112–113, 168n35; as cohort, 15, 47–48, 100–101, 117, 127, 152, 158; legally regulated, 22, 25; terminology for, 51–53; and species, 51–56, 59–62, 75–76, 78; and race or culture, 64–69; and animal husbandry or agriculture, 106–107
genetics, 40, 172n 4
Greenfeld, Liah, 71–72, 170n 28
Gregory, John, 91, 101, 150
Grotius, Hugo, 159n 3
Gustafson, Susan, 160n 9, 179n 23, 180n 37

H

Haller, Albrecht von, 36, 51, 100
Hart, Gail, 160n 9
Hegel, 13, 160n 3
Herder, Johann Gottfried, 10, 63, 68–73, 76–77, 112, 119, 170n 27, 176n 24

hereditary traits, 7, 43, 60, 64, 78, 89, 92
heritable disease, 35, 87, 102, 104, 118
Hilts, Victor, 173n 17, 173n 25, 174n 49
Hobbes, Thomas, 16
Hudson, Nicholas, 69
Hull, Isabel, 96, 109
hybrid, 2, 3, 9, 38–39, 52, 60, 67, 70, 80–88, 120–128, 158, 165n 65, 167n 32; monster, 24. *See also* bastard; miscegenation
hygiene, 10, 35, 85, 96–99, 110–111, 127

I
idiom, 5–6, 159n 10, 180n 44. *See also* adage
Illiger, Johann Karl, 52, 103–104, 167n 22, 167n 32
imagination, 11, 36–37, 112, 156
incest, 119, 122–23, 142–144, 154, 179n 31
infanticide, 16, 20, 26–31, 36, 97, 162n 5, 162n 9, 163n 18, 163nn 21–24; 165n 49
Iselin, Isaak, 86
Israel, Jonathan, 23

J
Johnson, Mark, 4, 165n 4
Justi, Johann Heinrich Gottlob von, 18–19, 22, 31

K
Kant: and illegitimacy, 16, 28, 34, 39, 142, 163n 16; and history of nature, 48; and species, 48, 50, 53, 55–61, 165n 6; and race, 62–68, 73, 77, 90–92, 168n 40, 169n 3, 169n 9, 169n 23, 171n 69
König, Dominik, 178n 12
Kord, Susanne, 163nn 21–24, 178n 13
Koselleck, Reinhard, 158

L
La Vopa, Anthony J., 71, 170n 30, 170n 32
Lakoff, George, 4
Larrimore, Mark, 64, 66, 169n 9, 169n 13, 169n 23
Latour, Bruno, 2, 157
legal fiction, 14

legitimacy, 7, 13–14, 17–18, 20–29, 33, 52, 62, 103–104, 113–117, 120, 128, 141–144, 154–155, 161nn 32–34, 161n 36, 161nn 39–40, 162nn 1–2, 163n 18, 180n 51. *See also* bastard
Lenz, Jakob Michael Reinhold, 176nn 27–28
Lessing, Gotthold Ephraim, 10, 128–155
Linnaeus, 44, 165n 6, 166n 13
López-Beltrán, Carlos, 96, 172n 5, 173n 25
Ludwig, Christian Friedrich, 60, 63, 73–76, 85–86, 102
Luther, Martin, 31, 50, 167n 31

M
Majer, Johann Christian, 35
Marcus Aurelius, 43, 45, 57, 165n 7
marriage, 8, 15–22, 27–28, 31–35, 87–91, 98–103, 109, 116–126; and impotence, 36, 112; and infertility, 112
Maupertuis, Pierre Louis Moreau de, 92
medical enlightenment, 96–98
medical police, 10, 19, 35, 96–104, 105–108, 126, 173nn 33–34
medicine, 35–36, 96, 97, 104, 105, 172n 10, 174n 34, 174n 45, 175n 64
Meiners, Christoph, 76, 81–82, 171n 63, 171m 66
Metzger, Johann Daniel, 10, 55, 63, 165n 48, 174n 57
Meumann, Markus, 161nn 33–34, 163n 17
Mills, Charles, 63, 169n 3
miscegenation, 37, 52, 67, 88; mixed-race, 83, 127, 167n 34. *See also* bastard; hybrid
monogenetic species concept, 59, 61
Montesquieu, Charles Louis de Secondat, baron de La Brède et de, 8, 16–17, 20
Moser, Johann Jakob, 13–14, 20–21, 160n 16, 161n 31, 162n 2, 164n 40
mother, 3, 7, 8, 11, 15–20, 25–40, 87, 99–100, 102, 106, 112–113, 118–120, 142–44, 160n 16, 161n 34, 161n 39, 163n 22, 164n 28, 164n 37, 164nn

200 Index

41–42, 167n 31; as monster, 30, 162n 7; mother-tongue, 3
mulatto, 52, 124, 167n34
mule, 38, 52, 167n 34
Müller, Adam, 9, 15
Müller-Wille, Staffan, 156
Muthu, Sankar, 70

N

nation, 2, 10, 49–51, 55, 62, 66–73, 76-, 90, 115, 126–127, 158
natural children, 18–21. *See also* bastard
natural history, 9, 41, 46–49, 60–63, 67, 74, 77–79, 94, 104, 167n 22
Nicolai, Ernst Anton, 95
Nussbaum, Felicity, 57, 84, 165n 7

O

orphans, 20–21, 97, 103, 116, 133, 144, 161n 33, 176n 30
Osterhausen, Johann Karl, 97
Outlaw, Lucius, 169n 3

P

paternity, 8, 31–39, 95, 134–143, 164n 37, 180n 35, 181n 70
perfectibility, 65, 85–85, 99, 158
Pestalozzi, Johann Heinrich, 27–29
physiology, 7, 11, 14, 36, 39–43, 47–49, 55–56, 77, 83, 87–89, 93–96, 100, 112, 120–126, 138–140, 146, 173n 15
Planert, Ute, 71
Plato, 14, 116, 165n 4, 176n 30
Ploucquet, Wilhelm Gottfried, 9, 32, 36–40, 95
polygenism, 41, 59–61
Porter, Roy, 173n 33
preformation, 100
pregnancy, 20, 28, 32–33, 36–37, 163n 14
property, 7, 12, 20, 34–37, 116–117, 159n 3, 162n 2

R

race, 2–6, 9–10, 37–38, 42, 49–94, 101–104, 109–110, 114–127, 158, 167n 24, 34, 168n 40, 169nn 3–4, 170n 25, 171n 63, 176n 48
Raimerus, Johann Albert Heinrich, 107
reproduction, 35–39, 47, 52–54, 86, 91, 100–101, 106, 109–117, 121–127, 158
Roman familial practices, 14, 26, 33
Rougemont, Joseph Claudius, 10, 95–96
Rush, Benjamin, 92

S

Saße, Günter, 177n 2, 178n 4
savage, 66, 69
Schaarschmidt, Samuel, 95
Schiebinger, Londa, 38
Schiller, Friedrich, 4–6, 159n 4; and *The Robbers* [*Die Räuber*], 4–6
Schmidtmann, Ludwig Joseph, 106, 109,
Schwab, Dieter, 162n 4
semiotic science, 35–36, 39, 165n 48
Seneca, 57, 162n 7
Serres, Michel, 3, 12
Shaftesbury, Anthony Ashley Cooper, Third Earl of, 8, 150
Shell, Marc, 131, 162n 1, 164n 35
Shell, Susan, 48, 67
Sloan, Phillip, 48, 77, 166n 19, 169n 4, 171n 70
Smith, Helmut, 69, 72, 170n 32
Sørensen, Bengt Algot, 178n 10
species, 2–10, 38–95, 104, 109, 112–115, 121–126, 151, 158, 166n 16, 166n 19, 167nn 21–22, 168nn 35, 168n 43, 169n 23
Stahl, Georg Ernst, 95
Steele, Richard, 10, 87–90, 172n 8
Steinke, Hubert, 173n 15
stepparents, 19
Sterne, Laurence, 123
sympathy, 150–151

T

temperament, 87, 89, 91, 95, 112
Tissot, Samuel Auguste, 101
tolerance, 11, 128–130, 151, 153, 176n 38, 177nn 1–2
Turner, Mark, 4

U

Unzer, Johann August, 97, 101

V

Vandermonde, Charles Augustin, 10, 92, 112, 119, 120–121, 126, 173

Vick, Brian, 71
Vico, Giambattista, 8
Vila, Anne, 126
Voegelin, Erich, 166n 13
Vogel, Samuel Gottlieb, 105
Voltaire, 38, 52, 72, 167n 33, 178n 12

W

Wächtershäuser, Wilhelm, 160n 30

Wessels, Hans-Friedrich, 177n 2, 180n 44
Wheeler, Roxann, 89
widow/widower, 32, 103, 116, 164n 32

Z

Zammito, John, 77, 181nn 69–70
Zantop, Susanne, 91, 171n 63
Zimmermann, Johann Georg, 111